SOCIO-POLITICAL ETHICS

Practical and Professional Ethics Series

Vol. 1: The Primer of Applied Ethics
Vol. 2: Environmental Ethics
Vol. 3: Bio-Medical Ethics
Vol. 4: Educational Ethics
Vol. 5: Economic and Business Ethics
Vol. 6: Socio-Political Ethics

About the Author

Dr. Debashis Guha, teaches Ethics, and Phenomenology and Existentialism in the Post Graduate Department of Philosophy, Ranchi University, Ranchi. After doing masters course in Philosophy from Delhi University in 1980, he was conferred the Ph.D. degree of Jadavpur University in 1988. Dr. Guha takes interest in Philosophy of Religion, Social and Political Philosophy, Philosophy of Science and Analytic Philosophy. He taught at the undergraduate level in a constituent college of Ranchi University from 1981 to 1989 and was then asked to serve the Post Graduate Department. Dr. Guha is teaching Ethics for twenty-four years. He was awarded the Visiting Associateship of the U.G.C. (1994-96) in Jadavpur University, Calcutta, where he worked out *An Inquiry into the cases of Pain and Suffering,* which has been published. He was further awarded U.G.C.'s Major Research Project (1997-2000) on *Applied Ethics in Indian Context,* which has been now shaped in Six volumes, of which the present work is the sixth one under the series: **Practical and Professional Ethics**. Dr. Guha has fifteen papers to his credit. He has presented philosophical papers in different Seminars, Symposia and Congress, two of them were presented in International Congress; one in the Platinum Jubilee Celebrations of the Indian Philosophical Congress, 2000-01, and the other in the XVth International Congress of Aesthetics in Tokyo, Japan in 2001. During his Major Research Project work, Dr. Guha has talked to many people from different walks of life, interviewed them and also arranged ethical dialogues leading to resolution of value-laden practical problems of urgency. Dr. Guha envisions people's participation in Practical and Professional Ethics.

Practical and Professional Ethics

Volume - Six

Socio-Political Ethics

DEBASHIS GUHA

CONCEPT PUBLISHING COMPANY, NEW DELHI-110059

Cataloging in Publication Data—DK
Courtesy: D.K. Agencies (P) Ltd. <docinfo@dkagencies.com>

Guha, Debashis.
Practical and professional ethics/ Debashis Guha.
v. 6 cm.
Includes bibliographical references.
Includes indexes.
Contents: v. 6. Socio-political ethics.
ISBN 13: 9788180693144 (set)
ISBN 10: 8180693147 (set)
ISBN 13: 9788180696022 (v. 6)
ISBN 10: 8180696022 (v. 6)
ISBN 13: 9788180696039 (pbk.) (v. 6)
ISBN 10: 8180696030 (pbk.) (v. 6)

1. Applied ethics. 2. Professional ethics. 3. Environmental ethics. 4. Bioethics. 5. Medical ethics. 6. Moral education. 7. Business ethics. I. Title.

DDC 170 22

ISBN-13: 978-81-8069-314-4 (Series)
ISBN-13: 978-81-8069-602-2 (H.B.)
ISBN-10: 81-8069-314-7 (Series)
ISBN-10: 81-8069-602-2 (H.B.)

First Published 2009

Published and Printed by
Ashok Kumar Mittal
Concept Publishing Company
A/15-16, Commercial Block, Mohan Garden
New Delhi-110059 (INDIA)

Phones : 25351460, 25351794
Fax : 091-11-25357109
Email : publishing@conceptpub.com

To my Teachers—

Sr. Rita Mary, Sr. Anis, Sr. Cecil,
Mrs. Purnima Das, Fr. W.J. Proost,
Fr. G.P. Lawlor, Fr. C. De Brouwer,
Dr. Luteshwar Jha, Dr. Margaret Chatterjee
and
Dr. Tapan Kumar Chakraborty

RAM DAYAL MUNDA, Ph.D. (Chicago)

- Chairperson Working Group on Empowerment of the Scheduled Tribes, Planning Commission, Govt. of India
- Chief President, Indian Confederation of Indigenous and Tribal Peoples, New Delhi
- Former University Professor and Vice-Chancellor, Ranchi University, Ranchi

Foreword

I feel greatly honoured to have been asked to write the Foreword of the present volume, the last of a Series of six volumes on Practical and Professional Ethics which is, Socio-Political Ethics, written by the author. At a time when human evolution has reached a stage which can be sustained only through a perceived self destructive process of greed (cessation), it seems only a principle of development guided by morality/ethicality can ensure survival of our planet with its structured complexities. The fast pace of the process of globalization with which it is moving is indicative of an extremely polarized future world in turmoil unless checked and mitigated through a well planned institutionalized moral/ethical force. The recent developments in the U.N. with all skepticisms on the sides, do give a hope that a functional base for People's Ethics could be formed for a global human and environmental well being: Towards this, I feel, the author's present discourse on Practical and Professional Ethics as People's Ethics with its theoretical justifications, is most welcome in the present context of the world.

The author and the publisher deserve congratulations for this monumental timely endeavour.

Ram Dayal Munda

Preface

Reaching the climax of an arduous effort is always pleasing but it is mixed with the feelings of dissatisfaction and fear. Dissatisfaction comes naturally because one feels that much needs to be done which, nevertheless, should have been done, and fear comes because one feels that not much justice has been done with the people, who were the backbone of this work which is for me "people's ethics". The Series of books on Practical and Professional Ethics is thus an account of People's Ethics, an ethics that blends theoreticism and activism, balanced largely. The Series is also a testimony to Application of Ethics and Professional Ethical enterprise in the Indian context, by means of balancing the most needed universal elements of both application of ethics and professional ethics mostly portrayed in the discussions. The unavoidable activism on the part of an Indian to apply ethics and to get involved in the resolutions of professional ethical dilemma is thus prominent. Application of ethics and Professional Ethics as aspects of People's Ethics are thus theoreticism and activism combined in a whole. There is no doubt that People's Ethics should not be apathetic to the ethical conceptions and interests of the global population, but it is pragmatic to be somewhat constrained in such activism when we focus more on value-laden issues troubling the Indian diaspora. Intersubjective corroboration is, therefore, universal in nature, but needs safe application by concerned people at different places as a means to ethical application, which might cover the professional fields as well. No one has prevented it to be equally useful as a means to resolve the occupational ethical crises, if occupational ethical enterprise is well under People's Ethics. The Series, *Practical and Professional Ethics,* stands for considering extremely important ethical discussions pertaining to society, polity and legality as well because without considering them People's Ethics remains incomplete. Hence, we are now poised to discuss Social and Political Ethics as a climax to Practical and

Professional Ethics, with risks of unfinishing a vast and challenging work with some injustice done to a number of issues and to many ethically charged contributors who were so kind to be in the same boat that swayed in the rough weather of value-crises.

Contents

Introduction

People have two extremely bad habits, one is to forget the past, even the very ugly ones, not always out of carelessness, but owing to a cunning act, which is distasteful. The other bad habit is not to tell with pride and without fear that the present has been infested by ugly elements though good prevails as emphatically as ever, and that the future is extremely important if that has to be lived decently by some of us who are or who will infest the world in future. Standing at the present epoch, we thus find many callous people forgetting the incivility, sufferings and turmoils of the past; to be precise, callous people forget the disvalues of the past or the value-degraded past. Equally true is that these people forget a harsh but real story of rising of the human and the humanhood from the ashes or the ruins of the past turmoils and abject valuelessness. We forget the belligerent story of the survival and moral evolution of the outwitted people, who became either valueless or morally bankrupt, the most dangerous viruses of society. We tend to forget that as we stand now throughout the globe, many among us are still fighting a battle against the moral viruses, and the humanity and humanhood is still bubbling with some energy at least, in many cases, incomparable to the most horrific parasitic humans of the value-degraded past. The cunning people are very deft at an act of justifying a primitive agenda that the past was morally glorious and we are by our act running to a doomsday. Whereas the truth may be that, we were always trying to fight the doom to see a glorious day. Hence, let us not be sceptics and hopeless, let us take the truth as it is. Let us face the challenges posed by the moral viruses that are stronger as ever. Let us have faith that the fight to crush them is on and it should go on. Hence, let us cultivate a habit of evaluating the morally good, bad and ugly of the past and the present, and strive utmost to prevent the rise of the bad and the ugly in the future. Let us be courageous to tell the morally ugly on the face that we will defeat you by our might, whether it happens or not, is unprovidential. Another śāstric clamour is that 'the good shall win over evil'. This is simply an ethical call for what ought to be the case, that is, we ought to be good evaluators of the disvalues of the past and the present and try to outwit disvalues together by ways open to us. A way open to all of us, the scientists, the artists and the philosophers alike is to come together in a social activism about which I was harping in the five volumes of the series on *Practical and Professional Ethics*.

Clearly, ethical value degradation and finding ways to counter them is a "human affair" in the "human society", which is governed by either an authority or authorities under a body of rules and laws, whether well framed or arbitrary. Most of the so-called human social agglomerations having an authoritative governance whether under well-framed or arbitrary rules and laws is fast vanishing or they are pushed to the brink of extinction by the power of people globally (and locally) because there has been apart from many evils, most ugly form of moral degradation under the shadows of authoritarianism. However, this is not to say that the so-called human societies having collective governance under well-framed rules and laws are not morally ugly. Even in case of the most glorified democracies, the governance of the people can be morally ugly by virtue of the value-degradations at the political and legal strata. The same may be the case in a communist society or in a socialist state. The reason is that having a society, polity and legality does not guarantee ethicality. Being a democracy, the Indian society, polity and legality remains unguarded from moral corruptions or value degradations. No one has really stopped us to this date from being killers of girl child in the mother's womb or after their birth or after they are married. No one has really stopped us to be dirty hands in politics, being rampant in election clichés, murderous in the share of power, bullish in bribing and anti-people in creating riots, famines and economic crises. No one has really prevented us to frame laws for a class or for the powerful, and to manipulate and distort them to suit our greed. Hence, having long years of independence, a free society, polity and legality do not imply that the society, polity and legality are morally sacrosanct. With the Indian people and others throughout the world being perennially both pro and con moral good, right, just and obligatory, the society that evolves are perennially pro and con to such things. The tension maze of social, political and legal ethics, the maze of pro and con moral good, right, just and so on is, therefore, never static; it is essentially moving through the ages, always seeing the ashes of the moral good as the phoenix rises or the rise of the moral good as the phoenix is crushed. Human societies always nurtures moral utopias in some way or the other that remains probable for us pushing us thoroughly from within to win in the tension scenario.

This final work that tries to bring out the theoretical and the active aspects of social, political and legal ethics by considering the nature and justification of social, political and legal ethics along with a number of value-laden or ethical issues and cues for their resolution. It is exactly in these contexts that we have discussed and attempted to resolve a number of value-laden issues such as reservation in jobs, modes of political protests and capital punishment.

I really do not know how to thank the number of students, teachers and people of professions and occupations who have helped me in many ways. Special thanks to the staff of the National Library, Kolkata, particularly Mr. G. Kumarappa, the staff of the I.C.P.R. Library, Lucknow, the staff of the Ranchi University Central Library and the Seminar Library. Thanks to my students Mr. Rajendra Singh, Mr. Purushottam Kumar, Mr. Pradeep Prasad and Ms. Sushma Priyadarshana. I thank Dr. T.K. Chakraborty of Jadavpur University, Dr. Ahmad Sajjad, Dr. C.R. Laha, Dr. K.K.L. Karna, Dr. P.V. Lakshmi, Dr. Bimla Kumari, Dr. S. Mishra and Dr. R.B. Prasad of Ranchi University for helping me in many ways. I thank my most efficient and meticulous typist Mr. Sanjay Singh for ensuring that all the volumes comes out right in time. Special thanks to Mr. Ashok Kumar Mittal and his colleagues of the Concept Publishing Company to bring out this series with great care and courage.

1

Nature and Justification of Social Ethics

The reader of the Series on Practical and Professional Ethics have been gradually betrayed by me since I wrote the Second Volume till the Fifth one in so far as details of the nature and tasks of ethics were not been provided by me. For this, I have a (good) excuse though, that is, much has been said in the First Volume, which being a Primer on ethical matters, dealt with the nature and tasks of ethics to a great extent, and in the four volumes to follow I became precise in this regard. Yet, I was not able to deny the truth that "ethics" suffixed to "environmental", "bio-medical", "economic", "business", "administrative" and "management" needed some clarification for its nature and tasks for the readers of these volumes, who were otherwise either not interested in or could not get hold of the Primer for the needed details about Ethics as such. Hence, the scrappiness that has been a reluctantly shaped out betrayal should continue without much regret in this last volume on Socio-Political Ethics. Clearly, the readers of this volume may not refer to the nature analysis of "environmental", "bio-medical" ethics, though they need to have an extremely rough idea about Ethics as a starter because without it we will be in no position to follow what "socio-political ethics" amounts to. Hence, in this chapter, we neėd to find out first what ethics as a branch of philosophy takes up to consider and then analyse what exactly it amounts to when "ethics" is suffixed to "socio-political". In any case, as was seen before, nothing is clear to us if "socio or social" and "political" as prefixed to "ethics" is made clear for their nature and significance. We will see shortly that though the title of the book mentions only "socio-political", wide-ranging "legal" discussions, particularly in association to ethics is included in this work. Truly, then the work should read without any precision element in the title

"Social, Political and Legal Ethics", which depends for its nature on the analysis of the meaning of "social", "political", "legal", and as I have said, "ethics". In this chapter, for instance, we are at hand a job for the clarification of the meaning of "social" and "social ethics" (which for some unintended parsimony ended up in "socio", meaning thereby on the one hand that many political and legal issues are deeply related to "social" issues, and on the other hand that political and legal issues are seldom disjoint as social issues in the very wide connotation of the terms, though that does not amount to their synonymy or equivalences). At the end of it all environmental, biomedical, business, economic, administrative and management issues are in some sense or the other "social" issues, meaning thereby the interrelation of the said issues which are nevertheless different, and that in a wider sense, the issues are seldom disjoint as social issues, where "social" might vary for its meaning from "human society" to the "society of existential" or what I have referred to as the "ecological community" (see Volumes 1, 2 and 3).

Let us take up "ethics" first for clarification of its meaning and tasks. Ethics signifies a branch of philosophy that considers in the main the *analysis of language* unique to ethical discussion; the *explanation of the standards or norms* of evaluation of human intentions, decisions and actions for their moral worth or ethical value, which is also a cue to the moral or ethical utopias or ideals and the moral or ethical means that enable us to realise the ideals; and the *application of our ethical experiences and knowledge* for the analysis and resolution of value-laden or ethical problems we face in our societies. It is thus extremely important in ethics to find out the meaning of value-concepts such as "good", "right", "just", "duty", "obligations" and so on and to discuss why value-assertions are meaningful, as well as to indulge into the logic of justifying norms, which comes under the purview of "metaethics" or the "second order task" of ethics. The "first order task" of ethics is "normative discussion in ethics", which conceives of the basis or bases of worthwhileness of our intentions and actions that affect our lives and other beings and things in many ways, either desirable or undesirable. Such norms are in the main, those of teleology or deontology, the first conceiving a number of "teleos" or purpose of our intended acts, which are touted as valuable higher ideals or ends of life, whereas the second one conceives of the value of intended acts as such or on their own or inherent values, which becomes the only ideal for our intended acts. Finally, in the applicative and practical part of ethics, apart from many theoretical jobs essentials to it, such as the discovery and justification of "models" of ethical application, we try to resolve a number of value-laden practical problems that people of different professions and occupations face in our societies. As offshoots, professional ethics and occupational ethics, environmental, biomedical, economic and business ethics, apart from specific theoretical tasks, undertakes resolution of value-crises unique to them. Of late, in ethics, we thought to revive old trends found in the Greek, Indian and many oriental ethics to discuss about the need and value of *being virtuous* and to find out what they are and which among them count most for inculcation or "value basing". This is unlike theoretical analysis, normative inquiries and application, 'being virtuous' by our own efforts or being helped by others is of great importance. This is what we call "virtue ethics". Many ethicists think that it is also important in ethics to discuss about the psychological factors influencing our actions, which is a discussion about the "psychological basis of ethics". Others think that analysing the empirical aspects of our moral behaviour and their impacts on social and ecological life are of some worth. In any case, ethics as we know it now, is extremely interesting, growing, thought provoking and useful. It has given philosophy an added dimension, that is, the free play of its ontological, epistemological, logical and linguistic tasks with regard to the issues of ethical values, and the access to enter into different non-philosophical disciplines for a value study (which is also opening its closed doors for the entry of disciplines alien to it). Ethics has absolutely no problem, therefore, to assume interdisciplinary tasks, and exactly in this sense, we shall find that it has great liking for the social, political and legal fields, though exclusively with regard to the issues pertaining to ethical value. However, it is extremely important to keep in mind the truth that the free use of "moral" for "ethical" does not amount to the same as what pertains to the moral dogmas, traditions, beliefs and so on because ethics is in reality "moral philosophy" and not "morality" or "moral science" or "social and moral trends or dogmas". The philosophical scrutiny (or critique) of morality apart from many things includes the scrutiny of the trendy social and moral beliefs, dogmas, traditions and so on. Hence, to think that ethics is nothing but what is given to us by a great society as a "value system" from time to time, is an unfounded idea because the idea itself may be a serious matter for philosophical inquiry or ethical criticism under the careful eyes of sound logic but not whims. As such, "social ethics" should be read as "aspects of ethical inquiries pertinent to social affairs" and not, "what societies give us as ethical value systems".

From this it should be fairly clear that we need to have a clear conception about what exactly do we mean by "social issues" or "social matters or affairs" about which there may be ethically relevant discussions. This is to deal with the "social ethics", which further enable us to find out what exactly do we expect to see in this field. It is interesting to note that analysing the meaning of "social", "ethics" and "social ethics" by way of deconstructing their tasks in the main, is a specific *metaethical enterprise* because it deals with the analysis of the expression or concept which is the focus of our study. Hence, it is always important to remember that an ethically relevant study called "social ethics" demands primarily a second order study of conceptual clarification than jumping straightway into normative and practical discussions regarding social matters. It is due to this that the present chapter and two others to follow concentrates most on knowing what exactly do we mean by social, political and legal ethics and what things are done under these fields. Equally true is that this chapter attempts at *justifying* systematically why ethically relevant inquiries about social matters make a strong case *in ethics*. Hence, we are at hand the discussion of "Nature and justification of Social Ethics".

Let us now analyse the meaning of "social" in "social ethics". Common sense calls us to realise that what relates to society is "social". Hence, what relates to human society and the numerous phenomena of its growth, developments, changes and convergences and divergences in opinions, faiths, beliefs, dogmas, economies, politics, administration, decisions, plans, and values are "social" phenomena. Yet, one might still inquire about "society" or "societies" when one refers to the "social" because we have just seen that the basic concept is "society", whereas "social" as a qualification reminds us simply of what is about society or what pertains to society. Naturally, therefore, we come to the concept "society". Philosophers approach this problem in two ways; one is to treat it as an *ontological problem*, which is to discover the ultimate objectively true reality that society is, that is, a concrete existence in space and time conceivable and perceivable by our empirical powers, whether by senses or intuition. In this sense, one is seen busy in arguing society as a "whole" that is conceivable at least in real terms because the "parts" of the whole, the individuals who constitute the whole, are perceivable entities, the real ones. That the individuals constitute a whole termed as "society" is not a verbal affair; it is real or concrete in essence, because the whole may be conceived intuitively or by means of simple reason. Nevertheless, other philosophers do not consider the problem as an ontological or even an empirical one (as we have seen that the ontological conception easily drags us to the question of knowledge of the objective reality); they treat it as a conceptual or a *linguistic problem*, the meaning of which is a matter of logical analysis. The meaning analysis may depend mainly on the way the concept is used, for instance, in the sociological, political and ethical parlance because the problem in consideration is verbal and not real or ontological, though any attempt at meaning analysis in terms of the reference of a "society" in no less ontological in nature. Thus, it may be a misconception to refer to something out there as society or to refer to something out there that constitutes it. We expect of an ethicist, who has learnt the basic lessons fairly well, not to indulge into defining "society" arbitrarily in concrete terms as a matter of well-founded ontological discovery. An ethicist should better take the course of analysis of the meaning of the concept in use, which is enormous in a broad sense but one might narrow down the scope to the specific use of the notion in ethical contexts, and then find out what relates to society or what is "social" and what is "social ethics". However, one must be careful to enlist how "society" is used variously or has been used commonly, that is, what are its usages or how social scientists stipulate its meaning for their convenience.

"Human values in society", "Human values and society", "Human values and a society" as well as all "Ethical values" instead of "Human values", make good cases for the analysis of the meaning of "society" (and thus "social") in a somewhat narrowly, that is, in the context of ethical use, which gives us an idea that even broadly speaking, "society" apart from having many uses, is used "abstractly" and "concretely". In an abstract way of using the notion as in the first two assertions, "society" does not refer to entities either particularised or distinguishable. Rather, it conveys the idea of the existence of beings called "humans" possessing certain dispositions or values which have some relation at least to "society" though the relation is not physical as among individual or individuals and animals. The first assertion thus conveys the meaning of "society" as an abstraction that becomes extremely vital to conceive once we speak of values unique to humans and thus most expectedly, actions unique to humans which refer to worthwhileness (or value) but not worthlessness (or disvalue). The said actions thus bear the specific dimension of being "social" and not out of it or not being political, economic, or religious and so on. The second assertion apart from the use of conjunction instead of preposition, is unique for its recognition of the distinction of the realms of "values" that humans possess and the realm that society as an abstraction is, though notwithstanding the distinguishable "realms", some relation of the said values in society and thus the social aspect of the worthwhile human actions and dispositions cannot be ruled out. The assertion thus tells us what the general relation between human dispositions and actions and the social dimension as an abstraction is.

Other assertions are different because there is a conception of "a society" bearing the sense of "particularity", distinction, and identification in physical or concrete terms or within space and time as "out there". It is exactly in this sense that we refer to "an Indian society" than "an American society". The sense of the Indian and the American societies "out there" is not identifiable as in many physical cases, though India and America as political entities or states have identifiable population, government and well defined free territory. Yet, these physical identifications do not constitute the sense of "a society". Taking a cue from above it may be said that particular societies are nothing but organisations or a system of settled forms of life or a system comprising patterned actions of individuals within a range of situations. In this sense, though "societies", Indian or American are non-identifiable existential out there, owing to the use of the abstraction called "society", there are nevertheless, identifiable existential involved in patterned ways of life (intentions, decisions, actions, reactions and so on), which constitute unique "systems" or "organisations" out there, each recognisable and distinguishable in terms of what they think and do in a range of situations. In this sense, "Human values" within a "society" are patterned values of individuals within a society, a system of worthwhileness so to say, easily identifiable and distinguishable in terms of what individuals think and do therein given a range of situations. It may well be that discrete human values are identifiable in a system; thus in a typical Indian society discrete human values are noticeable given a range of situations. It is due to this that the conception of what is worthwhile in the intentions and actions in the context of killing and consuming cows in India might vary greatly, and some conception of worth may be well in tune with another society, for instance, an American society. This does not allow us to say that the like conceptions of value or worth and the like actions or ways of life make a unique Indo-American island of value-conceptions. Rather, given a situation of say eating cows, there must be identifiable or patterned ways of thinking and acting in cases of "cow eaters" and "abstainers". Such groups do not mingle with other organisations having same value-conceptions because despite the similarity, they continue to be identifiable within a society for a cluster of values unique to that society, which in a range of situations bear a family resemblance so to say and therefore, "particular" or "concrete". In this sense, then "Human values *in a* society" gives us the sense of "a society" as an organisation having some identifiable patterns of values, norms, rules and roles for its members. There are thus paradigms of values (human) in a society, whether it is Indian or American or in a Zaroa society or a Kashmiri Brahmin society in India. Not exactly the same, but quite akin to it is to speak about "Human values *and a* society", in which despite the exclusivity of human values and a society, a reference to a system of values within a typical society is, clear enough. In one sense, the assertion does recognise more clearly the variety of human values in a typical society with the use of "and", which may be calling our rationality to note that "a society" need not be an organisation of uniform ways of life and values rather, there are conceivable sets of values of humans as members of the society. In any case, all four assertions tell us clearly that in the typical ethical parlance, with regard to society, whether in abstraction or concreteness, we speak of neither "non-human" or "inhuman" or "anti-human" values because "inhuman" and "anti-human" are disvalues but not values, and "non-human" values such as malleability and vaporization of some solids do not count in the ethical parlance. However, among many human values, we do speak of the value of valuing non-humans of great worth. Hence, in the ethical parlance, we speak of identifiable set of values pertaining to humans among which are "social" values, or values of humans in relation to an abstraction called "society" and values of humans in relation to members of a society that reflect a pattern for bearing resemblances. "Social" or "pertaining to society" thus amounts to "what pertains to an abstraction the meaning of which is clear in terms of complex relations among humans and other beings and things where humans act and are related", and "what pertains to an identifiable organisation of people bearing a family resemblance in terms of their roles, norms and ways of life". In both cases, we shall find that "ethical" or being ethical makes great sense, though given the discussion thus far one should not imagine that ethics discusses nothing else than "human values".

We will continue with the meaning analysis of "society" a little farther because both accounts dealt so far have half-truths when they are taken separately, but each of them is confusing if it is taken seriously. So what can be another reply? The other replies (not a reply) take us to different planes. They inquire that either "society" must be explained in terms of "individuals", in terms of a "collective", or as a "whole". This may not be the same as equating "society" and individuals or collective rather, *explaining the meaning* of the term in relation to other terms. This must be perfectly well if ontological tendencies are carefully avoided. There is no harm in allowing one to explain what "society" means in terms available to him or her that is understandable. The meaning analysis of "society" in the *individualistic* terms can be seen in the views expressed by Thomas Hobbes and Karl Popper. Without going for any synonymy between society and individuals, they say that though the term "society" is loaded with the conception of the "collective" because without collection of humans a society is unimaginable, the truth is that the collective is itself unimaginable bereft of "individuals". Hence, for Aquinas, the reductionist thesis allows us to say that "society" should be analysed for meaning in terms of "individuals", their relations, functions and so on. It is important to notice that Popper has not been eloquent in using the term "reducible" in this context because he prefers a better term, "analysed". For instance, Aquinas says that society is "A multitude of men are made of persons, when they are by one man, or one person represented… and unity cannot otherwise be understood in multitude"[1]. Moreover, Popper says, "Social phenomena, including collectives, should be analysed in terms of individuals and their activities and relativism"[2]. Though both opinions are "individualistic", the "unity" in Aquinas' position and "analysed" (in terms of activities and relation) touch on important aspects. The reductionist thesis in any case is not the one of linguistic synonymy rather bears the sense of reduction of "proposition about collectives" for their meaning to "proposition about individuals". Alternatively, the analysis of meaning of "propositions about collectives" should be *based on* or may be *reduced to* without any distortion in meaning to "propositions about individuals". Hence, analysis of meaning of "society" is reducible to analysis in terms of individuals but not the abstract "collective" or "whole". More important is to note that the individuals that constitute society are *not* discrete entities, aloof and unrelated; they are rather related in a "unity". This Platonic conception of "society" as "a unity" which demands ethically charged just actions (cf. *The Republic*, in the context of debate with Thrasymachus), is clearer in Popper's words when the unity is deconstructed for its concreteness in terms of actual *relations* individuals hold (and thus binds them) in words and deeds or intentions and actions that are amenable to the sustenance of "society" or for its existence. Hence, "society" is understood not just in terms of individuals, but how they are related through constant flux of intentions and actions, which is in Plato's term "just" or in our parlance, "ethically desirable" for the existence of the society. It may not be awkward to believe that the reductionist thesis (of meaning) has something to think in concrete terms because the thesis is individualistic; however, it is *synthetic* as well because ethicality of individuals leads them to the conception of society wherein there is unity among the discrete individuals. However, the individualistic analysis for meaning of "society" is not foolproof.

In his essay on "Society", A.I. Benn mentions about a critical analysis of the above said "individualistic" view by Maurice Mandelbaum. He says that though it may be largely true that "society" is an agglomeration of discrete individuals related by means of thoughts and actions, it is *not* necessarily true that all statements about thoughts and actions of individuals are equally true about the society. Without going into many details, we can see an apparent problem in the reduction of one statement into another for its meaning. The problem is that though the reduction does not necessarily amount to a synonymy or having same truth-value, it certainly tells us that statements about individuals would be both necessary and sufficient for the meaning analysis of statements about society, which is not the case because many statements about society or what are statements of "social facts" such as "modern banks are soft money lenders", might not be analysed properly for meaning by replacing "banking" and activities such as "money lending" exclusively in individual terms or in terms of what one or more individuals such as a bank manager do without any reference to the institutional activities, decisions, and so on. This may be true of many institutional and organisational decisions and actions, because a number of "social facts" are not properly understood for their meaning exclusively on what individuals think and do in social groups. The reductionist thesis thus has its problem in the main in downplaying the societal references in analysing the meaning of "societal facts" and "individual acts" as well. However, does this amount to say that the societal facts or statements about such facts are overwhelming in meaning analysis? Does it cover all individual references making is redundant? A view is that it does, which is the "holistic" view on this matter. Let us turn to the "holistic explanation" of "society".

The holistic explanation does not beg the conception of an abstract "totality" that transcends the concrete individuals. Rather, any statement about individuals refers to a statement about the totality or the society. Hence, meaning analysis of individual facts refers to facts of totality or sociality. Now, taking this thesis to an extreme, *holists* hold that individual facts *necessarily and sufficiently* refer to social facts and not the *vice versa* because going by the basic *organic theory* of relation between parts and whole, the whole is not only greater than and subsume the parts, what is true of the whole is true of the parts but not *vice versa*. Hence, parts or individuals of the whole or society do not make any logical ground for the derivation of truth of the whole, the other way round is true, nevertheless. In this organic theory of whole-part relation then, *only* social statements are needed may be true. This is largely the position of the Hegelians and of Plato (in his explanation of justice in the state and in the individuals). Scathing attacks are stored for such organic holism. Among other defects, holism is based on a misconceived individual-social relationship, the misconception stems from biological theory in which organs constituting organisms have a less value or that for their value depends on the organism. If this biological conception is dragged in case of society and individuals, it leads to the politically and sociologically repugnant theories of "totalitarianism" and "authoritarianism", both reminding us of the disvalue of a Nazi outfall of such thinking. The cursed legacy of the "social contractarians" (like Hobbes in *The Leviathan*) and the Platonic "Philosopher King" have been charged for relegating the so-called petty "organs" or "individuals" of society to non-entities because the whole or the totality rules supreme. This is why the Platonic King armed with a "contentless conception" of the Idea of the Good (cf. Karl Popper in *The Open Society and its Enemies*), becomes a Ruler by birth, thus crushing the individuals and with them the democratic spirit. Hence, if individual-talks beg social-talks and nothing else, we are encouraging the idea that the study of wholes or societies as wholes is possible forgetting the truths that nether social wholes are absolute entities nor are they theoretical constructs. Society as a whole can never be or rather should never be taken as theoretical construction, which does not progress or grow with the teeming individual activities and should be thus seen as absolute entities. The whole for its explanation then needs references to individual facts. This brings us closer to an understanding of "society" in terms of both social-talk and individual-talk. It may well be that both talks bring us closer to ethics-talk but we shall come to it after a while. For now, it is important to understand that "society" is an ever evolving whole in which discrete individuals despite their unique identities, goals, aspirations and so on come together in a milieu that is *functional* and not static. If this were true, societies are identifiable in having a way of life, which may be a combination of a specific ways of life despite a way of life of that society. Societies may be thus looked upon as embodiments of human functions identifiable for their uniqueness in a *holistic* and a *distributive* sense. It is true that the Indian society is identifiable *as a whole* as a *secular society* representing a unique way of life, whereas *on the whole* it is uniquely identifiable as a body of discrete faiths of discrete individuals and sects, each identifiable in a "distributive" sense as "having a faith" or "having faiths" or "having no faith" or "having no conception of faith". Hence, "society" is body of discrete ways of life "on the whole", whereas at the same time "as a whole" it may be identifiable for *its* own way of life. In both cases, the "way or ways of life" necessarily refers to a *lassiez faire community* and not a *status quo community*. This may be crucial in an understanding of the ethical as opposed to the unethical way or ways of life, and thus in understanding the ethical, unethical and anti-ethical society or societies. Equally true is that "society" may be conveniently seen as non-fortuitous or non-accidental agglomeration of humans, not to be seen as a "mere association" or "a herd". A society is not "a herd". It is a whole or a *community* not an association of individuals coming together and disassociating without a common and larger goal or a purpose or a vision without subjective whims. On the other hand, it should not be seen as an association, which is a body of individuals coming together to fulfil *their* specific goals, needs and aspirations. In this sense, speaking in a "distributive" sense, "society" is a body or a community "on the whole" having discrete individuals and their associations identifiable for having goals, needs and aspirations to fulfil, though "as a whole" identifiable as transcending the features of the "herd", becoming a community having wider, larger and deeper goals, to use other terms, having widening, heightening and profoundness of human intentions, decisions, functions and aspirations. Arguably, as against the "herd", "society" is the one that *should* have wider, larger and deeper and simply, *ethically desirable ways of life* than in its distributive sense of the "herd" when it is a body of ways of life much like a mixture of the ethical, non-ethical, unethical and anti-ethical. This may be a good basis to understand why "society" should be better seen as "having a culture" as a whole than having none of it though on the whole, it may be a transversality of cultures, the latter may be seen in smaller sects or in fortuitous units as well, even in case of an association of regular local train commuters who have become "much like a society of commuters". Alternatively, can we imagine a society of gangsters? The *use* of the term "society" freely as we wish does not justify the use itself because a goose club or group of gangsters or a herd of commuters do not make cases for calling them a "society" for the obvious reason of the above said "ethical-cultural identity"; and of course, the functional identity of society may not be taken as any function that goes on whether in terms of individuals, groups, sects, political bodies, even the state machinery. It should be identifiable as a *desirable constituency of functions*. A *system of values* may be most important aspect for calling a collective, a "society" than merely having a polity, economy, fixed boundary, demography and so on. The functional aspect of the collective may be crucial in realising "ethics-talk" with regard to "social-talk".

We may now concentrate more on the aspect that takes us gradually to "social ethics". By this time, we have analysed the meaning of "ethics" in terms of its tasks and the meanings of "society" in terms of deconstructing the basic features. It is proper to understand the nature of "social ethics" by putting the above analysis together. Things are not so simple because putting them together may take us nowhere. In fact, "social ethics" is *not* understandable if we put together what are the tasks of ethics and what society consists of. It may be nevertheless understandable when *performatives* in ethics relates to social matters and when social matters relate them to ethical performatives. However, in any case, *knowing* what "social matters" pertain to ethically relevant inquiries is most important in understanding what social ethics amounts to though many people doubt that any matter pertaining to society being factual rules out value related inquiries because they belong to different categories of inquiry. We thus have two points to clarify—one is "what matters pertain to society" which are relevant in "ethical scrutiny"? And, the other is "why matters pertaining to society" belonging to a unique category of inquiry make good case for yet another unique category of inquiry, that is in essence non-factual or rather, "value-related"? Answers to both these questions enable us to understand what is the *nature and scope* of "social ethics".

We have seen that socially relevant inquiries are those that relate them to the dynamics of well-defined, well-bounded and well-organised community of humans having patterns of or ways of life "on the whole", and thus identifiable cultures and value systems of the discrete individuals that constitute the whole, and a way of life "as a whole", and thus defined culture and value systems that is reflection of a unity in diversity. The impacts of the individual, group, organisational and institutional dynamics that despite some discreteness transcends each other and transverses as well making the society a body of organised humans which is nevertheless, neither purely self-goal-oriented nor fortuitous association nor passive, but awaits thorough understanding of the said dynamics of the individuals, groups, organisations and institutions. Hence, socially relevant discussions cover a wide range of discussions pertaining to individuals, families, classes, clans, groups, associations, organisations and most importantly the major and minor institutions. Social-talks are extremely wide ranging as we find now, they range from the micro to the macro levels of human existence, their lives, cultures, behaviours, customs, rites, rituals and so on. These talks mingle easily with the correlative political and economic talks because political and economic dynamics happen in a given society or societies in fleeting time. In few words, if we wish to be simple, in "social ethics", "what pertains to society or what is socially relevant" is "individual-cum-community dynamics". Socially relevant talks or inquiries are thus "talks of individual-cum-community dynamics". Talks or inquiries about individuals, their families, the institutions in which they are members or are influenced and guided by the groups they constitute come under socially relevant inquiries. The question we now face is whether the said "social inquiries" await "moral inquiries"? The question as we have seen before is latently sceptical if that means to ask: whether moral inquiries at all make any legitimate entry into the realm of social inquiries? Replies in the negative fails to *justify* "social ethics" and with it we fail to clarify its meaning. Hence, before taking on the case of meaning clarification of ethically relevant inquiries of the numerous social inquiries, we may take on to face the challenge that there is perhaps no "relevance" in such a meta-inquiry. I call it a "meta-inquiry" because the inquiry transcends the mainstream social inquiry as well as normative ethical inquiry. So let us find out why or for what *reasons* we can legitimately talk of an ethically relevant inquiry of socially relevant inquiries.

First, let us know why the sceptics should believe that ethical-value inquiries have nothing to do with social-factual inquiries or social scientific inquiries. Such questions are popular among those who make a sharp distinction between "is" and "ought" or "fact" and "value" on the one hand based mainly on the idea that social scientific matters are in essence different from matters of worth or value because scientific matters are "factual" that relates to the happenings of the world, whereas the latter pertains to what "should" or "ought" to be the case, or what is an "ideal". Hence, logically speaking, value derivations from facts, and factual derivations from value conceptions are ruled out. On the other hand, the sceptical questions are owing to the idea that being scientific or factual inquiries social inquiries are like positive scientific inquiries, *value-free* or *value-neutral*. Hence, the above derivation or a logical relation of the two has to be ruled out. In fact, any arbitrary relation that draws values from facts and the other way round must be fallacious, the much-touted fallacy being the "naturalistic fallacy". Nevertheless, the cause of disagreement is whether the said sciences are at all distinguishable for their subject matter on the fictitious ground of "value neutrality". It may well be our prejudice or illogical thinking that the positive sciences *per se* must be value free or value neutral, whereas social sciences must be of the same nature *qua* science. This would take us to believe that *per se* science are value free and should remain like that, and any attempt at deriving value from scientific fields should be strictly ruled out. We must be then staring at the face of nature of "science" itself for pertinent answer. But why should some people like Max Weber think that positive sciences, unlike social sciences is necessarily and sufficiently "value free", and the prodigal sons that the social sciences are, should be "value free" as well? The conception (or misconception!) comes from the idea that the positive scientific inquiries do *not* fall in the trap of subjective selections of matters of inquiry or what is the object of inquiry, and is thus in essence, "objective inquiry" preventing the entry of any element of "subjective" and "relative" considerations as in the selection of social scientific inquiries, which becomes *undesirably* "value-loaded". Nevertheless, *qua* science, social scientific inquiries should remain value free and for that, matter should refrain from relativism in selection of matters for inquiry. The sceptics thus emphasise that socially relevant inquiries are in essence value-loaded for (as Weber says), such inquiries are "culturally" grounded and thus deals strongly in human affairs, the person dealing them are drawn towards subjective selections causing the said corruption of the social science. It is a matter of concern that in the midst of such thinking, the positive sciences have been safely ruled out of value-content and value related inquiries. Can arbitrary conceptions of "science" itself as field of "objective" inquiry bereft positive sciences of value related inquiry or can it be not value-related as we say? The question that ultimately takes us closer to rebuttal of scepticism becomes all the more interesting when positive sciences are wiped out thoroughly for an ideal cleansing to make it a spic and span *non*-cultural or *trans*-cultural or even non-human affair, if the latter means nothing but an affair of mechanical *selection* of matter of inquiry and following an ideal objective *methodology*. Can all this not be read as an imaginary conflict between scientific methodology as subjective and as objective? It is really the case if to this we add the idea that subjective and objective is unrelated and non-relatable conceptions when it comes to methodology. I will now consider this problem briefly, for which two papers by Chhanda Gupta (1989) were of great use.

The proponents of the *causal* theory such as Carl Hempel and Karl Popper hold that the methodology of sciences (all of them) should be uniformly *objective* as against subjective because the subject of inquiry or the one that has to be explained (explanandum) in an explanation owes to certain *laws* which are assertive of uniform connections that ensues from repeated observation and not to the person who chooses to explain something in the way he thinks to be correct or which is based on no objectively valid law. Hence, scientific methodology in the *causal sense* must be objective because any explanation of facts depends invariably on the demonstration of a fixed set of laws as cause of the explanation. This idea of objectivity as against the subjectivity was somehow pressed on the sciences as necessary and sufficient though Hume had noted rightly that the "why" of an event (or what we call effect) happened in one way and not in another way is to show "how" an event is constantly conjoined to another event but not on how an event as a law stands as a cause. There is thus the "how" of an explanation that enables us to move away from the causal thesis of "objectivity" explained above.

Nevertheless, the casual theory argues that the "how" of an event should refer to the observation of constant conjunction between events or an invariable regularity among events, which is the "causal law" in a different name. If this were the case, those against the objective status of social inquiry as scientific inquiry charges that human dynamics in society cannot be explained adequately based on causal regularities or what is the observation of invariable regularity. Objectivity and explanatory adequacy must be crucial in the explanation of dynamics, such as the social dynamics.

Countering the causalist explanation of objectivity in sciences, many thinkers like Croce, Dilthey, Collingwood, Windelband and Dray said that actions of humans that build the social dynamics is certainly different from actions that are performed by the natural entities or the non-humans because the latter lacks in freedom of will. Such free actions of humans are thus not under the compulsion of causalistic laws rather for their explanation we need to reflect on the motives, intentions, will, determination and inner factors like these, which do not make much sense with regard to non-human dynamics. Though it will not be proper to assert that these inner factors are causes of human dynamicity, they are still not the same physical laws of causation that control natural dynamics. We thus have a "psychological" or "subjective" explanation to the human activities and thus to the social activities making them unique cases for subjective interrelation than the stark factual interpretation advocated in the natural sciences which are "objective" in the sense of contingent on observable causal explanation *vis-à-vis* non-observable inner explanation. This would amount to say that the non-naturalistic scientific explanation found in social scientific parlance in no case have conception of a law or laws, or cause and effect and thus no deductions from laws that constitute an explanation, which will be a dismayed account of science itself. However, the social scientists like Dray retorted that the rejection of "objectivism" is not call for an unscientific temper to scrap the conception of law in explanation, rather to scrap the idea that explanation necessarily and sufficiently begs observable law or laws. The debate of objectivity-subjectivity thus runs into a rough weather when absolutists' tendencies appear to hold that either sciences (all of them) are natural or else at least some sciences (barring the natural) are non-natural. However, both positions may be overstretched absolutism-scientism (the former) taking nothing but causal deductivism to be true thus ruling out the humanistic (the latter) or the non-causal thesis of interpretation of social dynamics as everything but a science. Equally true is that the 'quasi-scientific' status of the social scientific explanations cannot completely trash causality or the laws because the so-called psychic or the subjective factors in the social scientific explanations may be considered as causal in nature.

At this point of stiff absolutism that sees no end to the controversy, Donald Davidson in his work *Essays on Actions and Events* (1980) and in some of his papers holds the position of "a bland monism" or *Anomalous Monism* which rules out the stance of scientism that every other social explanation is causal in the sense of publicly observable phenomena touted in the natural sciences, and rules out the stance of humanism that every other social explanation is mental in the sense of non-observable; rather he tries to show that a bland monism justifies that the mental events are not anomalous or lawless, and are thus *real*, whereas the physical laws cannot be touted as the only real laws just because every other event can be shown to be under laws that are stark facts. Davidson argues that the mental events are "real" as far as such events are subclasses of *physical brain processes*, only these events are *described* in unique mental or psychological terms. Clearly, being the subclass of the physical events, the mental events are subsumed under physical laws; they are not anomalous or lawless. This is also the basis to understand the monism with regard to the explanation of the matter and mind. What Davidson asserts may be stated simply as a unification thesis reminding us of the "semantical monism" of Feigl and Karl Popper's "interactionism without tears". This is to assert that though social sciences might deal in subjective explanations or those pertaining to an agent's perception of things, which is largely inner or mental, it is not to be taken as lawless, rather subsumed under physical laws of brain activities, they are nevertheless, *described* in unique mental terms, which is why we call them "mental events". In this sense, mental world is a subclass of physical world, and there being *interaction* of the worlds of same class, there is neither dichotomy nor any mystery. However, it may be thought that in such interaction, freedom that is basic to human dynamics and basic to explain social dynamics, gives way to *determinism* of physical laws. Davidson saves the case by saying that explanations that are subjective or those calling subjects' mental realm as important should be nevertheless seen as "rational". Hence, rationalisation is a species of causal explanation that at the same time assures of freedom of agents.

Nevertheless, the critics of Davidson charge him at the points of "identifying" the physical and the mental (because what is mental is physical), thus presenting us with the odd physicalism or scientism. If the identity is not respected then psychologism or subjectivism will be the odd alternative to accept. Hence, the *blunt* monism of Davidson must be either physical or mental, but not what he strives at, "interaction without tears". We are then hardly at the brink of understanding why the "subjective" fixed to the social scientific inquiries be not detached essentially from the natural scientific inquiries called "objective" on the grounds stated earlier. However, as we stand now, it is of great importance to justify that the social inquiries are "scientific" without any fuss though its "scientific" nature does not guarantee only the odd naturalistic objectivism, rather the interaction of the "subjective" and the "objective". It may well be that such subjective-objective fabric of the school of inquiries lay in the fact that the psychologically grounded aspects in such inquiries refer to "good reasons" that agents have, which are banked mainly on "good or strong inductive evidences" that agents have by virtue of participating in the natural (including the social) milieu incessantly. These inductive evidences turn out to be *law like* generalisations observable publicly, thus granting the needed non-wishful, objective status. Hence, the subjective-objective combine owes much to the aspects or non-arbitrary good reasons in the social scientific talks. This line of defence of social-talks as scientific in the naturalistic as well as humanist sense is well noticed in the views of J.L. Mackie (1974) and portrayed nicely in the essay on this issue by Chhanda Gupta[3].

As we now stand, there is hardly any artificial dualism among the sciences: positive and social as far as the former is objective, whereas the latter is subjective, and that the former be called a science and the latter a pseudo-science. Thus far we know that social sciences embody a fine balance between the objective and the subjective methods in inquiry basic to it, and in no case can its subjective method be touted individual perception and predilection causing impregnable relativism preventing any objectivity in the inquiries. If the inquiries and talks of the social sciences bear the same scientific temper as bears the natural sciences, it should be little too much to say that the former deals in facts but corrupts it with value imputations whereas the latter deals in facts and remains aloof in value imputations. That factual inquiries of the sciences may be happily related to the value-based inquiries (and not mere value imputations) without any corruption of the field is the point to be taken up now. The way subjective-objective duel has led us to dismayed thinking, the fact value duel might do the same if we do not consider the issue whether fact and value are unrelated and unrelatable particularly when we are considering the cases of sciences, positive and social.

First, we must turn to the Weberian conception that though social scientific inquiries should be value-free it does not remain so for its obvious selection of subject matter, which calls for subjectivism. We have just seen that the subject matter of social sciences are not absolutely subjective and not objective if that means the inquiries conducted by agents in cultural contexts which nevertheless, considers objective facts basic to the law like generalisation established for the inquiries. Earnest Nagel argues in *The Structure of Sciences* (1961) that the "selection" of subject matter in social sciences like any other science is neither arbitrary nor accidental, it is well thought out. The point that some such "selections" are "value-laden" as in the case of social sciences but not in the case of the positive sciences is an unfounded idea because scientific inquiries are focused or guided in nature, they are in no case arbitrary or subjective, meaning thereby wishful inquiry of the inquirer. Such inquiries in the positive sciences being culture dependent have a deeper significance, which takes us to its aspect of value-loadedness. The positive scientists, for instance, focuses on or selects one hypothesis than other, they move with courage in the discovery of a truth that might conflict with those well established or those having a might of absoluteness, they would be catholic towards the quantum shifts in scientific findings whatever degree of iconoclastic zeal they may have. These are the few deeper "values" inherent in positive scientific inquiries. Hence, to call it value-free and the social scientific as value-laden is unfounded. Hence, Ernest Nagel thinks that in so far as the *stance* or the *method* of inquiries are concerned, both social and positive sciences are value-laden, but not so in the fact that is selected for inquiry by these sciences. With regard to the subject matter for inquiry, that is, its object, the positive sciences differ from the social sciences in the selection of value-neutral facts. This is much in tune with what Weber said before and thus not contrary to it. What Nagel refutes is that positive sciences are not value-neutral when we speak of its method and culture relatedness. It is interesting to note that armed with what Davidson has said, Gupta argues in her paper "Value and Social Science" that "the sharp division is not maintainable even with respect to the received view that facts are colourless in the sense of being devoid of value."[4]

Gupta argues that the idea of stark facts of scientific inquiries being value-neutral comes from Humean subjectivism in which any value assertion that is an assertion of evaluation of facts is nothing but discretion of speaker's *states of mind*. Hence, to call anything a virtue or a vice does not mean that the thing so-called has a virtue or a vice but is imputed with a value or a disvalue by the speaker. Hence, it is descriptive of what one merely thinks. However, Gardiner and Foot argue that in such cases of evaluation and evaluative assertion concerning facts, description of speaker's state of mind or feelings are not important bereft of the matter or the fact concerning which the description is. Hence, it is the "fact" that becomes crucial in the moral evaluation because certain facts unlike others call for such attention for their intrinsic value-loaded nature. Facts may not be thus wholly value-free or value-neutral. This must be true of the facts concerning human intentional activities. It may be due to this that the stark factual study of biology or physics may be value-loaded in terms of both method (which we have seen) and *subject matter*. The subject matter of the physical study of star wars or biological study of biological warfare may not be wholly value-neutral as a culture-dependent and intentional act. To say that physics or biology as such have no 'value-agenda' in defining its subject matter, it takes on mere facts as they are in nature, and unveil what they are and why are they like that, is to forget that though the agenda need not be artificially fixed, it is a perspective towards the subject matter as opposed to some other matters that are not like that. The study of the deadly anthrax virus or fission-fusion of atoms as they are, may be value-neutral, but the same is not the case with the perspective of the dynamics of anthrax virus loaded bombs or fission-fusion bombs in war-fields. Hence, to call "facts" devoid of value elements will be out of wits, they make good cases for value-inquiry when they appear in sciences, positive or social.

That facts are not value-free is taking us gradually to what we have left behind that is, the justification of an ethically relevant study of scientific facts, particularly social facts, which in turn takes us to justify "social ethics". However, we are still not completely out of the clarification of nature of what "socially relevant talks" are Interestingly, we are at the brink of understanding a socially relevant talk that also drags us to ethical talk which is the talk about the meaning of "society" and "social", and the nature of "social science" including meaning clarification of "science" as well as the meaning clarification of subjective and objective sciences. We are now dealing in whether such sciences can be value-laden. However, to suspend it for a while will be pragmatic, as we have to continue with the idea that the factual sciences are not value-neutral. Gupta goes along with Davidson to argue that those events or facts cannot be cleaved into an imaginary dichotomy wherein some facts are stark, whereas others are apparent. It is not that facts in them are value neutral, whereas apparent crust of fact-world is coloured with our value perceptions. To continue, the former belongs to positive sciences and the latter to the social sciences, thus ruling out any value ascriptions or any value agenda in the former case. For Davidson and Gupta "facts as such" is as empty a notion as "values inherent" in some facts. Some facts are neither intrinsically value-neutral nor are some of them intrinsically value-loaded. Facts are rather parts of "life-world", which in turn is a "cultural world", the anchor to all sciences natural or social. Gupta goes on: "The sciences view the same life-world and facts therein though in a different way. Human sciences view the same facts from a different perspective—that of needs, interest, passions, life-styles and ideologies"[5]. Hence, it will be completely out of way to urge for an ontological thesis that facts inherently belong to the natural sciences or to urge for the reality or objectivity of "value properties" as queer entities says, J.L. Mackie in *Ethics: Inventing Right and Wrong* (1977). However, Mackie argues to the "perspective thesis" saying that "value attitudes" towards facts and matters of natural sciences is perfectly well. This is then a good way to understand why study of stark facts can be value-laden and not value neutral. Well, this must be true of social sciences as well, if we shun the typical ontological conception that such sciences are merely culture dependent, relative, subjective or that they are subjectively value-laden. The truth may be that some social talks may be perceived in the *value perspective*, whereas in many other cases this may not be possible.

Though we are not in a position now to enlist which things should be put under socially relevant discussions that need ethical scrutiny, we are in a position to say that some discussions pertaining to the human and social life, which are matters under social sciences await ethical or value related perspective for a fresh set of study that is, social ethics. The moot point is "why human and social dynamics should be put under the ethical scanner?" We may say that a strong justification for the same is with us, that is, social dynamics raises some such issues that should be better resolved in the perspective of ethics. Hence, certain social issues need to be analysed in the perspective of ethical values or that both these things should be related for a fresh set of study. This is to say that some social issues raise questions of value not because the issues are by nature like that rather without taking note to the ethical or value questions, the issues may not be pertinently answered. Hence, these social issues need to be analysed from the perspectives of ethical desirability, good, just, right, duty, obligation and so on rather than focusing on the factual perspectives. In social ethics we thus have a unique way to look at social issues, which otherwise if left aside to social science, would never reveal these pertinent and pragmatic inquiries conducted *de novo*. However, to tell this will be a little unsatisfactory because social ethics as ethically relevant inquiry of social matters need more justifications—why should there be such inquiry at all?

What I get from this discussion is that the social dynamics cover the individual dynamics "as a whole" but never dilutes it because "on the whole" society of discrete humans are dynamic too, maintaining their freedom and unique features. Both the individual dynamics as "discrete phenomena" and the social dynamics as "collective phenomena" are thus related in a whole of what we have just seen, the "life-world", which is nevertheless, a "moral world" as well. This idea of "life-world" as "moral-world" is expressed differently by different people giving us the needed justification of why should there be moral scrutiny of social or collective life. Graham Keith, for instance, justifies nicely that the life of the collective calls for ethical care when it comes to the question of "practical rationality"[6]. For instance, discrete individuals constituting the collective needs to rationally choose his or her ends of life; they decide, intend and act likewise, which in turn partly affects the agent and other individuals, families, groups and society. The practical rationality of the individual may be seen as the *inner core* of the society, which awaits value-based scrutiny for the desirability, good, right, just, and so on. Hence, the practical rationality of the individuals in a society becomes a matter pertaining to the "core" of society, which in turn is deemed to have a "moral" way to *understand* such dynamics, and for that matter, comes in the purview of social ethics. Moving beyond the core, to the groups, sub-groups, large or small collective entities, the said group (not a herd) have their own rationality to decide, intend and act, which affects the group, its core (individuals) and the associated sub-groups, groups or other large or small collectives, again a matter to be *understood* in *ethical perspective*, thus giving space to social ethics. Graham thinks that more often than not the *external* dimension of the collective may not be seen as different from the *internal* dimension or the "core" of it when it comes to the moral perspective of understanding their dynamic rationality because moral evaluations of the groups or collectives may not be completely possible without the evaluation of individuals' moral evaluation. In this sense, the individual aspect in understanding value matters pertaining to society may be different from (or may be identical with) understanding value matters pertaining to society. This makes social ethics possible for sensible inquiry externally and internally, most intricately and in all complexity. However, complexities do not destroy the basic conception of ethical inquiry into what we call the collective as a whole; where individual identify their dynamic rationality with that of the society or the collective. It is exactly here that the ethical inquiry into "self orientedness" of the individuals and "other orientedness" as well as "social orientedness" comes to the fore. Social ethics is thus a meaningful inquiry when we delve into the aspects of individual good *vis-à-vis* social good, though that is in no case abstaining from personal good because we cannot forget the truth of rankings in common social condition. In the climate of ranking, individual interests, goods, hierarchies and benefits cannot be forgotten, nor they can be banished; the ethicality of the idea of contributing to the interest of the common should not be forgotten or banished because without these the lucky few do not "constitute a collective", and their rationality may be at stake for such inherent unethicality. This analysis makes a good case in social ethics. Naturally, the "free rider" problem in civil societies justify that there is at least one strong social issue that takes us to its ethical scrutiny.

This is how, the realm of social ethics unfolds and with it the justification of such study. Take the case of "free rider" a little farther. It becomes even more interesting from an ethical perspective to inquire whether the ethically cursed "free riding" is owing to its inherent egotism. It may not be so simplistic a case because none of our individual rationality demands a maximization of our own goods and benefits to be taken as a case of blunt egotism and thus unethical because in this case, says Graham, "rationality had been identified with individual's interests. It is not necessarily identified with self-interest... the free-rider problem does not depend for its substance on a definition of rationality in terms of egotism."[7] Hence, the dynamics of individual's rationality within the dynamics of the rationality of the collective (the whole) makes a good case in social ethics to know whether gain and loss through individual decisions and actions and through corporate decisions and actions are ethically desirable. The problem also takes us in social ethics to inquire whether it is at all ethically relevant to study how individuals and collectives behave. Alternatively, whether it is ethically relevant to inquire how *should* individuals and the collectives behave. It would further take us to ethically relevant inquiry whether the "ought" of the collective behaviour should take precedence over the "core" behaviours of individual as "supra" entities. Social ethics unfolds this way for its meaningfulness and subject matter. However, we now have on the one hand the ways in which social matters that includes "core" matters open for ethical intervention, that is, the trans-factual ethical inquiry though such intervention relates to factuality on the other hand because the field of social matters is amenable to value neutral analysis for a sound inquiry. However, what exactly is this "trans-factual ethical inquiry"? This is the final point in our project of justification. We shall wait for it until we clarify that social sciences as value-laden is not the same as the field of value-inquiry which ethics is, because in the former case, we are just referring to the *stance* we can take owing to the unique features of the factual issues which distinguishes them from those of factual issues that rules out taking any such stance. Whereas in the case of ethics, we are considering the *features or dimensions of the stance*, which may be taken, when the factual issues awaits a value-related stance. The ambiguity that arises in such conception may be dispelled by saying that the "value ladenness" of social sciences refers to the ethically relevant questions that the factual science raises or are capable of raising, which needs some care on the part of another field that is beyond (*transcends*) it, which is ethics for it has the necessary components of such inquiry with regard to relevant practical matters. We will come to these components later on.

For the time being, we will be involved in the justification of social ethics in terms of socially relevant matters amenable to or relevant to ethical scrutiny. (Moreover, we have said that with this, we know what social ethics amounts to or what some of the ethically relevant social issues are). We have just seen that value based inquiry into social matters hovers mainly around the intricate relations among individuals in society, and between individuals and society, as well as among individuals and societies, and individuals and the international community. To be precise, social ethics justifies itself as an interesting field of inquiry into patterns of relations in "core-whole" dynamics. When we keep this in mind we find different ways in which social issues await ethical perspective for a thorough analysis. We can enlist many of them and justify social talks as ethically relevant. However, let us be somewhat choosy in this regard and take a few examples. First, we must begin with the cases of marriage and family as basic social institutions and then take up the cases of population and racial relations. The family as the basic social institution objectifies the physical and psychological wants of man. It serves the social, biological and spiritual aspirations of humans. Family thus serves the purpose of the propagation of human race, brings common people of societies to interact closely, and gives them an active life, civility and culture. Family gives us love, sympathy, camaraderie, entertainment and compassion. Families are often in existence owing to the institution of marriage in society. An institution binds motivated male and female sexes to participate in a life of caring, sharing, and satisfying most of the above-mentioned needs said above. Seriously, even the hermit would not suggest to not having a family life and a married life. However, marriage is not an essential institution for having a family life because unmarried people too live in a family. An important way in which families have changed in the modern times in the developed and the developing countries is that they now have "nuclear families" consisting of husband, wife and children, and in the recent times families without biological children, that is, either having no children by choice or adopting children by choice. The concept of a family without marriage is not altogether alien now as live-in relations under a roof or even husband-wife relations without institutional marriage or unnamed cohabitation without institutional marriage is all in existence in our societies. It may be that cohabitation is sexually motivated but not necessarily linked to procreation. There may be consensus between grown up men and women to have sex but they are either secret or open in a covenant to not to have any children of their own or adopted. They may be moving in such a relation as easy as a dating relation, in which no institutional bondage allows them to settle under one roof for a long period. The changing nature of family and marriage in our societies have seen a family of gays and lesbians either demanding for or having obtained legal permission from the society to cohabit with specific form of consensual sex leading to have no biological child, though they may or may not adopt child or, may or may not go for artificial fertilization if one of them happen to be a woman or both are women. A family may be a unique one having gays as cohabiters though one may change sex, that is, cohabitation existence in society may be as bizarre as having partner having changed sex (at least one of them). Reports are there that people cohabit in a family of eunuchs or in a family consisting of a eunuch and sexually able partner. The institution of marriage is bizarre in the changes that it has undergone. Obviously, we had from early age's most informal marriages, and through the formal ones reached the more civil of them, the court-marriages, that is, the most legalised formal marriage. As we stand in most of the civil states now, such marriages have become imperative for all practical purposes. Reports are there that long term formal social marriages following racial customs have to register for remarriage so to say through the legal court-marriage. However, *courtship* is different from institutional form of marriage because in the former grown up people of opposite sex take time to mix closely, know each other before having a family life of either living-in type or any of the types stated earlier. No one sees any problem if such courtships allow gays and lesbians to participate if that is allowed by social/racial culture or by the law of the land.

Where do ethics come in here? Truly speaking at several points, but the most important point is that the constant dynamics among the population that has changed perception of marriage, a life after marriage, sexuality, cohabitation, procreation, having offspring and many other things related to family and marriage as basic social institutions awaits a fresh perspective through which these phenomena should be evaluated, that is, analysed, criticised and appreciated for worth or value. We have seen that the "another" perspective should be the one that is not the biological, sociological, legal perspectives rather the "moral or ethical" perspective, not because these questions are by nature inherently value-questions rather they are capable of raising unique questions for their moral worth and should not be left aside but analysed in that perspective. The question of cross-cultural marriages, for instance, should be seen from the angle of what is ethically worthwhile, that is, in what sense are questions pertaining to such social phenomena be seen from the angle of ethical good, right, just, desirable and so on. This is to say that these phenomena are not evaluated for their biological, social, political, economic, legal and pragmatic worth or value, but for their being morally good, bad, right, wrong and so on. This is to say that the evaluation of one form of marriage and family life from biological perspective or sociological perspective may not be necessary and sufficient ground for drawing the ethical conclusions. In this sense, though it may be worthless to evaluate such marriages on cultural grounds or on the grounds of social mores, yet, the same may be stiffly debated for moral worth irrespective of both the perspectives or the grounds available to us. This may be the case as biological worth and social worth are not the same as moral worth, or the one cannot be the necessary and sufficient basis of another. Moving far from biological worth, we might reason that cross-culture marriages are ethically worthwhile because they enhance *universal racial cohesion*. On the other hand, we may reason far from the sociological angle that such marriages are worthless because it is *intrinsically good* to care for our own racial good. In any case, we may not easily settle for an absolute answer in this regard, but we do have different perspectives to face these unique questions emerging from socially relevant discussions about basic social institutions. This is one way to understand what exactly we expect from a socio-ethical discourse and that social ethics is justified for making a good case of meaningful inquiry. In the following chapter, we will take up the value-laden questions regarding marriage and family in more details for a likely practical resolution because that is the major theme of this work. Here it is sufficient to mention that most important ethically charged questions in marriage and family are centred around the conceptions of human *freedom* in the selection of a life he or she should live; the way he or she should perceive sexuality, its value and satisfaction; the objectives of a married life and family life and their worth in society; the way opposite sex should be viewed and treated as "other" essential in society; the value if any of honesty, obligation, rights, duty, bequeathing, swearing, contract, faith, mutual trust, psychological and physical satisfaction in marriage and family. Most importantly perhaps are the problems concerning ethic of love and cooperation in marriage and family. Closely related to these are the ethical worth of social and legal interventions in marriage and the worth of divorce if any. Many hot social debates follow owing to the methods in getting a divorce and the role of authorities whether personal or impersonal in such matters. We cannot perhaps skip discussing the ethical worth of religious intervention in marriage, divorce and ways of leading a family life. The latter might face the wrath of racial and legal authorities, which is, however, a matter of ethical scrutiny. It is but natural that in the ethical scrutiny are grinded the ethical issues of racial obsessions, trends, traditions, and social mores.

With marriage and family, we move closer to wider questions pertaining to society, important among them are those of population and eugenics. Population cannot be cursed for inherent evil nature because we have just seen that procreation is natural to all living beings, big and small, humans inclusive. It is of great importance for that ecological balance there is a steady growth in human population though for that other beings and things cannot be ruined. However, the tragedy is that the envious human prowess to procreate round the clock and several biological, medical, social factors that have boosted the procreative genius with steady increment in birth rate with correlative increment in life span have steadily corroded the ecological balance. It has put a tremendous pressure on ecology and natural resources, the crunch in energy balance is visible and people now find the population boom as a curse for it is showing signs of eating up humanity with nature in a near future. This is not to say that pressure on land, water and other natural resources are uniform in the world owing to population boom because at many places it is still not grave owing to the lack in human existence or what is now fashionably called, 'human resource'. In this part of the Asiatic world, we are finding the heat a little too much, China and India the worst sufferers. Naturally, there must be some clamour to check or stop the menace, which invites many problems, social, political, religious, psychological, economic, and so on. Hence, the growth of population and equally the lack of it, and the call for control or its boost along with ensuring increment of human life expectancy, gives us a number of tough questions, no doubt factually grounded, having clear social significance, but they are distinctly value-loaded, that is, they raise questions of desirability, good, and so on. At this point we need to clarify whether social ethics amounts to deal with social issues in the ethical perspective meaning thereby nothing but the hackneyed study of what are desirable, good, and so on in the growth of human population and related issues. There is vagueness in presenting the case like this. We need to be clearer in explaining what perspectives truly constitute an ethical perspective. The issue has two aspects—one is that ethical perspective means being anchored to the *tasks of ethics* so that we can find out whether such task-performances make inroads in social issues like family, marriage, population, and so on. In that case, we have to find out in which ways metaethical, normative, virtue-based and practical ethical enterprises in ethics make ways to take on social issues because these issues invite such enterprises. Another aspect is that ethical perspective amounts to the clarification of *nature and dimensions* of those social issues, which are distinct from being starkly factual because they may be explained and resolved in non-natural or non-scientific ways or in the way of the substantive ethical. I have assured the readers at two places that the former ethical perspective will follow only after the latter is considered. We are now engaged in the latter perspective.

Let us continue with the population and eugenic issues in this perspective with a nice little passage that reflects what we intend to do: "During the past century philosophers have rarely dealt with crucial social issues. In the past decade, this attitude of being neglected has begun to change. Various philosophical views, especially in moral philosophy, have significance for population issues. Reasonable resolutions of most population issues require clear conceptions of the moral concerns involved. While philosophers are qualified to clarify the issues involved and the standards and principles relevant to their resolution."[8] Anyway, most of the value-loaded issues in population are issues concerning migration, death rate and birth rate and correlative to this are issues in eugenics, particularly those concerning state and other authoritative interventions either controlling the birth rate or enhancing birth rate. In any case, same interventions may be to enhance life expectancy defeating the death rate or in some bizarre cases to keep off from defeating the death rate or to participate in its increment, which is reported in the cases of killing girl child even to this date in many states in India. With this comes the value-laden issue of gender selection, infanticide and pre and post-natal neglect towards newborn babies and their mothers. Closely associated to these are the issues of partisan approach in health care distribution in rural and urban areas, particularly when it comes to the allocation of funds for extensive and intensive health care for poor mothers in expectancy or after birth of their babies. The issues of class-based population care *vis-à-vis* mass-based care make good cases for ethical intervention. The matter of state support towards care of the aged, which is again an important factor in seeing that the death rate of the population does not supersede or greatly increase than the birth rate in a country causing alarming situation for the demographic balance. In any case, it is believed that the care for mass health, to ensure the radical decrease in child death rate though a well controlled birth rate and to ensure the dignity of the aged masses to live a longer life free from threats of physical pangs, all become extremely important issues in ethical scrutiny. One might wonder how death rate can be a value issue in social ethics! The point is that "death rate method" can be an effective population controlling method, which is a much fine-tuned method than direct intervention to ensure that a chunk of the mass is assured of death than live longer. This is deliberation on the part of the health care planners to abstain from rigorous prevention of diseases, mostly if they are fatal. It may invite us to go slow in sanitation measures and to curtail medical treatment to the elderly if they are ill or terminally ill. These things bring to the fore the questions of desirability on the part of the planners and health care takers, the replies to which certainly do not end up in theoretical-practical jargons but to why certain steps are ethically justifiable over others, that is, what distinct ethical reasons do we have to justify that a going slow method is good and not bad. Most of the time these reasons are well noted in normative ethics as overreaching principles and secondary rules of morality. Nevertheless, there are always counter-views which provide reasons in favour of the negative method stated above because some of us think that futile efforts to prolong the miseries of a natural death of elderly corrodes the genuine and paying efforts to provide health care to the young, who have a long healthy life to live. This tension may be all the more acute when it is considered in not so well off countries. However, another view may be that death rate method is as useless as deadly wars, epidemics, diseases; in fact, nothing have really stopped a population crisis because birth rate is very high.

The crucial ethical issue in population, therefore, hovers around *birth rate*, that is, the methods that can affect the rate in a more or less acceptable humane or ethical way. Can there be a human face in controlling the birth rate? Can it have any ethical basis so to say? Well, it can have if the controlling method is not imposed but an authority is left to his or her free will. The ethical aspect of population control thus involves the questions of freedom. The couples are thus left free to have child or not to have one. Everything is thus left to the conscience of the grown-up people to evaluate the social and demographic situations and plan their families. Con-view of ethicality in birth control at freedom is quick to remark that this does not happen practically as the controlling measures are too slow to cope up with constant increment in birth rate. Ethically speaking well-off people who do not depend much on the grants of the welfare state find them free to have more children. In this context, some people come up with the ethically based conception of a method of coercive control in agreement, but what exactly is such "coercive" method is difficult to ascertain. Some fanatics even call for a more ethical project to educate the masses for a control of mind to control sex urges than controlling families as an *external* method. Why this method is too unpragmatic at the present scenario is not difficult to understand.

Ethical issues in population cover, as we have seen before, the question of *equality* in distribution. To this, we may add the issues of equality in targeting a group or a class or a section of society according to their apparent ruthlessness in or lackadaisical attitude towards population boom. In India, the problem gets worse with the introduction of religious taboos related to the control of population. Interestingly many countries may face this problem. In the midst of the ethical controversy with regard to freedom and equality, we face the problem of "rights", that is, the problem of curbing and/or intervening in the enjoyment of "right to procreate". On the other hand, the issue of "right to limit the population" perhaps for the maximization of the good of the aggregate, which becomes an important ethically charged agenda for the state authorities, is well debated. In fact, the problems of freedom, rights, and equality in the context of population control are closely related to the ethic of a quality of social and individual life *vis-à-vis* social and individual life evaluated for the quantity of benefits without associated conception of a good-life or life where well-being is more or less assured.

Ethically relevant issues in population centres around the duties, obligations and responsibilities we owe as humans towards others. The case becomes unique when we come to our duties and obligations towards the well-being of the underpowered, particularly the "migrating" masses, which may be a social phenomena around the globe owing to disparities in physical facilities, resources, employment, security and so on. This may be acute in cases of wars, famines, economic recessions and political unrests. India is one of the worst witnesses of ethical crises owing to migratory trends across its borders. It has seen the cases of trans-border migration and associated population pressure that puts the society in a terrific moral pressure as well. This was noticed during the Bangladesh War for liberation and during post-Bangladesh creation when some sort of a backlash of ethnic security, employment and so on was troubling us.

The trend of migration continues opening fresh pockets in the Northeast owing to the Maoist-Democrat power control in Nepal. The tremendous population pressure is causing havoc in a society bursting under population. Nevertheless, the point is whether we are ethically just in protesting the migrants or retort to send them back. Will it be unethical on our part, somewhat egoistic and inhuman, particularly when we look at our brethren who are ready in flocks to migrate to Europe, America, Australia and Canada a for their good? Do we not say that the developed and the developing countries have some obligations towards the world community? The case becomes more interesting when we consider the requests for political asylums. Do we not feel ethically responsible towards some people who are fighting for a cause, which we approve best for humanity? However, some of us argue that self-sacrifice is not living in an edifice of fools. It is foolish and unethical to allow our funds to crunch and resources to deplete for the good of others. Beggars should not be economic saviours. In any case, we get a distinct idea of what ethically charged population issues can constitute—they constitute meaningful discourses in social ethics.

Population raises ethical questions in other ways, that is, when we consider the cases of over-population, population explosion and optimization of population. In a civil welfare state, the conception of well-being of the population goes along with any of the three cases in principle, but how do we optimize welfare in the face of optimum population and population explosion? Such crises may be faced even in case of under population owing to serious lack in the contribution of human power in development. It may be argued that optimized population can ensure optimization of welfare of the population because optimum population is the most desirable characteristic of population in terms of its size or number in an area available for habitation. However, the optimum is a vision; it is not optimized but optimizable. Hence, there are needed changes in the population at the present epoch for gaining the optimum level. The point is how to determine which changes are ethically desirable in the optimization of population? If it is to encourage freedom in procreation for the optimum good, can that be ethically just? What if that turns out to be a quantum shift to population explosion? Hence, the counter ethical view may be that over-population is desirable state wherein you are able to work out programmes for an optimum level. However, that needs curbs though neither amounting to mass killing nor mass neglect for health care so that death rate is maximized. Contesting ethical arguments thus takes us to an interesting area in social ethics.

One of the most ethically challenged areas in eugenics is the "desirable *methods* in birth control". In a multi-religion, multi-lingual, multi-cultural, and multi-racial society, it is challenging because social habits of the masses just seem to be impossible to handle and the idea of control straightaway goes against the natural powers of humans. The question of methods tinged in ethical hue becomes even more interesting when we consider some way at least to stop a live birth by means of contraception, sterilization and abortion (which does not mind foetus being put to death). These drag us to questions ranging from playing against nature, god, human sentiments, physical abilities, sexual urges and killing a person (if foetus is a person). The simple ethical stance is that as moral agents no one enjoys the moral authority to deliberate and harm other agents by means of either killing or disparaging their natural powers and aspirations because "harnessing" is a way to corrode the social structure from within, it breaks social unity and causes irreparable harm to its existence. Most of the believers around the world argue that "contraceptive" measures in birth control goes against the "nature" of humans, who are creations of god, and therefore, it goes against the design and purpose of god, which is an act to be shunned for obvious harm done to humanity. However, one might retort that what is "natural" to the humans is to procreate though contraceptive measures are not forced on us, it is our will to impose on us when our "natural" urges need some limit or needs to be checked for our good, which is not against Divine Will or Divine Purpose. God perhaps would not love his creation to go berserk in destroying the balance in nature, to overpower His creations and then destroy them. Contraception invites other interesting ethical questions with regard to its "artificiality" and "naturalness", that is, whether chemical interventions such as in the form of contraceptive tablets may be called more or less natural interception in comparison to unnatural interceptions in intercourse by using condoms and copper-Ts. The moot issue becomes the "unnaturalness" in human intervention towards "intercourse" and not merely in procreation. Many religious bigots do not think that there is anything ethical in humans intervening in natural intercourse. We can smell the obvious counterpoints on ethical grounds that make this an interesting socio-ethical issue. A number of ethical questions are raised in cases of sterilization and abortion. Sterilization on its face value appears to be more humane than contraception in any form provided uninhibited "intercourse" becomes the cause of disagreement. However, it may be argued that the act is grossly unethical in mutilating the organs given to us by god or by nature, whatever it may be, and we have no moral authority to do so. Nevertheless, those arguing for its ethicality might argue that the so-called mutilation of organs is consensual and the act does a lot of personal and general good and thus ethical. Abortion on the other hand is a hotly debated ethical issue. I will not indulge into the detail because much has been said in this regard in *Biomedical Ethics* (vol. 3 of this Series). Briefly stated, this is value-laden social issue as far as abortion is deliberate act that becomes not a part of any arbitrary human decisions for the trauma, it is rather a well-planned *medical termination of pregnancy* at physically permissible state of a woman to control birth. There may be strong social, economic, biological and practical reasons for doing so, but in the midst of all the ethical ground is the overall good of the woman which is possible only after some "spacing", and that in consensual sex, other preventions did not work or were not taken seriously. Most of the theists and medical practitioners might agree to the overall good of woman and the pragmatics of spacing, but not to the act of abortion after conception at any stage due to the strong ethical reason that rather than overall good, it does a lot of evil to the woman by causing harms, biological and mental. Most importantly, the foetus is a "person" aborting which is not allowed in medical code of conduct because it amounts to killing unless the *defined cause* of abortion is not pro-woman, biologically and practically, that is, when there are serious maladies in the foetus. Anyway, in each of the cases of population and eugenics, my intention was neither to give factual details nor details of ethical positions. Here I was trying to justify that these factual issues in society ask for ethical scrutiny, and for that matter social ethics makes a good case for study in ethics. With this, we also have some idea about the *issues* are before us in what we call, "social ethics".

We have an idea that society being an intricate body of human relation, cooperation and unity in diversity depends much on the ways in which humans are respectful in the recognition of the value of the relation, cooperation and unity, which may be so crucial in understanding the basic moral knowledge of humans to be caring and sharing if at all they want their own well-being. Obviously, we do not want that our well-being is not assured but equally true is that we tend to forget that this cannot be or should not be done at the cost of the well-being of fellow citizens, who in our association constitutes this society. Hence, we must be extremely caring about a society in which optimization of well-being is at least in principle taken to be probable, and moral agents, institutions and organisations about whom we have been concerned thus far, function in tandem. Despite all care, if the moral care is neglected, we have been arguing that the individuals and the society are bereft of worth or value, and certainly no one prefers an uncivil and disvalued society full of worthless individuals. There are two strong cases of moral care shown by us in societies in our own times at least, the care for *human rights* and the care for *social justice*. This is not to say that care for "non-human rights" do not make a good case in society, particular when moral care envelopes this as well. Equally true is that economic, political and legal rights demand care, our moral care in particular. What we are justifying now is that social ethics as a meaningful ethical enterprise calls for some attention towards the problems in human rights and social justice because these problems may be approached differently by showing how they open up for ethical scrutiny, that is, the scrutiny of their desirability on ethical grounds. To start with, we are here concerned with "human rights" wherein "rights" should be understood as "claim rights" or "entitlements" or "what is due" to a person or persons in societies. Moreover, "rights" should be taken not only as natural or practical or economic or legal or moral in narrow sense; here, we are speaking of what we expect a person or persons *qua* person or persons should enjoy in civil societies or what we expect is due to them, the lack of which is amenable to "claims" by the deprived and *must* be met by others who owe to them whether voluntarily or coercively by an authoritative intervention. Though there is a distinct fervour of "legality" in interpreting rights as claims rights in civil societies which must be nevertheless, met with success, "human rights" are not merely "legal rights" because the former are rights that are due to civil citizens, which are not always met with success by the court of justice owing to formal legal interventions, they are met with success by other social and political institutions, agencies, organisations and so on or by the moral agent themselves or by an interventional forum. The moot point is "why call for rights need not go in vain or should be met with success?" This point may take us to the *ethic* of having rights, making a claim for it and meeting the claims for rights. If this be the wider sense of rights that humans should enjoy and should be ensured of, there is no point in thinking that such rights do not cover the

scapegoats, and if individual rights are forgotten for social rights, it ends up in some sort of totalitarian thesis that is unethical for being anti-liberal and against ordinary men in society. However, it may be argued that "general welfare" is a concept covering "individual welfare" and therefore, there is no apparent hitch between individual good and general good. Drawing some strength from it we may say that if human right is seen in the context of the "general welfare" of humans in an extremely broad way, there is perhaps no way to imagine why it may not be "natural" right of humans as well because no one would imagine in an alien land or wherever, humans should not enjoy the right to *their* well-being but with some caution that "their" welfare is guaranteed *institutionally*, though not keeping individually and collectively callous.

Justification of social ethics in terms of sensible ethical scrutiny of individual and social rights takes us closer to related conceptions of individual and social obligations and duties as well. Garvin thinks that it takes us to individual and social justice as well, to which we will turn shortly. For now, we are reminded of the realm of rights and ethical way to deal with those rights. The greatest ethical issue in this context is which rights as human rights should take precedence? Now, this is a problem of "just classification" of rights provided we abide by the basic idea that though individuals and groups deliberate on their rights, they come to be institutionally guaranteed or are assured at social level. There must be then a basis or some bases to evaluate the numerous rights we can imagine we should have as humans, which is however, a difficult task for any individual and a society because most of the time the classification and subsequent grading (for relative importance) are debates not for mere pragmatics but for moral value. If "general welfare" that includes the concept of justified "liberty of individuals" be the well accepted basis to classify which rights for humans are justified for value and precedence, social ethics still debates whether such and such rights are primary than others. The universal urge to recognise a realm of rights that is well graded and acceptable has been pressing on us, as we have been elevated to universal morality than remaining racial or local. Still, the urge to have such and such rights at the racial levels or what is more localised (in the sense of national being), which may conflict with the overreaching universal urge of morality. Hence, stiff moral disagreements cannot be ruled out when we come to classification and gradation of human rights "locally" and "universally". The moral conflict is obvious for our obsessions with local, social, political taboos and economic conditions.

Hence, grading human rights depends on many factors outside moral scrutiny of the matter, though each of these factors may be seen under the moral scanner, otherwise it will be very difficult for us to justify why or for what reasons should a totalitarian grading of human rights be not accepted over a communist or a democratic grading. On the other hand, why a capitalist grading should not be scanned for value *vis-à-vis* a socialist grading. Through the years therefore, throughout the world we have been debating about the "realm of human rights", that is, among the social, political, economic and many other conceivable and justifiable rights (universally speaking), which we should enjoy, and which should be pronounced keeping in view universal welfare of humans, and for what reasons. It is not by virtue of a magic spell or whims that the Universal Declaration of Rights has emerged, which is not a sacred text remaining unalterable after constant moral scrutiny. This must be true of all "local" declarations of Rights, which often becomes a part of the sacred constitution of the "locality". No one has perhaps stopped us from ethically scanning these declarations because we know that with time our moral wisdom tells us to change the classification and grading of rights. Our sacred constitutional Rights are amended just for that matter. This becomes an interesting area in social ethical inquiry. (Readers should now excuse me for not indulging any further in this Declaration of Rights because my purpose here is by far clear now. I would not take the charge to discuss why or why not should Right to Private Ownership take precedence over Public Ownership in business, or why or why not should armed rebellion be a right for us.)

Lucius Garvin succinctly puts that there is no social ethics without individual or personal ethics, and there is no personal ethics if social ethics is not conceived because there is no conception of individual good and well-being if individuals live all alone, and there is no social good or well-being if none of the individual members have attained their well-being. Similarly, rights, duties, justice are individual as well as public virtues. One important aspect of social ethics is to discuss about these social virtues, among which "justice" plays an important role. We have already seen that the concept of rights is closely related to those of duties, obligations and justice. If there is a claim right to wages out of the labour we invest, it is just for a competent party to distribute the wage in equitable manner in due proportions and in time. We know that just distribution of wealth or property is related to what is someone's duty or obligation and related to the right a party holds to have some wealth or property and another party who holds the right to distribute it equitably. Among the ethically relevant discussion of social issues therefore, the issue of justice is extremely important, but that is a sweeping remark because we can speak of social, economic, political and legal justice in the social context. However, in the social context, when we are concerned more about *procedural fairness* on the part of some responsible parties such as the executive and the legislature (the two organs of government), who seek fairness and equitability in the distribution of goods and benefits, social and political, we say that we are concerned with "social justice", covering thereby "personal justice". It appears that "social justice" is a very broad conception of "justice" in which the socio-political benefits of individuals and the community they constitute are fairly and equitably distributed by agencies responsible to do so, thus make us believe that social justice is no "justice done to oneself" or justice done to one's own family, groups and so on. It is justice done to all as far as practicable, though ideally probable. We tend to come nearer to such justice, which does not happen suddenly, or with a stroke of decision. Clearly, such justice conceives of "other than my own decisions and actions, fair towards me" though "I may be equally decisive and active in all fairness towards others". This is so because given our nature and position in societies, we tend to be best judge of ourselves, that is, best to judge our good, which often neglect those of others, which is detrimental to social good at large. Hence, we need competent persons and institutions to do *our* good, which is pathway to social justice. Obviously, individuals disagree on doing well, but they agree too, which is basic to social justice. In any way social justice is highly *relative* in so far as what is good for persons of a society and when is good done to them is variable. Such an evaluation of goal of good is thus context dependent. It is very difficult, therefore, to conceive of universal or international justice. In fact, differences in political ideals, social goals and moral perceptions, the conception of justice done to people differs. It differs in a society even with the fleeting time.

An important aspect of social ethics is that ethical scrutiny of social matters naturally drags us to the matter of justice done to all the sections of a society though "inequality" appears to be natural course when it comes to social distribution of material goods, educational opportunities and to lead a civil life enjoying benefits due to that life. Social justice is thus a basic issue to reflect on the ethicality of human conditions that has been created out of unjust decisions, actions and schemes of the responsible legislative and the executive. The point becomes ethically so relevant because society is looked upon as a personal and comprehensible entity that imposes necessary moral burden on its members to not only legitimately enjoy the benefits given to them but to act consciously and morally charged to rectify the wrongs that have permeated the masses and thus the society. Social justice, ethically speaking, is some sort of correlative measure on the part of the members of the society to see whether wanton wrong doings have been taken care of. To take care of the legislative inaction, malfunction and wrongness that cause injustice in society, we need to go for legal justice because such injustice cannot be corrected without an institutional intervention. Truly, the institutions being parts of social super-structure, their interventions should be treated indirectly at least as social intervention, but not in an unorganised, uncivil and unmethodical manner. Hence, in social ethics, we discuss the ethical aspects of nature, purpose and limits of legal justice in the context of social justice, taking it to be a truism that both are neither mutually exclusive nor necessarily correlative. In the words of Wojciech Sadurski, "they (social and legal justice) apply to different phases of the social process. Social justice applies to work done by a legislator, legal justice is work done by a judge (or any person acting authoritatively in applying rules)"[12]. What is of great theoretical interest having far reaching practical implication is whether the legislative and the judicial grounds (or rules) for justice are different because social and legal justice are in fact different forms of justice. Well, the debate drags us further to the deeper *ethical* issue whether it is desirable or *ethically just* (on ethical grounds available to us) to imagine that what law enacts in society as just will be good enough to settle any issue of social injustice. Alternatively, other way round, is it ethically just to say that what the legislature enacts in society as just will be good enough to settle issues of social justice? The problems are really about the ethical validity of the assured unilateral just acts of the "judiciary" *vis-à-vis* those of the "legislature". The point is who *constitutes* judicial laws in the society for justice? If the institution or the authority is a sovereign social authority, not a person or group or association, it represents largely the ethical approval of the masses through moral churnings and practical repercussions, the focus of which is to maximise social good or social well-being. In this sense, though laws are constituted by the people, for the people that aims at well-being through broad spectrum justice to the people, the judiciary as an organ of the government protects the law, they are the trustees or custodian to these sovereign laws (because they are just and good). Hence, the function of the judiciary that does "legal justice" though relies heavily on the just laws that have been constituted for social good and thus on what *bases of justice* legislators provide them, they try to *protect* laws in the real life hard case for ensuring social justice depending on many things that are beyond what the legislators provide. They rely on facts, evidences, justifications instances and many other things. This way it is ethically just that the judiciary acts custodian of laws for social justice being free from the dictates of the legislators though not overlooking the spirit of the law enacted and facts available. In another way, it is ethically just that the legislature constitutes law to ensure social justice being free from intervention of the judiciary though not overlooking the aspects of legality and pragmatics of the law when enforced. In yet another way, it is ethically just that the executive enforces what the legislature and the judiciary demands for ensuring social justice. The moot point is that for all the three organs of the government, "social justice" is vital and such justice is to maximise social benefits or goods in quantitative and qualitative sense. It is important, therefore, to note that though *functions* of legislature, executive and judiciary are mutually exclusive, non-interfering and unique, they are nevertheless, in close relation, act in unison because they guarantee social justice only in doing things that way and they keep in view that in doing so they have strong ethical grounds available to them. It may well be that all of these organs of social governance do not agree on all issues in practice. But if they do not lose sight of social, distributive, legal and political justice as what is ethically jut as well because they are conducive to the maximisation of social well-being, they realise that though differently they "function" and independently they "decide and act", they are in unison. This idea of acting in unison than conflict must be ethical itself.

However, in social ethics, interesting ethical questions about the above-mentioned simplistic view of justice (social and legal) are further put to deeper ethical inquiry. The central point of the debate is whether any law that assumes to do social justice should be really taken *ethical as such* because in any case, non-arbitrarily framed laws are for social good, constituted by the people, for the people. If it were true, "All laws are intrinsically ethical or just". In the "simplistic" opinion, "all laws are intrinsically moral and not immoral or unjust" and for that matter it is ethical on the part of the legislature to see that the laws are framed for social good and the judiciary sees that the laws are put to practice as and when necessary for social good. Hence, the "unison" opinion has nothing to offer in terms of the possibilities of either the framed laws are unjust or that the laws are just though legal justice is stupefied in individual cases. In any case, we have to conceive of non-sacred laws, those that fail from within for many reasons and thus cannot be intrinsically just in all cases, and we need to conceive of non-sacred legal justice that fails owing to many reasons in the individual cases and thus cannot be ethical as such. In the view of Lon L. Fuller[13] a truly intrinsically ethical law need not be failure in any of the two ways because laws are, much like the "sacred optimum", intrinsically ethical, it does not fail in any case. This must be right in favour of the *logical possibility* of laws assuming to do justice, but fails to do so or are *formally* so constituted that they fail to be cogently ethical, foolproof ethical, so to say, and yet are "law". Such laws are "ineffective" and largely unethical, when evaluated for value from a perspective other than the *positivistic perspective* seen above. Hence, "having a law" does not necessarily and sufficiently beg to "have a law that never fails to do justice substantially and individually". "Having a law" does not imply "having an intrinsically ethical law", though it is expected of a law that it is *judged for its ethical value* on the given *teleos* of social well-being. This appears to disparage the *deontic* view that among many things of intrinsic value, we must conceive of "law", but tragically, all *constituted laws* are on ground reality not intrinsically good ideally, we have been merely expecting laws to be universally intrinsically good. This may be refuted by a *deontic* argument that though laws constituted by *us* are contingent on *our* wisdom and severely dependent on *teleos* of the law, if they were not intrinsically good, we would have not bothered for any law that is in principle ideal or unfailing. Laws being bereft of inherent value are thus not deemed to have any purpose (*teleos*) whatever. Our urge "to have laws" in society shows that among other good things, laws are good even if they failed in some cases or they did not. Nevertheless, even in that case, "to have laws" is not to have "just laws" always. Having just laws always is contingent on so many things that do not depend on abstract laws but on concrete factors. It may well be that our wisdom takes us to the "conception of law" that is just intrinsically and the conception of "a law" or "laws" which are judged for ethical value teleologically. However, to forget the truth that legal justice can be valued for ethical worth, on deontic and teleological grounds is to forget that such justice often conflict with social justice. Moreover, in many cases of social justice, particularly when we come to justice done to individuals in society, the conflict is too sharp, unredeemable or rather not to be redeemed at all because such "injustice" on the part of the legal system is demanded for "substantive social justice". Sadurski writes, "Impartial and strict implementation of legal rules may lead to injustice in individual cases, not the magnitude and diversity of social situations cannot be grasped by legal rules in such a way that their application will always lead to socially just solutions."[14] Hence, "Avoiding injustice requires sometimes departure from rigid rules: to prevent a situation where social justice demands legal injustice, various legal systems "open themselves" towards moral considerations and include direct appeals to moral judgements into the legitimate operation of the application of legal rules."[15] Such a view of social and legal justice amounts to conflict with the thesis advocated by Ronald Dworkin,[16] because Dworkin seems to suggest that the social justice is an *integral aspect* of judicial justice, and as such cannot be the basis for the value-judgement of legal rules, and that Dworkin seems to argue that social justice is not an evocation of the moral perception of a person because for a judge in the court of justice, social justice is within the legal system, and for that matter does not beg any moral basis beyond it. It is important in social ethics to evalsuate this con-view about moral basis to social and legal justice. On the simplistic unison thesis, the thesis of Fuller and Sadurski, it may be extremely difficult to agree with what Dworkin says because it may be argued that both social and legal justice *involves* moral perceptions of persons in society. In other words, the talks of justice, social and legal, involve *cases* of social and legal justice, "justice" conveys the sense of "procedure"; whereas and in the case of moral justice, it conveys the sense of "desirable" or "good"; but nevertheless, "procedural justice" does involve questions of "desirability" because "procedural justice" is nothing but mere evocation of persons involved in such justice, those are well thought out and planned methods in giving certain things due to us in society, which asks for evaluation of *worth* on basis that is not limited to legality and legislation. In fact, the legal and the legislative decisions, principles, rules and actions are never beyond moral scrutiny, for which interesting moral theses such as the teleological and the deontological have already surfaced.

Social ethics as a meaningful ethical enterprise takes us to consider the *methodological* issues in distributive, social, political and legal justice. The way in which different forms of justice opens for ethical inquiry is whether such forms of justice follows a "method" that is "ethically just". If the forms of justice have a definite aim for them, that is, if procedural justice in many conceivable ways aims at doing what is "just" in the society, it must not be ambiguous. The ways in which justice is done cannot simply state that all of them aim at "doing what is just" because we need to clarify what it is to "do what is just". It may be said that all forms of justice aims at ensuring the due *benefits to its optimum* to the public that constitutes the society or in ensuring the rightful claims or goods to the optimum. If this were true, all forms of justice does not merely aim at doing what is just, they aim at maximisation of rightful benefits to the public. It would be a little awkward to say that justice in any form must not be linked to an explanation of benefits because losses cannot count as just for humans. However, it may be said that "benefit maximisation" is a *physical* concept, involving mostly the criterion of "quantitative" benefits and associated calculus. This may be true in case of distributive or economic justice largely. Though social and political justice cannot be said completely beyond the physical-quantitative conception of justice, for which definite "scientific methods" are deemed to be most suited, which are still as elusive as the ideal of justice in any form. No amount of Noble prizes until date to economists has given us at this point a method of physical-quantitative economic justice. The sociologists and these political scientists are in a similar situation, but all of them are after the ideal. However, not all among us would agree to the idea that "benefit maximisation" is purely physical-quantitative because more often than not justice is taken as distributive justice in which fairness and equality rules supreme, but this is only one aspect of justice, not the whole of it. In the recent times, there have been important ethical discussions among economists about the validity of measuring benefits on purely quantitative terms. Many of them have argued that holistic justice apart, even economic justice is done when "well-being of individuals in society, which is a way to look at what are benefits", is attained. The "well being" or a "happiness" index that does not merely count on physical-quantitative benefits has become a point of discussion though what amounts to such a besnefit is more or less ambiguous to many of us. Some western economists are at awe when they find that people in abject poverty in India as so "happy", some of them are not happy owing to physical conditions, resources, money, and wealth and so on but many of them are happy on queer "qualitative" grounds such as the metaphysical, spiritual and so on. Is it important to inquire into such qualitative forms of benefits? If at all they are important, how do we maximise them? On the other hand, are these benefits non-optimal, are they intrinsically valuable or optimally good *per se*? In social ethics it is important to inquire whether such intrinsically valuable benefits for humans are really so or do they not make any sense? No doubt there has been quantum shifts in the utilitarian conception of physical-quantitative conception of benefit maximisation as justice done in the society right from Hume, through Bentham to Mill. J.S. Mill does not only recognise the value of quantitative benefit maximisation as just action, he nevertheless, does not lose sight of quality of benefits thus maximised. This must be particularly inspiring for the ethico-spiritual thinkers of the east but not for the mainstream ethicists of the West or even for the mainstream economists of East and West, particularly those of the Freidman *gharānā*. Anyway, despite ethical imbroglio over which benefits *should* be maximised and/or encourage and why, the point of *methodology* remains stiff, and its stiffness is owing to the ethical imbroglio over *why should* such and such methodology take precedence over others.

It is very difficult to keep aloof from the Indian ethical conception of overall justice done in the society that considers seriously the quantitative-qualitative aspects of benefit maximisation in society. It speaks of the ethical view of justice done at the "social level" and at the "personal level" through quantitative and qualitative benefits, the latter taking us to the ethico-spiritual ideal realisation in life, which gives some solace to ethicists who do not equate any form of justice to the purely physical. However, the method of doing all these things is not so pronounced at one place. Some important thinkers who have contributed immensely with regard to the models of procedural justice in society that is ethically deemed to be stronger than physicalism and pure metaphysicalism, to combine the spirits of physicalism, Aristotelian eudemonism, contractarianism of Locke and Kantian deontology. Most of these models do not blindly work on justice as maximisation on utilitarian benefits, they move "beyond" utilitarian benefits or goods in society that combines the spirit of the above, though it does not in principle prevent our welfarist to combine some points of metaphysicalism that are awestruck as to why hungry people in India should still smile. Thinkers like John Rawls, Robert Nozick, Amartya Sen and many others have contributed in this field. We need not enter into the details of these models here, what is of our interest is that among other socially relevant issues that open for ethical critique, justice: social, economic, legal and so on, make good cases for their nature analysis, justification and methodology. In short, we can say that most of the models of justice invites us for the ethical critique of the conceptions of procedural fairness and equality in society by the government and its several institutions and organisations particularly in view of the rights and aspirations of individuals and the positions they enjoy by virtue of the advantages they have in life. This also brings in the ethical scrutiny of the advantages, aspirations, and rights and obligations the distributors of advantages enjoy in society. Another point is to rank the benefits of the masses for maximisation at the priority basis; this is also linked with the idea of quantity and quality of goods to be distributed on priority basis.

Thus far, we have been dealing with the nature clarification and justification of social ethics. The justification is possible in terms of unfolding the ways in which social issues are not to be analysed and resolved on scientific basis rather on ethical basis. This is to say that we were trying to justify social ethics as a sensible enterprise in ethics so far as hard social matters can be and, should be analysed, and resolved from the ethical perspective, that is, from the perspectives of the desirability, good, right, rights, just, duty, obligation and so on. Now we have the final task for us, that is, the justification of social ethics by showing how "ethical task-performance" shows relevance in social matters. To be clearer, we need to show how metaethical, normative, virtue based and practical tasks in ethics make perfect sense in dealing with issues that belong to social phenomena. This is nothing peculiar as we have already justified why factual issues might invite value related inquiries. On the other hand, it will be not difficult for us to show why despite tasks of ethics belong to a field that is in essence non-scientific should nevertheless, take up issues emerging in society, which is otherwise believed to be matters *related to* scientific analysis. Nothing prevents non-scientific inquiry being related to other fields which are scientific and analyse a few interesting things for us. The simple reason is that what ethics performs cannot by valid argument be limited to ethics itself and nothing else. If we take this line of thinking we will be much like old-fashioned analysts thinking that ethics is only logical analysis of language, and should be thus "limited" to the field of "language of ethics" and nothing else. We have seen that such limitation puts ethics in jeopardy, as we have to abandon normative, virtue based and practical discussions in ethics, which limits the linguistic analytic project of ethics as metaethics. Hence, we will abide by the conception of ethics as performing the four important tasks mentioned above and justify that such performatives make perfect sense when they take up social issues, thus justifying social ethics. In doing so, I will be precise in considering some examples from metaethical, normative, virtue based and practical ethical performances that make valid inroads in social matters. Let us start with the metaethical task and its relation to social matters. Skipping what metaethics undertakes, we can straightaway show that an important feature of metaethics is systematic justification of issues that are said to be ethically relevant. If this were true then what we were doing in this chapter and what we propose to do in other chapters is metaethical if we fail to justify that social ethics is a meaningful ethical enterprise, there is no point in writing pages about social ethics. If we fail to justify why social issues are value-laden and how they should be resolved, and if we fail to justify why ethical tasks apply themselves in social issues, there is no social ethics. In this sense, the entire chapter dealing in nature clarification and justification of social ethics is metaethical in nature. It is metaethical in nature because the discussion of justification is grounded on the "logic" that we have on behalf of an ethically relevant discussion about social matters. In this sense, demonstrating the "logical" basis of the entry of normative ethics, virtue ethics and practical ethics in social matters are metaethical in nature. Deeper as we move into each of these tasks of ethics, we have to find out the "reasons" behind considering an ethical norm or ethical norms that apply themselves to social matters. The same reasons are needed when we consider a virtue or virtues needed or not needed for moral agents who are social individuals and participate in a dynamic social life of thinking, deciding, intending and acting voluntarily. Equally true is that "reasons" are required for the application of either standard norms of ethics or not applying them at all to *resolve* social matters that raise questions of value. It may be said that as we go on discussing the normative and other functions of ethics and their application in social issues, in every stage we need to critically evaluated the "reasons" we have in favour of such application. Moreover, we know that an important aspect of social ethics is to analyse the nature of the crucial *concepts* such as "rights", "duties", "obligations", "social morality", "individual morality", "individual and social freedom" and many more because the concepts are the basic blocks in social ethical discussions. The analysis of concepts and the language of social ethics is metaethical in nature because here we do not deal in the nitty-gritty of social rights, for instance, rather we deal in what "social rights" amounts to when it is used in a body of language unique to social ethical discussion. Equally important is to note that the metaethical theory of *prescriptivism* advocated by R.M. Hare stresses on the role and importance of "reason" in arguments that are morally oriented though the moot issue may be factual. For instance, we may be arguing at length about the ethical validity of abortion or sex-workers' social rights but in both cases, the reasons we give, their strengths and weakness count most in the climate of agreements and disagreements among the public. Hence, the body of ethically charged language that concerns about factual social affairs takes us to the consideration of meaning and truth, and to the consideration of reason that interplays in the language of arguments. In his work, *Freedom and Reason* (1963) Hare writes, "Consider the questions... of whether it is wrong for a pretty girl to earn good money by undressing herself as a "strip club" for the pleasure of middle-aged businessmen... those who call such exhibition immoral do not do so because of their effect on other people's interests... one *reason* why it is wrong to confine the term 'moral question' by terminological fiat of questions concerning the effect of our actions upon other people's interests, is that such a restriction would truncate moral philosophy by preventing it saying anything about ideals."[17]

Let us now come to the ethical task of normative establishments for ethical evaluation of intended acts of moral agents, institutions and organisation, which is under what we call "normative" ethics. The standard first principles or ideal norms for moral evaluation available to us in ethics are teleological and deontological norms. Normative ethics in dealing with the clarification of nature of those norms and their usefulness, more often than not considers what bearings if any of these normative theses have on the value-laden social issues. In fact, a number of social issues become ethically problematic for us because those issues concern in the main the moral anomalies of the free moral agents in terms of what they think, decide, intend and do in real life influencing a number of people, other beings and things, and the community at large in *undesirable* ways. Hence, moral evaluation of such decisions and actions of the individual and the corporate on grounds available to us becomes important in ethics. However, most of the time our norms by themselves fail to justify why certain actions are of such and such worth and not unworthy because absolutism and rigidity of the monistic theories tend to be arrogant as evaluative first principles. The most talked about evaluative principle in the modern times is utilitarianism advocated by J.S. Mill and by a number of his modern day followers. Equally important is the teleological theories of egotism and eudemonism both having modern proponents in good numbers. We can refer to our discussion of justice to find that these teleological theories have deep bearings on the subject or issue. In any procedural justice, say for instance, distributive justice or social justice, the evaluation of their worth or value rely heavily on whether such justice is so-called because they tend to "maximise pleasures for maximum people" (utility) or tend to "maximise pleasures of the moral agent concerned" or "maximise welfare in society, that is, something beyond the feelings of pleasure and happiness". Obviously, these standards fight each other fiercely for fittingness to real life value-laden social cases, analysing them and showing us a way to resolution. For Stuart Hampshire for instance, utilitarian standard tends to justify a rogue political justice, which is a contradiction in terms because there is hardly any parity between "rogueness" and "justice". The suggestion is that utility principle may do political justice by mass massacre, destructive wars and evils like these. However, the point may be thoroughly refuted. Similar attacks on egotism are noticed because it champions rogue distributive justice, the justice of the monkey sharing a piece of cake as if. Later on ethicists like Bernard Williams and Amartya Sen, much like Hampshire, preferred to revive Aristotelian welfarism in their own ways in showing how the thesis does not support rogue distributive justice.

Deontologists such as Kant, Ross and to some extent Rawls do not agree that the monistic teleological theories are adequate evaluative bases because they fail to realise that the moral value of human decisions and actions (as well as the value of the cooperative decisions and actions), is *not* contingent on the "purpose" they serve because in case they fail to serve the desired goal, actions themselves are devoid of value. Hence, we will refrain from doing *desirable* actions if they do not serve a *desired* goal, though the "desired" may not be "desirable". In this sense, we will abstain from benevolence in society or do social, political and legal justice if they do not give us either personal pleasure or pleasure for the masses or general welfare, though no one contests the idea that if we do any kind of justice to individuals and masses, we should have the due pleasure, welfare and so on. The idea is that certain decisions and actions at the individual and at the cooperative levels are such that *in themselves* they are of worth or value, and should be done without any conception of desired goals and the calculus of consequences of actions. Hence, social justice, legal justice and distributive justice carry *intrinsic* value, they are good themselves and thus done as a moral necessity or an imperative, whether they please us or help in our well-being and any such thing. Such imperative justice demands that *qua* humans, we treat humanity of intrinsic worth, we do not treat them as means to our ends, and we treat them as our own and thus act as members of a kingdom of ends (not means). Hence, to evaluate moral worth of our decisions and actions, social ethics should take recourse to deontological normative principle. However, there is an epistemological problem of *knowing* that such and such actions are of intrinsic worth and performed for that reason, depends on our *intuitive* dispositions, the rational intuition so to say. Deontology thus begs intuitive thesis of knowledge of intrinsic value, but side steps problems of consequential calculus of the teleologists. The cultural relativists and the champions of non-intuitive empiricism are against such conception of evaluative standard in ethics because cultural differences show us that there are wide ranging disagreements about the intrinsic value of human decisions and actions. Those against intuitionism argues that there is hardly any universalisable secondary or derivative principle of morality which our touted uniform intuition draws for the benefits of choosing and doing actions that are binding on us as necessity or duty. However, thinkers like W.V. Quine and John Finnis are of the opinion that there are common value-intuitions in the human cultures despite wide variations. Anyway, social ethics assumes a justified status when we reflect on this absorbing debate about opting for evaluative basis of our well-intended social actions.

When we consider the virtue based ethical thinking, we are offered with two stiff options: either the first or the secondary principles of morality serve as the bases to morality or they should be replaced by the cultivation of the needed virtues and values in us. Virtue-based thinking chooses the second option because as individuals in society it is primary on our part to be virtuous than followers of principles in real life situations. No one really values actions as good or bad on teleological and deontic bases and does them in real life. It is another matter of theoretical interest whether an evaluation for moral worth begs a moral standard, but following a standard and deconstructing standards in act of evaluation are different things. Virtue ethics since the time of Aristotle through G.E.M. Anscombe has urged social beings "to be virtuous" than followers of norms in life. The cultivation of virtues such as benevolence, self-love and so on precedes following a principle of benevolence or self-love. Without *being benevolent,* we cannot imagine to be a follower of benevolence. When we discuss which virtues *qua* social beings precede norms and should be thus cultivated among individuals in society for a good social life, we are doing virtue ethics at the social level. It becomes more focused when we consider the problem of cultivation of virtues when stiff value-laden social issues approach us. When we are faced with the ethical aspects of social problem of *affirmative action*, for instance, it will be futile at the ground levels of reality to follow utilitarianism or Kantian deontology if first and foremost the responsible parties, the legislature and the executive in the main who are responsible in assuming such action for overall social welfare are not courageous, self-sacrificing and benevolent, that is, if they are not themselves virtuous in these ways. Hence, value problems in society demands that those individuals, groups, institutions and organisations who are responsible in analysing and resolving those problems should be bearers of some *aretaic* virtues (those of character) and *deontic* virtues (those of duty). It may well be that social beings need to cultivate in the main egoistic virtues, utilitarian virtues and deontological virtues, not anyone of them. However, it may be debated whether value-laden social problems such as affirmative action demands *cultivation* of one or more virtues in us because the entire project may be utopian and unpragmatic. There is no doubt that a benevolent person can practice benevolence but how is one sure that (a) benevolence is something worthwhile or a virtue, and (b) benevolence is something that he or she is worth of? That "benevolence" is a value or a virtue is said to be a matter of *intuition* because worthiness is *intrinsic* to it; or, it is a virtue because it produces beneficial consequences for moral agents. In any case, the value of benevolence begs normative theses. Moreover, the knowledge that I am benevolent draws its strength either from the beneficial consequences of some of my decisions and actions, or from the intuitive experiences of my character or what I intend and act. In both cases, we have to take recourse to normative theories. Hence, even if the ethics of virtue asks for virtue inculcation as most important among the individuals and the social institutions so that value-laden social issues are resolved, virtues some way or other are linked to what desirable *teleos* we have for us and strive for them and/or what *duties* we have for us and strive for them. In this sense, we may be striving for inculcating teleological, deontic, or both virtues in us justifying the fact that we cannot completely rule out the conception of normative ethics. Through the ages, wise people reflecting seriously on social issues, which call for urgent ethical resolution, have preferred that the masses in civil societies should be value-charged or value-oriented. For this, they have preferred value education and value based decisions and actions, but the moot issue remained unresolved whether value-orientedness can be ever a possibility without normative orientedness. The point is interesting as no one is able to pooh-pooh the idea that following any norm begs minimal inculcation of virtue to follow that norm and not another one or none of them.

Finally, we come to the justification of social ethics as practical-ethical involvements in social issues calling for urgent value resolution. Major part of this book deals with this aspect but here in the course of justification it needs to be said that while we are involved in practical ethics we may be said to do the following: (a) apply anyone or more normative theory explained above in cases of social value crises such as divorce or preferential treatment or population control and find out most pertinent resolution of issues under consideration, and (b) apply *our* moral knowledge, experience and sense by virtue of talking and debating with one another regarding social value crises and reach *moral consensus* that most pertinently gives us the moral cues to decision-making and acting. In both the ways of practical ethical involvement, our focus is to resolve social ethical crises. Of course, in any of these ways, we may be involved in resolving political, economic, business and legal crises as well. If we can show that ethical theories or our ethical knowledge can be *applied* or *practiced* on ground levels of social crises to resolve them, we have social ethics as a branch of ethics that apart from other things deals in ethical resolution of socially relevant value-crises. Nevertheless, social ethics as application of ethics in any of the two ways is highly debated. It is argued that social value crises should not be resolved *artificially* by applying any norm available to us by expert ethicists. Social ethics thus cannot justify itself as a practical ethical venture that plays with normative theories in real life cases and that too by expert ethicists. On the other hand, it is argued that social ethics can justify itself as practical-ethical enterprise if an only if common men, decision makers, ethicists and all other interested parties come together to apply their knowledge of good, right, just and so on in the context of stiff social value crises to resolve them and find out the moral cues in decision-making and action. However, the contra-view argues that there is either no ethical application in social cases or there is something like that only if the technical persons apply normative theories. Or else, we do not know what is applied in ethics. Laypersons are not said to have applied ethics in social cases. Countering the view (and justifying social ethics as non-artificial application of ethics), it is said that though application of *our* ethical knowledge of the desirable and the good is possible and resolution most likely, analysing the moral debates for normative inquiry, that is, to find out which theories are reflected in the common moral perceptions of the masses is another thing. Hence, refraining from norms can we apply ethics but having applied ethical knowledge, the dynamics of norms can be easily discovered. Any way, indulging into such arguments drags us to an interesting field of ethics, which is practical ethics, and when it plays in the field of social issues, social ethics emerges in yet another justified form. This much must be good enough to show what social ethics amounts to, why it is a justified ethical enterprise and what important issues are before it. Let us now move on to some social value crises and their resolution, which is an important feature of this book.

Notes

1. Benn, S.I quotes Thomas Aquinas in his seminal essay on "Society" in *The Encyclopaedia of Philosophy*, (Ed.) Paul Edwards, Vol. 7, Macmillan Publishing Co. & The Free Press, NY, 1974, p. 471.
2. *Ibid*, p. 471.
3. Mackie, J.L., *The Cement of the Universe*, Clarendon Press, Oxford, 1974 and Gupta, Chhanda, "Objectivity in Social Inquiry" in Krishna Roy, and Chhanda Gupta (ed.), *Essays in Social and Political Philosophy*, I.C.P.R. in association with Allied Publishers, New Delhi, 1989.
4. Gupta, Chhanda, "Value and Social Science", *Ibid*, pp. 82-92.
5. *Ibid*, p. 84.
6. Keith, Graham, "Morality Individuals and Collectives" in J.D.G Evans (ed.), *Moral Philosophy and Contemporary Problems*, Cambride University Press, Cambride, 1987.
7. *Ibid*, p. 13.
8. Bayles, M.D., *Ethics and Population*, Combride Unviersity Press, Massachusetts, 1976 p. xi.

9. Garvin, Lucius, *A Modern Introduction to Ethics*, Houghton Miffin Co., Boston, 1953 p. 485.
10. *Ibid.*
11. *Ibid.*
12. Sadurski, Wojicech, *Giving Desert Its Due: Social Justice and Legal Theory*, J. Riedel Publishing Co., Dordrecht, 1950, p. 36.
13. Fuller, Lon L., *In the Morality of Law*, Yale University Press, New Haven, 1972.
14. Sadurski, W., *Op. Cit.*, p. 43.
15. *Ibid.*
16. Dworkin, Ronald, *Taking Rights Seriously*, Duckworth, London, 1978 gives us a thesis about social justice/legal justice distinction and moral views of a person with regard to social justice.
17. Hare, R.M., *Freedom and Reason*, Clarendon Press, Oxford, 1963, pp. 147- 48.

2

Value-Laden Social Problems and their Resolution

In the previous chapter, we discussed about the nature and justification of "social ethics". We came to conclude that social ethics deals in some social issues, which may be analysed and resolved from "ethical perspectives". Among the ethically relevant ways of dealing in social matters are included metaethical, normative, virtue-based and practical ethical ways, which show us what exactly do we mean by social ethics and why is it justified. We found that there are a number of social issues, which despite being factually grounded raise distinct questions of "moral values" such as desirable, good, right, just and so on. These issues are thus "value-laden social issues", which await "ethical perspectives" among some other perspectives for thorough analysis and understanding. Ethical perspectives clarify what exactly we do in social ethics and why are we justified in getting involved in social ethics. There are thus two ways in the nature clarification and justification of social ethics. We have agreed that social ethics is *within ethics* (and not sociology) because here we are more interested in an ethically relevant study of social issues. All said and done, social ethics emerges as an extremely interesting and challenging field of study, but the point is whether metaethical, normative, virtue-based and practical-ethical analysis of social issues is enough? Alternatively, do we say that analysis of social issues that invite us for ethical discussions as a theoretical enterprise is enough? In fact, thus far, we are well within the limits of theoretical discussions that relate ethical and social talks. We have for now stronger challenges from the *practical aspects* of both social and ethical studies. The challenges are, whether social issues waiting ethical scrutiny end in a mere theoretical social study, and whether ethics entering social issues end as theoretical ethical enterprise. If we reply in the affirmative, in the true sense of the term there is no social ethics, because no social-talk relates to practical ethics and practical ethics does not relate to social-talks as pure theoretical enterprises. Hence, in social ethics everything is all right even if there is no practical ethical enterprise. What do we conclude then? One way is to say that though social ethics is a body of justified inquiries, there is no practical ethical scope for it. Another way is to say that though practical ethics is a body of justified, inquiries there is doubtfully any social scope for it. The former is *scepticism* about practicality of ethics in the context of social ethics whereas the latter is *agnosticism* about a practical ethical involvement in social ethics. Both scepticism and agnosticism are unwelcome, as they do not allow us to know properly about social ethics and in some sense about practical ethics. Hence, it is important for us to know why practical ethics as a "truly practical enterprise" is related to the social field and why social ethics as it is, should be seen apart from other things, a serious practical ethical involvement.

What is then social ethics *per se*? Social ethics as we know it must include practical ethics as practical venture for the *resolution* of social matters that are "value-laden" or those raising questions of ethical value. The reason is that by its nature social ethics constitutes a body of social issues that are not merely factual, rather they ask for resolution of some crises at the factual level which turns out to be all the more acute and urgent for being "value-laden" or raising questions of ethical value. Though most of the problems and crises at the factual level are important awaiting urgent resolution, some of them call for our special attention because these problems for resolution do not straightaway depend upon the nitty-gritty or what we may call ground level mechanics of resolution, rather they are or they should be preceded by the churnings of "why something *should* be done" and "how something *should* be done". For example, an urgent social problem awaiting mechanics of resolution is why and how do we activate the public distribution system of food grains. Nevertheless, it is an urgent and crucial practical social problem awaiting *ethical resolution* before the *mechanics of resolution*, whether to activate "preferential justice". As a social issue or practical social problem, this is not merely practical but "value-laden" because its "mechanics of resolution" is taken over by the "ethic of resolution". Hence, the ethical perspective or perspectives are awaited in order to resolve some practical social issues of urgency. In this sense, while "preferential justice" as a value-laden issue *awaits* ethical interference, ethics as practical *enters* the realm of social-talks such as this to resolve them. The point is what exactly we mean when we say that some value-laden social matters *await ethical resolution*.

Before answering this question, let us take up the correlative question, 'What is practical ethics *per se*?' Practical ethics is ethics put to practice, not simply to serve nature clarification and justification of issues like "social ethics", but to serve the actual demands of society to resolve value-laden practical problems such as value-laden social problems in which ethical dynamics precedes socio-political, legal and economic nitty-gritty or mechanics. Practical ethics *per se* is 'ethical dynamics'. In the field of social ethics, practicality of ethics is apart from other things, ethical dynamics in real life situations to analyse and resolve time tormented social issues, which are value-laden. It is exactly at this point that we get a reply to the question asked above, that is, what do we mean by value-laden social matters awaiting ethical resolution? Value-laden social matters are those issues or problems in society that need serious ethical dynamics for their resolution before we are involved in the minute mechanics of dos and don'ts. Hence, practical ethics as it really is, shall nevertheless, remain dynamic for urgent resolution of value crises of a wide range, such as value crises in society. In this sense, the value crisis of preferential distribution of public goods and services should be resolved and not nourished for they take us to terrible social strife and unrests. The resolution should be first and foremost at the ethical level because the issue is bubbling with questions that needs to be countered first with our ethical experience and knowledge to come to conclude why certain preferential acts in society are ethically desirable and how the same should be done, the latter smoothly takes us to the mechanics of dos and don'ts. More often than not doing and not doing something at the practical levels of social life without preceding ethical dynamics turns out to be impractical, unworthy and unethical. Not long before in India, even the economically well-off people got foodstuffs from the public distribution centres at heavily subsidised rates thinking that this is equitable act among the masses consisting of high and low, and poor and rich. Soon it was discovered that the act of subsidy in the PDS on the part of the government was impractical, unworthy and unethical because it corroded public fund, did greater favours to well-off people and not pro-public welfare in the true sense. Hence, the cart being put before the horse has to be put to the right place, the asking questions though not merely the impracticable and unworthy aspects of the "mechanics" but the ethical reasons for encouraging a mechanics of a particular kind. The point is why at all should we not *prefer* some sections of the population for distributing bare necessities to them because they are entitled to have those things though completely underpowered in view of what they already have. The question is why preferential act should be preferred than the erstwhile act of equitable justice in public distribution? Hence, ethical dynamics that resolves the acute ethical or value crisis first, should be at the first place, and then the mechanics should follow smoothly.

If social ethics is ethical involvement in social matters, it should imagine dynamic ethics. However, what it is to be ethically dynamic in social matters? Any attempt to answer this question shows that perhaps scepticism about practical ethics and agnosticism about the same dynamics has been taken care of. However that is not the case because we are not sure why the said dynamics is at all a dynamics in the true sense of the term. In fact, the mechanics at the social level compels us to imagine that without dos and don'ts there are no dynamics, and we do not conceive of ethical dynamics that reaches social matters. There is some lingering agnosticism. Similarly, we may think that as mechanics need tools or aids for mechanism, social mechanism need the same, and if ethical dynamics claims to be basic to social mechanism, it must be *aided*. Nevertheless, we are doubtful whether ethics has adequate aids except normative principles and secondary rules, which may be in anyway aid to social mechanism. Both the lingering agnosticism and scepticism now takes us to the consideration of the moot issue, that is, what exactly is practical ethics or ethical dynamics that becomes an aspect of social ethics. Let us face these questions: Do we know *what* to apply in ethics when it comes to resolution of social matters that are value-laden? In addition, do we know *how* to apply what needs to be applied in ethics when the point is of ethical resolution of social crises?

In the common parlance, the mechanical conception is that what are applied in ethics are norms of ethics and the way it should be applied is to empower ethicists as technicians of norms to apply one norm or norms in particular cases to resolve them. Alternative conception may be that we apply our virtuous dispositions to resolve tricky value crises and for that, our moral intuition and zeal are enough. Well, both options of ethical dynamics in social matters might sound great but they turn out to be not only unpragmatic but unethical as well. The mechanical conception of ethical dynamics that calls for normative application by expert ethicists is fraught with problems. The major problem is that there is hardly any reason for us to agree in favour of a norm or a few norms that resolve a social problem or problems of ethical dimension beyond any doubt, because most of the norms taken in isolation and as monistic standards have their own theoretical and practical limitations. Moreover, ethicists are not omnipotent and sacred agents who enjoy exclusive rights to apply one or more ethical norms to resolve ethical crises because others may not agree with their utter intellectual supremacy over matters that are close to every sane person's ethical sense of urgency to resolve value crises in society. Moreover, rather than picking a norm in a tricky situation it may be wiser to put our heads and hearts together to apply our ethical experience and knowledge that we gather in the social life of interactions to resolve value crises thus finding for us meaning of a life of activism in social matters. Hence, rather than ethical mechanism as aspect of social engineering, we may contribute in ethical dynamism through ethical debates and dialogues about value crises in society thus reaching *intersubjective corroboration* with regard to value-laden social issues. In this sense, agnosticism and scepticism are replaced by methodology of intersubjective corroboration. Clarifying what is applied in ethics and how should we do so, we need to apply our ethical experience and knowledge in cases of social value crises to resolve these issues by means of ethical discourses amounting to corroboration of views that takes us to the next stage of mechanics of dos and don'ts smoothly and naturally. We thus come to know that we do *not* have to rely on ethicists alone for ethical dynamism because normative application is unpragmatic and ethical intellectualism and mechanism are unethical for being essentially anti-people—it snubs common person's ethical powers by virtue of being a member of this vast community of ethical agents to resolve ethical crises. It is repugnant for those depending on the equitable distribution of goods and services and those involved in their distribution to accept that wise ethicists should unilaterally resolve the value-laden social problem of preferential distribution by using norms of their choice as sacred commandment. Ethical dynamics does not take place when all others shut up but ethicists keep going. Hence, ethical dynamics, not normative ethical dynamics is required in ethical corroboration after rounds of ethical debates about value-laden matters. Little needs to be said about the alternative conception of application of our virtuous dispositions such as honesty, dutifulness, nobility, cooperation and so on. No doubt, in ethical corroboration, parties should be honest and cooperative if not normatively obsessed, but that is not enough, ethical debates and resolution takes us to the application of knowledge in a *logical* way. It is a complete misconception to harp on the matter that first we apply our virtue of honesty in application because demands of virtues and having them do not guarantee applying ethical knowledge. A person may be utterly vicious in possessing virtuous dispositions but do not apply them; and interestingly, if our ethical knowledge is not applied in the real sense, how do we come to claim that we have virtues of honesty and to be logical in ethical application? Ethical dynamics demand on ground levels of reality that we come to cooperate and resolve crises through debates that are logically sound and not whimsical cacophony, and getting involved in the dynamics reveals a few virtues we have even though some of us were agnostic or sceptic or illogical or dishonest or simply, disgruntled and disagreeing intellectual snubs. Applying our ethical knowledge is basic to ethical dynamics that presupposes some virtues that we have or we acquire or we are pushed to have them, but applying ethics is not applying one or more virtues we have. *Having* ethical knowledge and applying them may be a great *virtue* but then we do *not apply* this virtue called 'ethical knowledge and application of such knowledge'. Conclusively, ethical dynamics in social matters is the application of common ethical knowledge of sane people in society to resolve value-laden social matters to resolve them in cooperation through ethical debates amounting to the corroboration of views and subsequent mechanics of duties or the mechanics of dos and don'ts in association.

If social ethics is social matters opening to ethics and ethics coming to social matters, it surely covers ethical application because social issues invite dynamics of our ethical knowledge and ethical knowledge comes out of the theoretical comfort zone to counter social issues awaiting ethical resolution. Social ethics is thus not a purely theoretical enterprise, it is practical because it demands social matters to be analysed, understood and resolved from *ethical standpoints* (which is not the same as normative standpoints). One questions what at all is applied in ethics if norms are not applied in social matters? It appears that the question must be scepticism's last citadel. The counter question is 'Why at all when norms are applied should we call it applied ethics?' We are definitely not by any imagination applying metaethical theories to resolve the crisis of preferential justice. We are also not applying virtue ethical theories here. Can it be application of normative theories of Kantian deontology or Mill's utilitarianism or the like? It can be (and often it is the case), but we are in reality applying *our* (the concerned parties') ethical knowledge which reflects a number of such normative thesis, logical systematisation of the same is an enterprise undertaken by a few trained philosophers by virtue of their genius. Normative theories are reflected in the moral opinions of ordinary sane people the who possess the knowledge of evaluative standards by being participants of this vast ecological community where they intend, act, influence, and are influenced, and where they reflect on what is desirable, right, just, and so on. Hence, public participation in moral dialogues about matters like preferential justice reveal public moral scrutiny of the matter, which on careful analysis reveals the normative characters inherent in them. It is due to this that without being preoccupied and obsessed with norms, concerned parties in our society can participate in the dynamics of ethical resolution of social matters, provided these people are invited to go through an "organised dialogue", that is, a debate that is oriented towards considering ethical perspectives of people for value-related matters and not oriented purely towards intellectuals' artificial theoretic mechanism or theoreticism. The ethical orientation of the debate has to be taken up by either trained ethicists or those interested parties who desire to be *ethical corroborators*, but this is not another intellectualism because *organising debates* and *conducting* them as corroborators with the aid of select *questionnaires* of moral orientation may be "non-structuralist", when ethicists and others mingle in the public, talk to them, read their views and then cutting through the cross-sections of the populace invite criss-crossing moral perceptions to freely disagree and agree on moral matters in debates. The questions are thus not intellectual manipulations, they are formulations of ethical corroborators who are *de-classed* or those who learn in and with the public to know which morally oriented questions are best for stirring ethical disagreements and agreements on social issues. The corroborators have no normative prejudice; the same is reflected in his questions and in his attitude during the debates, where he or she acts as able moderators, careful analysts of opinions and efficient corroborators when the house tends to agree on moral issues. If we follow this, we come to know what is applied in ethics. It is our moral knowledge, our moral prowess, our moral arguments that are put to practice for moral resolution on social matters. However, no one has prevented the ethicist or the corroborator to take on further *post-corroborative theoretical analysis* of debates and consensus to find out the dynamic aspects of normative theories. This analytic work may be an aspect of practical ethics; as practical ethics we have seen before takes other theoretical interests, but practical ethics as such is practical if it involves people's activism for moral resolution.

If social ethics is not handmaid of pure theoreticism, there is assurance for some ethical dynamics in it, we have to show our readers how well it happens in real life. For this, I will follow a pattern. First, I will take up two value-laden social issues and analyse them in the typical Indian context and find out questions of value they raise instigating our moral perspectives to activate. Second, I will produce the questionnaires I have used for ethical dialogues and leave some hint towards normative findings. Third, I will leave many opportunities for my readers to work out their analysis and construct questions for debates they would like to arrange. Finally, I will consider one case in entirety, that is, its analysis, debates and points of corroboration and post-corroboration normative analysis of the debate. I have selected for my purpose the issues of "Caste, Class and Marriage in India" and the case of "Divorce" both related to the micro-social existential that is, "family", the status of women (also men) in it and the number of ethically relevant questions needing understanding and resolution. The problem that awaits complete treatment in this chapter is "Affirmative Action" or "Reservation" at various spheres in India. Let us start with the social issue of "Caste, Class and Marriage" and try to know the value-questions that it raise for resolution.

Family according to me is the primary social institution in which a few or a number of individuals thrive to constitute the intricate coherent fabric of society. In the recent times, we are pressed hard to believe that a family need not necessarily and sufficiently depend on the fundamental *institution of marriage*, which is in the common parlance a more or less customary covenant between two sexes, male and female, who normally assume the status of husband and wife. This conception of existence of families without marriage is in fact brought to our modern psyche *de novo* with the advent of what is called, "live together", but the truth may be that families having transitory or unstable relation among men and women, and even unorthodox relation among men and women staying together in a household, having a way of life is not new. Any way, leaving aside the squabble about marriage as basic to family as an institution, we can say that in a particular household, the co-existing man and woman, having a *way of life* unique to them, may be considered as a "family" if there is no completely fortuitous relation between the said parties, not extremely unstable and transitory, having no social or religious or legal sanctions and customs that binds them for a more or less stable co-existence until they call for a quit in relation legally. This is an explanation and not definition of what a family is most likely to be in the world, granting any degree of queer exceptions. It may be noted that as marriage is a debated social institution that is basic to the existence of family, having children may be equally debatable for calling an existential a family because adopting children or having none of them in a household where man and woman coexist may be called a family. The sub-nuclear family (if that is an acceptable expression) is thus a social existential consisting of man and woman cohabiting. The nuclear family may be relatively complex with the introduction of natural or adopted child or children. Macro-family is more complex having complex relations among its existing members by virtue of natural, biological, or hereditary ascendance. Joint family is a huge body of relations, natural in the main, particularly known for its joint holding of property, assets, income and so on. There are however, intense arguments among sociologists whether to 'live together' amounts to a family not because there is no marriage and there is no social, religious and legal covenant between man and woman who live together. The extreme opinion is that in the lack of legal approval, men and women cannot "live together" and enjoy the rights of a family, for instance, to be called husband and wife and get an identification card for them mentioning a particular household, though they may be seen as two individuals *staying* together for some time or for a longer time like fortuitous living in a dormitory or to be harsh, in a brothel! Nevertheless, softer people believe that legal interventions are useless for two grown up man and woman living together than marrying and constituting a unit and be known by traditional names, identities and addresses. Living together both parties may enjoy equal rights to have ration cards, telephone connection and so on for them. They may have sex, even have a child naturally or if doctors allow them, through fertilisation techniques asexually. Weird social relations have made marriage something of an item in ancient warehouse; can family be a lost treasure in the warehouse? Most probably no, because we need legal approval for marriage, live together needs the same, family as a social institution for sure needs a legal approval for relation between a man and woman bound in a way of life until they want legal separation. It may well be that all families are not existing owing to a legal covenant; there may be social acceptance or approval or even religious approval or both. However, in civil states, such social and religious approaches of families are fast taken over by legal approvals. In fact, civil societies are quickly shifting to the legal basis to the existence of both marriage and family (and even living together). A family is thus a micro-social institution that *should* be based on definite legal sanctions of relation of a man and woman existing in a household, having a way of life unique to them, enjoy social, political and economic rights due to them, they can fight for their claim rights jointly or singly, and have children biologically or in other ways permissible to them. The unit of family may be nevertheless, transitory lest there is a social or legal intervention to see through the break up, but *desirable* is a legal process to break up the said unit.

Though a family is constituted out of a relation between a man and woman of a particular legally permissible age, the relation as we now find should be legally accepted, and the best way is to have such relation through a legal form of marriage. Marriage is not a necessary and sufficient institution that is basic to the existence of families; it is nevertheless, desirable that legal forms of marriage brings into existence legally accepted families. Hence, no one has prevented grown up men and women in our societies to marry without a legal approval and constitute a family, such marriages may face rough weather when they tend to break or break in reality, and with it breaks the families. In fact, none in the society can uphold the rights of members of families except the legal institutions. Hence, in cases of separation and consequent hitches in the sharing of property, assets, incomes etc., it is the legal back up that is needed. Hence, legal marriages can help us in enjoying all legal rights that are correlative to such relationships and should be thus enjoyed, but in the Indian society legal marriages are late starters. There is much confusion, misconceptions and prejudices about the legal form of marriage until our people are pushed to an extent to go for it for some obvious favour. In the recent times ardent champions of social-religious marriages or customary non-legal marriages reluctantly accept the legal push on them particularly in cases of settlement of entitlements and rights, and other favours such as requesting for a visa and so on. However, for many Indians the idea of legal intervention in marriage and family matters is repugnant as the saying goes: "Marriages are made in Heaven." The divine nature of the bondage of love, compassion and camaraderie in marriage does not go along with legal sanctions. For many among us the sanctions and interventions are external, not giving the needed freedom to the moral agents to come into a deep relationship. The evolution of the human character and self is jeopardised. The natural course is thus the socio-religious or customary non-legal marriages whether that is "arranged" by the families of a man and a woman coming into that relation or by virtue of "love" between the parties intending to solemnise it through marriage. The starting ethical issue in marriage must be then the evaluation of goodness of "interventionism" in marriage. If "interventionism" or "externalism" in marriage is carried too far even family and society becomes redundant, irrelevant and unethical because the decision of solemnisation of a relation through marriage is open legitimately to those who desire to come into that relationship and no one else. Hence, carried too far, "arrangement" is a form of "intervention" in marriage and thus against the *freedom* of man and woman who want to come to a relationship. In this sense, religious ceremonies or solemnisation whether in public or in an extremely closed atmosphere is "intervention" of another type as it is semi-legal not exactly legal in any case. It is much like *bequeathing* in the quasi-legal interventions of the sacred texts and authorities, which is a threat to freedom of persons or a reminder to them for life that the breach in bequeathing may be *punished* by the quasi-legal authorities or by Divine fiat. However, not all among us would agree that like legal intervention, social and religious marriages are interventional in nature or are quasi-legal and thus unethical for being anti-freedom of humans. If any form of marriage is solemnisation of some kind at least, whether by law or social-religious customs, it may be seen as unethical owing to interventional nature of the act of solemnisation. Hence, there may be only one ethical form of marriage when a man and a woman are let free in our society to choose *their* way to solemnise their relationship and constitute a family. Nevertheless, this is not to be seen as living together or a form of unsettled dating or arrogant sexual liberalism. The ground for ethical disagreements spread like wild fire. In the former cases of legal and non-legal interventionism and in this case of non-interventionist liberalism, we debate which form of marriage is ethically desirable. What exactly then is marriage, that is, what exactly do we expect from the institution that it *should* be like? Or, is it more ethical to have no social institution of marriage because that is closer to the ultra-liberal conception of ending "closed social institution" like "marriage" and the correlative "family", and just be together till it suits us best and thus be at liberty in sexual acts and in the choice of having children. The simple matter of marriage is not so simple when the ethical scanner starts scanning or when the social phenomenon of marriage is deconstructed to some extent at least to discover that it opens for ethical scanning for reasons obvious to us, that is, it raises questions of desirability, good and right of marriage as such or forms of marriage or ways to institutionalise marriage.

We shall further discuss about what many Indians express in these matters and thus fall in line of moral debate. The reason is that in India the case of marriage assumes queer status when the factors of caste and custom are dragged in this regard. In fact, the moral questions pertaining to marriage becomes stiffer when the social factors of caste and casteism are related to marriage. We have to find out what these stiffer ethical questions are when we consider marriage particularly of the legal or social-religious types, notwithstanding the fact that the non-interventionist type of marriage faces the heat of caste, and casteism to equal proportions apart from the traditionalist (interventionist) snubbing.

Without going into the historical details of casteism in India, the threadbare *śāstric* analysis of "caste" and the great Indian debate over who dominated whom and did what wrongs on humans, let us first accept that the caste system in India as we find it now with the tentacles of problems that it has already spread, it has already seriously jeopardised social justice, protection of human rights and extending equality of opportunity to the masses. Hence, the strong ethical reasons to root out caste system are expected to hinge on these three factors, which constitute, "social welfare". In this sense, caste system may be touted to be unethical because it is anti-human and social well-being. However, the charge may be countered as myopic owing to the maladies in understanding the conceptions of *varṇa* and *varṇa vyavasthā* in India which dates long back not merely to *Mānava Dharma Sūtra* of Manu but to the *Upaniṣadas* and Epic philosophies, particularly *Gītā* and to a great extent supported by the *Sāṅkhya* psychological thesis of *triguṇas*. It is said that the basic conception is ethical, as it is pro-human and for social well-being. The system is based on the idea that humans should be classified for their social duties according to their *guṇas* or character dispositions evolved through a number of ways than the advantages owing to birth or fortunes or favours, and therefore, the castes of the society should go on performing their allotted duties with a sense of obligation and non-infatuation towards the results of what they do. This way of doing what we should do takes us to an elevated platform of self-realisation that assures our well-being to its fullest. Hence, the caste and the system had nothing in it that is unethical or against humanity and human welfare until the feudal state powers in connivance with the *dhūrta* priests exploited the masses by creating a hierarchy among social castes, thus creating classes of power and fortunes, which is, however, unethical as the whole idea is not only anti-human and anti-social, it is complete distortion and cunning act of manipulation with a social philosophy that is good in itself. If this has to be believed, there are two courses of action: the *status quoist* which calls for abstention from rooting out castes, the system and the inherent social philosophy but let people know the truth and value of the philosophy, and the *activist* calling for (a) social, constitutional and legal radical changes and policies that fights the evil to root it out with its philosophy and (b) the social, political (constitutional) and legal reforms backed up by a philosophical rejuvenation that castes out unethical philosophy. If the former course of action is pacifist and tolerant but largely toothless, the latter is some sort of reformist liberalism that either calls for a shake up of rudiments of a social philosophy that has somehow come to the focus of the debate or to rejuvenate it as well. Any ethical debate about caste and caste system in India should thus hover around these opinions. It may be argued that *status quoism* is ethically good because without proving beyond doubt that the cursed social philosophy of the Hindus is to be cursed because it is anti-social, and that emotional charges does not disprove a strong thesis, it is most urgent that we stick to our system by advocating the logical grounds for doing so and the philosophical soundness it has. Though for all that state power must rise to the occasion to see that what is in our system is not abruptly overturned by any arrogance or violence. Hence, the protection of the inherent worth of a philosophy and thus a system that is pro-humanity and social well-being is ethically just. On the other hand the liberal reformist of the first type may argue that *status quoism* is essentially unethical as its touted intrinsically good philosophy of the caste and casteism is not really intrinsically good, it is a mere conception of a powerful class in our society that wants to find out some way to prevent the visible social changes and uprisings by glorifying a redundant thesis of the historically powerful class. Hence, the ethic of social reforms and changes is that the unprivileged, underpowered and socially degraded sections of our society should rise and the liberal polity should assure this in many ways, if needed by the use of power or privileges or preferential treatments. In any case, the liberalist call does not deem it ethical to take a revisionist step to glorify our social philosophy that has given us that caste system. Other things remaining the same, the other liberal thesis tries to adjust socio-political and legal reforms along with a philosophical rejuvenation that brings out the ethical crux of the caste system so that despite greater social well-being, any caste is not maltreated or a philosophy is not made a scapegoat. The ethical idea may be that holistic social well-being does not demand reforms and uprisings backed by government activism, which assures that erstwhile dominant castes are maltreated proportionately or that they surely come down. There is perhaps no ethics in social justice with qualified injustice, which was not needed as a matter of strategy or genuine help. Moreover, the ethic of qualified protectionism that prevents a complete ouster of a philosophy by use of reformist prowess is that it always gives us a chance to a philosophical revolution and critique of what was the basis of social justice.

Truly, in the recent times in the vastly changing Indian society we have been relatively more analytic in our evaluation of caste-system, its philosophy, the activism in Indian Diaspora and the rapidly changing conception of the Indians about ways of life, modernity and the visible trendiness all around. Indians now speak the language of globalism, open market economy, free trade and the radical social changes that are caused by economic new order. It is quite natural that the changing society evaluates its own value system and its ethical perception of caste, class and casteism. Trends in modernity caused by several economic factors must be responsible in the evaluation of casteism as well. Among the changing evaluation of the caste system is the factor of fear caused by the quantum socio-economic changes in India. The fear is of the tremendous force of modernity that has come up with the new economic order which is perceived to be unethical as it has changed or tends to change the *śāstric* conception of caste and casteism in all its glorious forms as well as the non-*śāstric* feudal manipulation of the same. The fear is that the Yankee modernity has invaded the Indian society to corrupt its people, society, culture, religion and its socio-religious tools such as caste system. Hence, rather than evaluating, the ethical grounds of having a caste system and protecting it in all humaneness, the pseudo-liberalists threat to overhaul and/or trash the system as unethical bigotry of the past. Is it ethical to evaluate caste system as based on an ethical perception that is new *avatār* of gross sensualistic egoism the closest kin being the said modernity? Such questions have come up for ethical analysis in our times when casteism is under consideration. In the light of what we have said about family, marriage, caste and casteism and related ethical questions awaiting scrutiny, we can now put things together. The point is that in India our families are more often than not identified by the caste hierarchy they belong. Naturally, the individuals of these families are equally known for their caste hierarchies. Starting from school admission to application for jobs, caste becomes distinguishable identification mark of a person. There are reasons because caste identifications are not for well or ill-treating a person or to avenge injustice in the society. Caste identification becomes a social tool for affirmative action, preferential justice and thus social justice on the part of various authorities, institutions and organisations. Now the obvious social mechanism to identify ourselves by virtue of our castes is not the same as caste identification becoming a tool for marriage that ultimately (in normal cases) forms a family belonging to a caste provided the married man and woman either hails from a uniform social hierarchy or they are unified in a hierarchy of caste by virtue of rituals. In both cases, the patriarchal domination is common; the married woman takes up the caste by either birth and ritualistic unification or simple transmutation through rituals without any hitch. However, there are exceptions; it may well be that in a typical matriarchic domination, caste transfers are in accordance to that system in the reverse gear so to say. Alternatively, in case of living together in a so-called family or a family in existence by virtue of love marriage, or in some cultures even in social marriage, if the caste transmutation is in the reverse gear, it may well be that caste hierarchies are determined differently. In a typical case of a family existing without any official form of marriage, it may be overenthusiastic to imagine that caste snare has been avoided. For all practical purposes in social life, it may be ration, jobs, voting and so on, caste of the existing man and woman may be identified as crucial. Therefore, in marriage caste and casteism do not appear to leave, not even if we are so bold to snub such caste-based queries or act iconoclasts. Then what to speak of marriage in India in the normal case—caste and casteism rule supreme in this regard, whether it be male-chauvinistic or female-dominated. The reasons for such nagging tendency to cling to our castes and their supremacies in marriage are many. Ethical queries in fact creep in now. One reason is *śāstric*, that is, by virtue of a sacred system it has been deemed proper that people of uniform character dispositions (*guṇas*) should be in a long lasting married relationship so that the family does not face obverse situations and the family breaks with broken people, mentally and physically. The following reason is that the progeny bears the caste heritage and should follow the same route by virtue of birth because contrary act will be non-*śāstric* and unethical. So the authoritative morality of India rules that caste based marriage, in the main female to male transmutation of caste, tells us that disseverance of authoritative morality is unethical because in cases such as these it is not the limited reason of ordinary humans that works, they should have faith and rely on *śāstras* of unique intuitive perceptions of truth about life and world. These are weak *śāstric* reasons to justify the ethical validity of caste based marriage, weak in the sense that the evident gappiness in reason allows us comfortably to charge camouflaging hereditary clanism and chauvinism of classes by birth in the garb of the theory of the *guṇas*. First, how can a man and woman belonging to different families though of same caste have the same *guṇas* if they are not hereditary or generic than an evolution of temperament or nature by factors that are non-hereditary, that is, social, economic, educational and so on? Obviously, two married people of same caste do not and cannot have same dispositional evolution, the same moral nature or character traits. Their progeny might not have uniform character-evolution and married to another one who is *believed* to have similar traits by *virtue of birth*. Hence, *caste* cannot be the ethically justifiable determinant in marriage; the *śāstric* authority thus does not enjoy absolute moral authority in this matter. In fact, hereditary conception of caste is more of chauvinism because it encourages the strict dominant hierarchies among castes and their power tracking in society. The power trackers in society thus give us the most unethical forms of casteism with associated conflicts. If marriage as a lasting human relation is based on such unethical hereditary chauvinism, it corrodes the society from within as more than two people of matching dispositions who might fall in a lasting relation of love, faith and dedication, two unmatched temperaments though of uniform caste-heredity are in a relation who stay together but not make a good relation. The stronger *śāstric* argument is that it is not the heredity rather the evolution of moral character that is an identification of a moral agent's caste and a *search within the caste* for social marriage (because love marriage does not beg such a search), should be ideally a search for uniform *character traits*. Hence, the *śāstric* authority does not act as dictator of morality but an able and wise guide, which tells us which traits, should be ideally matched within a caste. The truth is the ethic of unification of moral agent's character traits in a marriage relationship might comfortably take us to the ideal search of uniform temperaments *outside* a defined caste, which is a caste by birth. Hence, the last argument must have no problem with the acceptance of the ethics of social unity and non-violence embedded in *trans-caste* marriages, if by that we mean trans-caste-by-birth marriages when our so-called ideal search tends to fail within a defined caste system. If the *śāstras* rule out *asavarṇa* marriage just for the reason of undesirable and unmatchable character traits then such characters can be well found 'outside' a caste by birth. If this were the case, then better accept the universal ethical truth that marriages should be based on an ideal search for unifying moral character traits and temperaments for the reasons of filial and social harmony and a non-violent society of strong cohesion, thus marrying outside a defined caste system should be encouraged for the suitable ethic of social good, harmony and peace. Where heart and mind melts into a unity, there is an ideal marriage and an ideal family, which is then possible even in the search of a relation by moral agents who desires to come to that relation through healthy mixing, mutual understanding, sharing, caring, love, compassion, dedication and sacrifice. Is it not ethically desirable that even an ideal search within caste by birth, which truly clicks, should be left to the boys and girls of age? In his seminal work on ethics, Richard Brandt evaluates the use of moral authority in trifling social matters such as dating and marriage when we are considering two people of coming to an age but have not reached it. Surely, societies have intervened in delicate matters such as these, parents have been authoritative and this may be the case in the long run just because these people need some guidance until they come of age. Hence, *śāstras* or any other authority such as family or the society is useful ethical guide in matters of marriage only if we are too immature or we voluntarily rely on external sources. The point is that legally speaking, marriages (and not dating or living together) has a fixed age for boys and girls, of some expected physical and mental maturity. Hence, guiding immature people in finding matches for marriages does not arise. As far as we declare ourselves immature or voluntarily submit to authority for choice, only then people of age out of modernity perhaps dedicate their freedom in such matters, which may be nevertheless, a matter for close ethical inquiry. Hence, authorities are not to be blamed if they are allowed to assume that status but then they cannot have the moral authority to fall in the trap of choice as per caste by birth, they may assume greater moral status by transcending caste by birth, though no one has prevented them from a choice within one's caste by birth for an ideal ethical match. A stronger argument of the *śāstric* following is that marriages within one's own caste (by birth) is not exactly owing to the reason that they have similar character traits rather, they have uniform hereditary and genetic properties that is biologically speaking ideal for a match. Biologists believe that certain restrictions should be imposed on marriages for the biological well-being of couples and their progeny. Alternative ethical conception is that biologists in fact speak of trans-genetic and cross-cultural marriages, which are best for the biological well-being for couples and their progeny. Hence, it would be ideal for marriage to break away from fixed caste or castes by birth and of course, from some restricted biological matches and go for ideal cross-cultural and trans-genetic matches for marriage, which may be "arranged" or whatever that is irrelevant as far as moral agents have an agreement. In fact, marriages are looked upon as sacred and divine in nature by many Indians and any intervention of the *śāstra* or personal authorities are taken as normal because they are aimed at the good of the married people, but many Indians still believe that either interventions should be minimum or abolished and marriages be left to the decision of boys and girls of age who have the burden to find out an ideal temperamental and virtuous match for them lest they have the uncanny ability to take longer and bolder strides from emotions to gratifications and then to love and dedication.

The simple looking issue of marriage is not so simple when it drags us to unusual moral debates. The participants of such debates as they are in our society (if we have the urge to trace them), are ordinary thoretical-ethicsless people who never heard of a number of *śāstric* thesis or utilitarianism of Kantianism or Eudemonism, but they are ardent debaters coming at times to agree on many points. For this, that is, discovery of disagreements giving way to agreements on the ethical issues of marriage and thus resolving the social crises to an extent, we have to now follow our method in which preparation of questions for moral debates and selection of parties based on the information we gather from the public views, writings and so on are most important. And then of course, the debate followed by a closure in which ethicists have for them a role cut out for corroboration, and post-corroboration normative analysis. Bearing the title: "Caste, Class, Religion and Marriage—are we trapped in an unethical snare?" the moral debate arranged by me selected the following persons for the debate:

1. Mr. J.P. Sharma, Former District Registrar, Ranchi,
2. Sri Amol Bhattacharjee, Officer in the Central Coalfields Limited, having long experience in Hindu marriages as a priest,
3. Fr. O.K. Tirkey, Auxiliary Secretary, Bible Society, Ranchi,
4. Dr. V.S. Upadhyaya, Professor and Head, University Department of Anthropology, Ranchi University, Ranchi,
5. Dr. Binod Narayan, Reader of Sociology, University Department of Sociology, Ranchi University, Ranchi,
6. Dr. Asha Kumari, Lecturer of Home Science, University Department of Philosophy, Ranchi University, Ranchi.

The questions that were put in the moral debate are as follows:

QUESTIONNAIRE

1. Evaluate the worth of marriage and family in human society.
2. What is the moral worth in distinguished humans according to their castes and classes?
3. What ought to be desirable relationship between a man and a woman after they are married by any customary and/or legal way?

4. What is desirable and undesirable in fixing marriages, and fixing marriages based on caste, class and religion?
5. Evaluate the customs of dowry in marriage and widow remarriage on moral grounds.
6. Suggest some humane norms with regard to marriage in India.

First a few words about the selection of the panel of debaters. It is desirable that a moral debate should not include too many or too less participants. Rather, the most needed parties, that is, those most concerned persons should be accommodated in moral debates. The selection should be open and careful, not giving way to personal whims rather depending on one's gathered information about the issue while talking to people and reading important essays and articles. It is expected that someone who has the experience of a marriage registrar in public office along with a legal background should be selected for the debate. Mr. J.P. Sharma fits here for this reason. Mr. Bhattacharjee was selected for his wide experience as a Hindu priest for customary marriage. Fr. Tirkey was selected for having the same experience though as witness to a different custom but in any case thoroughly religious in nature. Both the teachers of Anthropology and Sociology were invited to participate in the dialogue for the matters pertaining to marriage and family fall in their academic domain. Dr. Asha was selected for two reasons, first in the capacity of a home scientist she has different perspective to share and because she was expected to share her ethical experiences about widow remarriage.

The first question attempts at studying the value system of the participants with regard to family and marriage in general. The second one tries to gauge their value perception about humans *vis-à-vis* their castes, classes and religions. We now need a question that moves deeper into the questions of human relations in marriage in the complex contexts of customary and legal forms of marriage and then move further to consider the cases of marriages fixed on the bases of caste, class, religion and so on. To evaluate the value perspective of woman in marriage, the cases of dowry and widow remarriage were needed. The last question aims at finding a synoptic view of decision-making rules in this regard.

I have deconstructed the method to some extent in this case so that from the next issue onwards, readers try to find out for themselves how a panel should be selected and questions framed. They also get many opportunities to disagree with the selection and the questions, which is always welcome in the relativistic and ever growing method of ethical application. As I have said before, I do not intend to provide here the details of what the participants argued because that detailing will be done only in case of the last issue for all practical purposes. However, our readers wanting to act ethical corroborators and analysts might move ahead in the direction of having another panel of experts and discuss on the moral matter. It is always good to infuse some practical interest than providing all the details every time. Anyway, I will have the moral responsibility to tell my readers about the most notable finding in the debate.

"The overwhelming stature of caste and class in marriage is *unethical* only in so far as that stature becomes anti-human, and anti-social, that is, instigates social disharmony. The unethicality lies in the complete neglect of basic human-values as supreme, which is again anti-social, anti-harmony and thus unethical. If marriage does not give many opportunities to grown up people to get some basic freedom in choice of partner and mode, it must be essentially deterministic and unethical. This is why there must be ample freedom in the widow and widower remarriage. It is evident that human and social well-being are the desirable ends which the social tool called marriage should aim at."

It is evident that the above finding may be disagreed upon; the desirable set of rules may be different and normative finding different too. We come to know more about the method as we consider the case of "divorce". Divorce does not come up as a natural consequence of marriage rather, it is an unnatural course of action on the part of the married couples to settle for divorce either arbitrarily or legally, which is nothing but a coercive or whimsical or well-thought out plan to break a relationship, and *breaking* relationship is not in itself a natural course of action in our society. Society, every organ of it is an epitome of cohesion, relation, organisation and unity. Moreover, in arranged and legal marriages agreement, trust, bequeathing, covenant and unification are well noted; breaking a relation is to go against these expressions of voluntary decision-making on our part before marriage. Divorce is thus a voluntary act to stay apart from the bond of love and compassion, the act is in essence against the spirit of socialisation. Marriage as a strong tool for our socialisation, harmony and unification apart from several need fulfilments is thus jeopardised by the act of divorce. It is not that divorced people are anti-social, they fail in socialisation, or that unmarried people are unsocial. However, divorced people are beyond doubt parties who could not stay in a unique form of social cohesion at the most micro-level of social existence and socialisation. There may be strong reasons in such breach of relation though surviving in cohesion were more desirable course for personal and social good and a sure step towards effective socialisation and moral evolution or moralisation. It may be said that both socialisation and moralisation are possible without marriage and with divorce, and that socialisation and moralisation through marriage and staying for life in that bond is still not attainable or even not desirable. However, the point is that though marriage and staying in that relation for long may not be necessary and sufficient grounds for socialisation and moralisation, divorce at will, cannot be necessary and sufficient ground for the same. No one is arguing in favour of marriage and the implied socialisation and moralisation, one is arguing in favour of marriage and implied socialisation and moralisation by virtue of a *deep cohesion* than a breach—a breach in married relation harms the said cohesion and thus harms the most strongly possible way of socialisation and moralisation though other ways are not contested. It may well be that on extremely strong grounds a woman gets divorced, and her socialisation and moralisation are enhanced, but the point is whether the said "strong grounds" are really "strong" on uniform perception and that other "strong" reasons and adjustments could not prevail owing to touted "strength" of one's *own* grounds. Hence, the case of "divorce" in society opens for us a can of worms immediately, the most noted one's that our readers have come across by the time being are, *intrinsic disvalue* of divorce versus *intrinsic value* of divorce, and the social-moral disvalue of divorce *versus* social-moral worth. The lines of conflict are drawn, which grows acute when we consider the typical Indian social setting and divorce therein.

Most of the Indians raised eyebrows a few decades ago when the case of divorce was discussed for practical and moral value because it was believed that the large Indian Diaspora does not imagine about things like divorce. It is said that though during the middle age married men and women became valueless in taking divorce without any social and moral hiccups whereas a few decades ago our ancestors were so noble and sacred not to imagine about such social and moral evil. As a philosopher I do not have sufficient information to pronounce any verdict in this matter but the social progress that I have watched and the news items, articles, papers which I have read have given me the common sense to imagine that in the ancient, medieval and modern India, in so far as marriage is concerned, divorce or something like that amounting to a break up of a defined relationship were always in existence. It will be very difficult to argue based on imagined data or *a priori* historicism that long ago people were good to snub divorce and now we are too bad to adore it. In fact, even today many Indians look it as social and moral curse, many take it in their stride and others think that it may not be either completely cursed or enjoyed, it should be evaluated for any value on legal grounds if marriage itself has a legal side. However, no one has prevented us from taking a legal side if marriages are customary having little or no legal side to it though in many cases two people were customarily married and they claim certain rights. It may well be that the legal side takes a queer social turn in so far as settling divorce is concerned because any imperative ruling is always less preferred than an amicable personal settlement not because Indians were sacred people or should be sacred now but for the reason that marriage and divorce are dominant social concerns, they involve individuals and families, their desires, trusts and understandings which may be easily settled at those levels than taking the precious time of the otherwise burdened courts in India unless the atrocities and primary and secondary oppressions against married woman (also againsts married man) does not demand urgent legal and security interventions. Are we then really worried with the Indian scenario in our times? Yes, it may be the case because there is a peculiar renewed interest in the Indian Diaspora to find out why are they so unethical or ethical, so anti-social or pro-social when a number of marriages are broken in no time or after a long time. It is disturbing to notice that many puritans and otherwise orthodox social groups, castes, classes and faiths are coming up with the theoretical and practical controversies due to what they call "growing cases of divorce". Many among us are doubly enthusiastic in such controversies when we are particularly interested about the new world and Indian economic and social order, and about modernity, feminist movement, human rights and social justice. Are the cases of divorce really "growing" in India? Is the growth rate alarming? In addition, if the answers are in the affirmative, what are ethical stirrings that might have a hold on the menace?

The social scientists in India insist that as compared to the pre-globalisation era, the Indian society is witnessing a steady growth of divorce cases on some worth considering and some flimsy grounds. The 'worth considering' or the more or less uniform 'strong' grounds of divorce are in the main primary and secondary oppressions of men and women resulting into many forms of atrocities, which are *undesirable personally* on emotive and physical grounds; *socially* on the grounds of disharmony and disorder and *legally* on the ground of growth of criminal acts. Interesting point is that the personal, social and legal undesirability of grounds of divorce, that is, oppressions and atrocities on humans are 'strong'. In fact, personal, social and legal undesirability which are main grounds of divorce can be evaluated as of Frankenstein measures because they point towards the basic unethicality of personal, social and legal disvalue of oppression and atrocities on humans. While a divorcee suffer physically and mentally, suffering is unethical as it maximises *personal* (egoistic) losses than benefits and while a divorcee suffers by being participant in division of a family, it is unethical as it minimises *social* (altruistic) benefits. In addition, while a divorcee is suffering owing to the effects of criminal acts on her, it is unethical because it threatens the *legal* structure and thus the *universal* element in civil life and civil well-being. It is believed that in India, the "growing" cases of divorce is an indicator of widespread morally undesirable acts causing personal, social and legal undesirable consequences. The sociologists are of the opinion that the rise in divorce cases is well noticed in the urban areas in India, among the young couples in particular due to the above mentioned strong grounds to be precise. Human atrocities are due to many flimsy grounds such as "intolerance" among couples owing to habits, customs and beliefs. There is no doubt that 'atrocities' and 'intolerance' are due to many factors in India. The social scientists are generally of the opinion that said genuine or strong ground of divorce are mainly economic and correlative changes in the perceptions of matrimony, sex and human relations. It is not difficult to find a growth in the number of divorce suits among urban population in the main, particularly among economically well-off people or among couples who are in the higher economic pursuits, cravings and expectations, and fall knowingly or unknowingly in the vicious cycles or affluent style of living and ways of life detrimental to the person and society. Those making flimsy reasons for divorce, that is, 'intolerance' are more often than not psychopaths who just do not cope up mentally and physically with people who do not abide by their personal whims, likes and beliefs. Let us not talk too much about flimsy grounds of divorce, but they are worth noticing because it is reported that in the judiciary many cases are of flimsy nature than genuine. One important aspect of "intolerance" is that the Indian Diaspora, the urban youth in the main, again appears to be *non-*

reconciling, that is, rather than resolving hitches in marriage, they are restless in settling the issue in great haste through a breach. It is equally true that the parents of the youth (urban in the main) have grown proportionately "non-reconciliatory". This may be again due to economic and other life-style reasons. Is it true that the growing intolerances and unrest are due to a feminist upsurge in India? We hardly contest that atrocities and intolerance (the grounds of divorce) are due to the age-old male chauvinism and patriarchal social systems. We will come to the feminist upsurge, but before that let us come to our study of "growth" and causes of growth of divorce in India. Reportedly, the Tata Institute of Fundamental Research has found that starting from mid-eighties, there is a steep rise in cases of divorce in urban India among the couples of age groups of 21 to 30. These young people are most of the time well placed, highly ambitious and persons of lusty pursuits in life. These trendy people championing Western modernity make our judiciary a happy hunting ground to settle personal issues. The Institute says that nearly fifty cases per day of divorce are reported. However, not all will agree that the urban couples are immoral and modernity along with affluence and growing egoistic hedonism are to be blamed. Almost the same grim picture though heavily parochial in terms of the urban youth is painted by a number of counsellors in the urban areas, who complain that the upwardly mobile young urban population is coming to the counsellors with bags full of nagging complains and habitual unrest than settling the marital hitches for a fresh lease of life. The divorce cases are mostly centred on the economic life-style and psychological problems that these restless people have. One imagines that this was not the trend in urban India a few decades back. Some overenthusiastic old nostalgic people complain that the dilution of social or arranged marriages, the family bonds that grew among the sacred rituals in India, and the over-hyped love marriage, inter-caste marriage, dating and legal marriages are the contributing elements in the entire phenomenon of matriarchic relation in India causing so many divorces. The argument may be extended to cover the growing sense of freedom or liberty of women among educated young urban womenfolk in India that contributes to divorce. This may be followed up by the argument that on matters of marriage parents should be relied because arranged marriage is the best. Women should be tolerant and accept their basic domestic role gladly to cooperate better with their husbands, and married women should not add fuel to the already kindled fire to achieve great pleasure in life. We know what happens when one supports this ancient perception about the role of women, their ways and life and their social contribution after marriage. We will not consider it now, but we cannot conceal the ethical evaluation of such perception *vis-à-vis* the liberal ones that we have not discussed thus far. Social scientists and psychologists are of the opinion that in India the growing rate of divorce cases can be also traced in the growth of the liberalist perception about extra-marital relationship. In fact, "nothing is unethical" is the clarion call of the contemporary urban India. This may take us to believe that "nothing is unethical in extra-marital sex" as well. More strongly, "nothing ethical or unethical" may be pressed too far in the contexts of marriage, sex life and extra-marital relationship. This must be a trendy affair, and expressions of liberalism and modernity. Are these perceptions in contemporary times beyond ethical evaluation? No, if we believe in the catholicity of ethical evaluation that does not take sides, whether orthodox or modern, whether conservative or liberal. No one really believes that liberals are so bad in advocating our sacred Indian women getting economic liberation. No one seriously doubts that women may be upwardly mobile at will and ability. Nevertheless, the point or ethical debate is whether upwardly mobile young women should play an ultra chauvinist role. What is unethical in the role-reversal of the women in India? The traditionally oppressed Indian women should now set free, they have right to equality and by virtue of that, they are equal with their husband and should thus enjoy the status, power, facilities and benefits but what next? Next is that if they do not get these touted things for equality with men, is it not desirable that they should 'set free', 'revolt' and seek divorce? The questions that crop up owing to the renewed ethical debate with the liberalists makes the issue of divorce even more challenging to face. In fact, the ethical perceptions about women, their role in family and society and their rights and justice invites us to consider them under social ethics as value-laden social problem.

The urban population also lacks in joint families, which is another concern for social ethics. These families are fast depleting even in rural India, which owes to economic and psychological tensions in families and society. However, it may be evaluated whether joint families really contributes to the resolution of marital hitches and prevent divorce which is otherwise not easy to resolve in nuclear families. Anyway, the growing trend of divorce in India invites us to conduct an ethical scrutiny, which we should analyse and resolve through the intersubjective corroborative method but for that apart from other things we need to evaluate the worth of joint families as well.

Nevertheless, before jumping in to the resolution through intersubjective corroboration, a few words should be said on the main complaints of divorce in our societies and take a close look on the ethically relevant inquiries with regard to these complaints. This is needed because in any moral debate, we are furnished with these complaints but the point is of resolution after ethical scrutiny. Our classification of causes or complaints of divorce stated before have to be thoroughly analysed because the causes of "oppression" and "unrest" of mind are somewhat vague. Most of the sociologists believe that the causes of divorce should be best classified from two perspectives: from the perspective of the husband and that of the wife. Now putting them together, we get the following: an important cause is the use of authority or dominance over wife and oppressions primary and secondary, which are worse as physical assaults, attempt to murder and incapacitation. It may be said that in stray cases, such oppressive authoritative behaviours are seen in case of a role-reversal in women. This is closely related to but a little different from assuming a dominant *personality* whether by man or woman. Covert oppression by man or woman is in terms of systematic neglect of family members. This is closely associated to the extra-marital relationship and correlative reversal of role of love, affection, spending and care outside one's own family. Oppressions also come in the form of *undignified* social behaviour such as drinking, addiction of other types and womanising or any form of extrovert infidelity. There are many causes, which are a bit different from oppressive causes. These are mostly psychological and physical in origin that causes wide range of unrest among couples or instability of mind. Prime among these causes are physical defects, mental illness and sexual defects and diseases. Others are economic insecurity, which may come with economic affluence and scarcity. Many forms of complexes of colour, creed, race, religion, caste and class cause divorce and in the recent times, workaholism is accused of causing divorce.

The rise of the liberal philosophy of giving women their due has emerged as a chief contributor to divorce among married couples. Before we take up this case in more details, we need to reflect on the ethical questions that come up in evaluating the so-called "oppressions" and "instabilities", because apart from the fact that oppressions and instabilities are undesirable on practical grounds, we need to have another perspective, the "ethical" one to inquire why or for what ethical reasons should or should not such oppressions and instabilities be called unethical and thus to be avoided carefully. Such an evaluation is all the more important in the recent times in the Indian society, which is moving towards a so-called global order, and in the context of which we consider the case of feminism and divorce. Without going into the details of the rise of feminism in India and the causes of the rise, we can say that the liberalist trend in our society is strongly supported on some ethical grounds, which are also helpful in the support of the feminist urge for a suit for divorce. Though feminism is a western *revolt* not only by women of that society but by all like minded people who thought that oppressions against women and loss of their freedom to decide and act in matters of great personal and social importance should be vehemently opposed and corrected because subjugation of women since a long time is *ethically* unacceptable. Hence, the revolt of feminism and the ethical basis of the revolt are related but different. It is important to note here that "feminist ethics" is yet another movement, not of feminists but of the ethicists, which we will not consider. The revolt dates back to the early nineteenth century Europe in particular but spread in America and other places, almost throughout the globe by the twentieth century. India was not left aside though the feminist activism here has not been exactly as it were in the west. Many Indians believe that the liberalist conception of rights of women in society and fight for it and for atrocities has been championed in our early *śāstras* and by many modern and contemporary thinkers. However, the point here is how far Indian feminists were influenced by the western activism and what significant changes are noticed here. We will not go into these details. What interests us most is that the Indian liberals were not far behind to champion the rightful causes of women and to revolt for such rights and liberties. It is important to note that even in the Indian society the feminist conception of family and marriage was hotly debated on ethical grounds, and this is what interests us most. It appears that the ethical debate centres around the western feminist conception of "humanity of women" which became correlative to save the "humanity" by means of "complete freedom as mothers" propagated mainly by Mrs. Philip Snowden and Ms. Ellen Key. It was further observed that the militant call for "complete freedom as mothers" is nothing but championing the cause of a woman who should be free at will to choose *asexual* and *non-maternal* life; she must not be subjugated to a male gifted sexual life and a family life of bondage. Marriage thus becomes equally meaningless male gifted life for her and must be against her humanity. It is not difficult to imagine that even in the late nineteenth and twentieth centuries such feminist call for liberation from male gifted marriage, family and sex life was not very catchy appeal for the orthodox, puritan, oppressed and relatively less educated and uneducated masses, the same is the case with enlightened people who will think twice about such "militant feminist humanism". Though some novels of Saratchandra and Tagore reflect on such matters, it is very difficult to say that the ethical evaluation of the militant thesis was bright enough because it was a "female-gifted" life to our women thinking that for women, everything will be fine if they are not pushed into maternal and sex life but what if no one really pushed them? The debate is interesting at this point because there is distinct ethical problem in a "push" on women in society, whether direct or indirect. The ethical call is that on matters of marriage and family women calls for liberty for decision-making and choice on such matters, they are not freak egoists or pervert individualists. If we get the points right, the ethical debate is hot. The heat is doubly felt when no less liberals (as in the west we have H.G. Wells and Bertrand Russell), who urged to refrain from the so-called "asexual and non-maternal militant feminism" because it is not call for a freedom of choice and decision rather, a freedom to ensure that marriage as a social institution becomes redundant. There is thus a tension between the conceptions of women enjoying freedom and equality by recognising the value of family, marriage and motherhood and the value of freedom to enjoy a life without marriage, family and motherhood or a life without marriage and family but not motherhood because it is not necessarily related to the conception of marriage and family. However, the militant feminists and Wells are of the opinion that women should enjoy "freedom of love" and is equal to men though there may be debates about the need of the basic social institutions. In a startling view W.L. George champions an ultra militant feminism calling for an abolition of marriage and family but neither sex nor living as couples and having children because women enjoys the freedom for "free love". This is again attacked on ethical grounds because it amounts to gross sensualistic egoism where fortuitous sexism and living together are glorified abolishing marriage and family. However, counter ethical view may be that the best way to save the humanity of women and stop atrocities on them is to avoid the diseased perception of free-sex and abolish the unknown and unfounded fear that marriage and family means curbing freedom and encouraging oppressions.

In the midst of the stiff ethical debate regarding the abolition of marriage and family, we should be nonetheless, reminded of the champion feminist J.S. Mill's urge for "economic freedom" of women and supported by others though with the alluring call for abolition of "home" and "home duties" by the feminists. A proper ethical evaluation of marriage and family will be possible if the non-militant and ultra-feminists all over the world take into consideration and understand four important ethical arguments inherent in these calls. First, feminism is an ethically justified revolt against the oppressions on women in families after marriage, whether arranged or legal because it is based on the conception of *liberty as freedom from constraints*, that is, to let women free from those undesirable constraints of husband, other family members, the society and the state which does not allow women to be moralised and to moralise our environment. This is certainly not to free women from family and marriage but to liberate from a constraint that does not allow her moral evolution as a free individual. Second, feminism is an ethically justified revolt as it is based on the conception of *independence* or *individualism* which sees the state and other agents as trustees to women's well-being, they are thus means to the good for women and should not act determinants of her decisions and actions or freedom which are the ethical means to fulfil the same good in her life. Women should not be thus seen as "household expert" whose good is to work there efficiently in many ways, starting from child bearing and rearing to cooking and other domestic jobs. Such conception of good for women is deterministic; it binds women in subjugation and constraints her contribution to society. Related to this is the third argument that feminists call for a renewed ethical look at her status with regard to a labourer after marriage, that is, what should be humane way to look at her "labour" she contributes in a household after marriage. Ethically speaking, it cannot be a physical labour moving in a vicious cycle of "bedroom to labour room to kitchen and to bedroom". If woman labour after marriage is perceived in this way, she is a commodity in a household, and the humane marriage relation that has been shelved here must be ethically undesirable to continue. Hence, if women are not free from constraints, does not enjoy individuality and their contributions after marriage are not valued in the right perspective, *divorce* becomes a rightful claim on her part. The same is the case when her complete evolution of moral character is jeopardised after marriage, it appears that divorce has a rightful claim or marriage appears to be suffering from a myopic conception of end of human life. The ethical debates about the feminist conception of marriage and divorce thus lull us to a tension maze where it is crucial that we look at the value of women in civil societies.

Readers now have an idea that before going for serious corroboration debates to resolve ethical issues in society one has to "learn from the masses" and of course, from the theoretical churnings about value-laden issues which we have in different forms. It is extremely important to keep our eyes and ears open to what is happening around us, and care for what people feel about certain things and what are the interactions about the value-laden issues in our society. A "non-structured" way to frame questions for moral debates by trained ethicists or others who are interested in these things demand de-classed persons to "learn and get involved" in intersubjective discourses. As usual, we need a panel and a questionnaire for settling the issue of divorce. In the year 1999, I arranged one such debate with the following persons aided by a questionnaire that follows next:

1. Mrs. Jaya Roy, Advocate, Ranchi High Court, Ranchi;
2. Dr. Maya Prasad, Professor of Hindi, University Department, Ranchi University & Women's Rights Activist;
3. Dr. Sandhya Sinha, Professor of Botany, Ranchi Women's College, Ranchi & Women's Rights Activist;
4. Dr. Md. Hasan Raza, Professor of Urdu, S.S. Memorial College (now in the University Department), Ranchi University;
5. Dr. Gaya Pandey, Lecturer in Anthropology, University Department of Anthropology, Ranchi University.

QUESTIONNAIRE

1. What in your opinion is the value of human relations in a free and fair society that builds by virtue of marriage?
2. What in your opinion is the desirable man-woman relation after marriage? What should be ideal or ideals of a married life?

3. Kindly evaluate the use of authorities and commands, personal, social and religious in a married life.
4. Kindly evaluate the importance of economic and other maternal need fulfilments as well as emotive and metaphysical factors in a married life. How do you judge the importance of a married woman in these regards?
5. Do you think that nothing is unethical in breaking a marriage relationship? What are the grounds for or against such breach?
6. Do woman and man enjoy a right to ask for divorce when they deem it necessary? Alternatively, do we say that the married couples are worst judges to call for a divorce though they have a right to do so?
7. Do you think that divorce should appropriately take care of rights of men and women wanting divorce? What are the appropriate steps and who should decide them?
8. Are social, political and religious authorities ethically permissible in the course of arranging and settling divorce and compensating the rights of men and women after divorce?

It is not difficult to understand why a moral debate about divorce (that is clearly related to the debate of marriage), should accommodate a lawyer who has a vast experience of dealing with divorce cases both as successful legal settler of the claims of parties and to counsel them to abstain from divorce. In order to evaluate the moral perceptions of champions of women's rights and even proper evaluators of liberty of women after marriage, we need one or two women's rights activists and persons of the feminist outlook (which luckily I was able to accommodate). The selection of a panellist belonging to a particular religion and most expectedly to have unique parallel legal, religious and social perceptions about divorce was natural. The accommodation of an anthropologist was also natural, particularly if he or she has good knowledge of the issue of divorce. It will be equally good to accommodate a sociologist, an economist, someone with a Marxist following and police personnel. However, a careful selection might take care of these views; for instance, an anthropologist may be good enough at sociological reading of the issue. A lawyer might fill in the gap of police personnel. A feminist might be of a Marxist following and a fair idea of the economic and social-political aspects of divorce provided the selection is careful. In fact, it is very difficult in a debate to accommodate many people because it may be lengthy, boring and difficult reaching a closure. Hence, the best way is to go on for many such debates throughout the country from time to time so that our policy makers and decision-makers are benefited by the ethical perceptions of people and the decision-making rules they suggest. In a democracy, this may be one of the best ways to resolve value-laden social issues. I have already hinted the readers to not to expect post-corroboration analysis of views here and thus not to expect the details of the debates. However, as usual, we can read the upshot of the debate, which is as follows:

The startling unanimous decision of some enlightened contemporary Indian men and women is that: "Divorce, when it is deemed to be necessary by the judgements of married couples, family members, other peer groups and legal experts, which cannot be or should not be settled by extra-legal ways, should be forthwith allowed by the court. The most important reasons for divorce are the acts of men and women, which are anti-human, exploitative and derogatory to human dignity and destroy individual, familial and social peace and harmony. Hence, divorce becomes a much needed, ethically justified social tool for it restores human dignity and social harmony which are deemed to be under serious threat without slightest controversy." It was argued that divorce cases should be adequately compensated economically and divorced persons should be allowed to remarry if that compensates their social, economic, physical and emotive damages.

We may now turn to the last issue that has put the Indian society in a huge turbulence, even today (2007). Let us consider the case of "Reservation in Jobs" in India, which is as broad to cover "reservation" of many types, such as reservation in jobs based on *caste*, *religion*, *gender*, *physical and mental handicaps* and *income*, which naturally leaves out a number of job aspirant who belong to the so-called "general caste", "major religion", "physically and mentally unchallenged" and those of "well-off class". Expectedly, while taking sides in appointments whether in the private or in the public sector, there are visible rifts among the job seekers, their families and those in different positions having occupations and professions in different institutions and organisations. And rifts among the population is not theoretical or intellectual, in reality they are very much active often expressed in forms of violence with associated verbal conflicts, which is another expression of violence. The so-called "protests" against reservation are hardly non-violent in nature. Hence, the protests and anti-protest or pro-reservation movements are both trouble-shooters for the social managers and legal heads. Often trouble-shooters need to be countered, that is, violence met with violence causing no less rift, suffering and hatred. From outside as onlookers, it appears to be "sporadic" as if nothing is abnormal in the country but the population is divided along sharp lines and they are in reality burning from within, wanting to go for an onslaught when situation demands—the violence truly has crept in the mind of the population. This may be the picture anywhere in the world. We will find shortly that in India, this is not only true, it is turning to be a real life civil strife after independence of a stature we have not imagined or are not imagining. How can we avoid this? Alternatively, should we avoid this situation being a responsible citizen? We should not do so because the problem should be settled between us non-violently first taking the basic ethical question of what if at all is desirable or good, just, or right in "reservation in jobs", and how it should be done, that is, what is the most desirable course of decision-making and action about reservation. Though I have considered the value-laden issue of "reservation in jobs" in India for all practical purposes, the value-crises in "affirmative action" and "preferential treatment" which does not merely deal in the reservation in jobs but in many spheres such as reservation in education, distribution of goods and services in the society, extending social benefits, welfare extending benefits to the minorities and even promotion in jobs. It also deals in reservation in view of colour or race or primitiveness or location or catastrophic conditions. Hence, "reservation in jobs" in India which takes care of factors such as caste, religion, handicaps, gender and income does not do complete justice with the more overreaching or broad issues of affirmative action and preferential treatment keeping in the broad spectrum of "reservation" in human societies at large. The readers might thus expect a full-length intersubjective corroboration debate that considers the typical value-crisis in Indian society owing to reservation in jobs, particularly in view of caste based reservation. I have now a duty cut out for me to do some justice at least by being more liberal in discussing other forms of reservation such as in education, distribution of social goods to the minorities and promotions in jobs and what are the ethical queries related to *preferential treatment and affirmative actions*. It is always good to move from the broadest issues in this regard that covers the main theme underlying all forms of "reservation" discussed above and then move to the Indian scenario of reservation in its broader sense and finally, to the crisis of reservation in jobs in India on the bases we have already seen.

Let us discuss about the ethical questions arising from the courses of affirmative action and preferential treatment provided we keep in mind that the moot question is whether both courses do any social justice and aim at social equality because often these courses of action in our societies are touted as doing social justice and equality. Other related concepts are "equal opportunity" and "discrimination". The points are whether the said courses of action are ethically just in extending equal opportunity to the masses having certain claim rights and whether that amounts to deliberate but ethically justified way to discriminate people for advantages and benefits. Hence, "reservationism" takes us to the issues of affirmative action, preferential treatment, equality of opportunity and social discrimination. This must be good enough prelude to what we discuss after this, that is, to concentrate more in job reservation in India with all the typical features that it has.

In a seminal paper "The Message of Affirmative Action", T.E. Hill says, "Affirmative action programmes remain controversial, I suspect, partly because the familiar argument for and against them start from significantly different moral perspectives. I want to step back for a while from the details of debate about particular programmes and give attention to the moral viewpoints presupposed in different types of argument."[1] And wisely, so because we have said that rather than the threadbare nitty-gritty at the outset we should first find out what is ethical in affirmative action. For Hill, in affirmative action, "action" is the key for its meaning analysis, and he obviously speaks human voluntary actions, the well thought out and intended ones, which have definite ends and means carefully chosen, the performance of which amounts to definite consequences, which reveals its value after thorough evaluation. It is very difficult to imagine some social being without choosing, intending and acting though the value or worth of our actions are not so easy to evaluate because it begs standards, which may be questioned for their validity. Hence, it is difficult to say whether our judgements of worth of actions are valid by our standards, such as consequentialism or utilitarianism or any other. The subjectivity of judgement of worth of actions or other ways to judge the same are trouble trodden. However, we cannot ever overlook the value of our actions, and this must be true of the actions of social institutions and organisations. In this regard, we can speak of a unique type of action which is "affirmative" which as usual has its own effects or impacts on the individuals, groups and society at large and the evaluation for its worth in terms of its ends and means as based on definite standards. The almost inevitable and unavoidable impacts of affirmative actions by a group or an organisation or an institution should thus take us to the moral question of their worth or value so that we can finally decide whether such actions are "affirmative" and desirable or some of its aspects or courses are undesirable and to be avoided. Hence, the question is why should we at all take an affirmative course of action? However, the primary question is, why do we speak of an "affirmative" course? The sense here is to imagine an intended course of action at the organised level in society that aims at larger social good by virtue of some *positive or affirmative steps* taken to fill the gappiness in benefits or advantages at the individual and group planes by means of selecting some people or groups of people for exclusive benefits or for their scarcity and needs, jobs, opportunities, honours, rights and justice. It appears that the actions taken are essentially "negative" and not affirmative because it negates the benefits and advantages of some individuals or groups of individuals for the sake of the same of others. (The saying goes that such courses of action are still called "affirmative" in so far as they affirm or bequeath an evident social injustice or disparities to be corrected by authorities who are morally obliged to do so to affirm or ensure complete public good and not partial public good.) Without going into any details at the outset, we find that such courses of action have deep impacts in society and we cannot jump into those courses without a scrutiny of their moral worthwhileness.

As we have seen above, the most widespread definition of affirmative action hinges on the conception of a good or value, which is "individual and social *benefits*", which is no doubt futuristic and obsessed with the idea that "good" is "benefit" and nothing else, though such "benefits" are matters of realistic calculus of the *consequences* of actions in the future which are probably or most expectedly to bring out greater individual and social benefits. In moral philosophy, such an ethical argument to justify the worth of affirmative action is known as the *forward-looking argument* advocated by the *utilitarians*. It is important to note here that old-fashioned utilitarians would say that affirmative actions are morally desirable as far as they maximise social happiness, though there is evident vagueness in "happiness" as the quantum of desirableness. Therefore, it is argued by neo-utilitarians, that affirmative actions are morally desirable as far as calculus of future consequences of such actions most expectedly maximise *social benefits or advantages* or maximises *social good than evil.* Obviously, if we imagine having a feeling of happiness from the said benefits or goods, it is altogether another futuristic expectation, but no one denies that having all benefits would leave us in a completely unhappy state in life. Among a number of benefits or good things expected to be delivered by the consequences of affirmative actions are distinct advantages to the minorities, women, children, handicapped, underpowered, old and weak, tribes and races, unemployed people, sufferers of income disparities and people distinguished for their colour and creed. For the forward-looking utilitarians as consequentialists and those inclined to the calculus of advantages it is important to answer why negative looking consequences of an intended course of affirmative action (mentioned before) are morally desirable. A consequentialist has to evaluate the negative effects of a said positive action. It is argued that the negative looking consequences are not so when we consider the overall advantages in the society though there is no doubt that those affirmative actions stir sections of people randomly so that entropic conditions are marked. Closely related to a massive protest and unrest is the fear that the calculus of benefits often overlooks the means we have obtained for benefits or at least we intend to have one which is nothing but causing an indirect harm to the underpowered or disadvantaged individuals or groups by keeping them off from real path of social progress and uplift thus not pushing them to the mainstream competition or fight for excellence and merely encouraging gratis and appeasement. Hence, what appears to be forward looking is in reality negative and thus undesirable. It may well be that there are some worth considering moral critiques of the utilitarian justification of affirmative actions which call our rationality to consider that though future benefit calculus is important for social decision-making, it may not be the whole truth.

This gives a chance to the *backward looking ethical justification* of affirmative action. For one thing, this is not "backward looking" in being a negative course of action. How can an obvious negative act be ethically good? In fact, what the forward-looking argument plays down is appreciated much for value by the backward looking argument, and where it looks is the "past" (and not the "future"). Hence, the backward looking argument is so-called because rather than considering the calculus of a future consequence of action for its moral worth, we need to look back to the past *events* that educate us what should be done or what course of actions should be "affirmed as our *duty*", that is, which affirmative actions should be performed irrespective of what are the good or bad consequences they might produce, the action *per se* is of value or worth or that it is our duty to perform the actions of intrinsic worth. This must be then a *deontic* justification of the moral worth of affirmative action. More simply stated, as certain events in the past suggest affirmative actions as of worth, they are nevertheless, irrespective of future consequences our duty to perform. Such an argument is influenced by Kantian deontology and advocated by W.D. Ross in recent times as the theory of "reparation" because at the social plane, inflicting injustice on our part is intrinsically bad and it becomes our *prima facie duty* to "repartee" or restitute what wrong we have done to others and thereby contribute to social justice. Hence, reparation is an affirmative action by virtue of being a duty or some course of action of intrinsic moral worth that we consider doing based on what we learn from "events of the past". Though the deontic justification is not foolproof, it is argued that the justification holds some distinct advantages over the forward looking utilitarian justification, such as the careful notice of the past *injustice* done in society which were found to be *morally repugnant* for its *intrinsic worth*, and to correct them now while we take an affirmative course of action in society for the restoration of social justice. The justification enjoys an advantage to look beyond the value of means and ends in so far as they were of our advantage, but to see that certain courses of action *ought* to be done for their worth notwithstanding the intrinsic worth of moral agents whether they are now bereft of some of their rights or some of them enjoy the same; no one really tries to take off the rights and advantages of moral agents. However, backward looking deontic justification has its own problems. As usual, a stiff epistemological problem to know beyond doubt that some events of the past were intrinsically evil or bad is really troubling. Let us take the case of wanton mischief and harm on the women of the past in India, the great social injustice they suffered. Even if we agree that the events suggested something unjust and evil, but how do we *know* for sure that the events *suggested* such evil and nothing but evil? The consequentialists have easy reply, for them, relying mainly on sense-empiricism, the effects of events of the past or the *consequences* that followed from some gross acts of humans on women inform us that they were of great disadvantage and loss (not benefit) to women, and therefore, unjust and evil. Hence, deontic thesis must rely on the consequences of past effects to be judged as morally repugnant as praiseworthy. However, the "intrinsic worth" of actions as our "duty" as suggested by events of the past is possible only if the knowledge of the same owes to our *intuition*. The universalisable conception of "duty" begs our weird intuition with a lurking danger of unjustifiable presuppositions, which are matters of stiff debate than universally accepted. It is an interesting point to debate whether an adult boy or girl of this age in India should look back to find gross racial injustice done on some poor people by the race to which they belong when they happen to be decision makers to reparate the ancient evil acts in exact proportions now. Can it be more trouble torn to calculate the proportionate justice to repatriate the ancient injustice now, provided the injustice "known" to us is intuitively, absolutely true?

In view of the relative merits and demerits, though demerits count most if we take any of the two views experienced here to be true, it appears that affirmative action cannot be an easily justifiable course of action. The crux of such doubt is that we are obsessed with either consequences of action or intrinsic worth of actions but do not care much for some individual and community values, historical conditions and values obtained from narrative accounts, which were truly emphasised by ethicists like Alasdair McIntyre, Carol Gilligan, Lawrence Blum and T.E. Hill. These thinkers justify the ethical value of affirmative action first, based on the life, thought and deeds of moral agents in a *historical perspective*, that is, by considering them in the perspectives of the past, the present and the future. It is important for us to evaluate our values across the periods and judge what courses of action were needed, desirable and to be carried on. This is much in tune with the evaluation of what *virtues* we need to inculcate across the historical periods in the capacity of moral agents who intends to value and act according to affirmative decisions. The champions of *virtue ethics* like McIntyre, who are in some sense critiques of normative absolutism of the deontologists and teleologists, justify affirmative action in this way. Pursuing a different justification we have the supporters of feminist ethics, such as, Carol Gilligan who argues that it is extremely important for moral agents to evaluate his or her *life stories* and find out at every epoch of past, present and future what were desirable courses of actions, whether affirmative or any other so to say as well as what are and what should be the most cherished values and virtues that also takes notice of the life stories of others as equally important because they cohere in a social organisation. It is desirable that what we value as justifiable courses of action at this point or in future, should nevertheless; take *care* of the other lives because we share a common history. Thinkers like Lawrence Blum argue that the ethical justification of affirmative action should be based on *community values* than sheer individual ones, though individuals must be seen as of great value. Stressing on individual histories, their life stories and their values, we often forget that doing justice in a particular case by affirmative action does not amount to affirmative action in the true sense of the term because we have overlooked the community life and community values. However, to consider the value of community life and community values in a course of action that is affirmative, we cannot differentiate individual cases or individual lives for their values and then "sum-up" to find what community values are. Consideration of community values is not to consider individual values and then add them to reflect community value. In any case, the upshot is that affirmative action draws ethical strength from care for evaluation of both individual values and community values in a "unity" considering the entire history of our lives. This has much to share with both the virtue ethical and feminist ideas we have discussed here, particularly the revolt to the normative deductivism that draws ethical courses of action from a standard theory without much care for individual values and community values. Based on the ethical justification of affirmative actions, which may be said to be contrasting justifications that are normative and non-normative, T.E. Hill first draws this conclusion: "I suggest that some of the values that give affirmative action its point are best seen as cross time values that fall outside the exclusively forward looking and backward looking perspectives. They include having a history of social and gender relations governed, so far as possible by the ideal of mutual respect, trust, and fair opportunity for all."[2] Hence, for Hill, the ethical validity of affirmative actions is derived from certain values in our societies, which should be seen as universal despite cultural, racial, and linguistic and many other differences along with differences in individual histories and life stories. These values, he says, are "mutual respect, trust and fair opportunity". Why does Hill filter out these values as paradigmatic in shaping courses of affirmative action? Perhaps he believes that with the growing trends in the democratisation of civil states it is the power of the public that matters ultimately for any state to flourish, and the power of the public lies in the "unity" or "cohesion" despite obvious relativism and differences. Actions that are affirmative then do not disunite or at least should not attempt to do so. Hence, actions must be unifying in nature, "binding" so to say. Naturally, therefore, affirmative actions draw moral strength from the public cohesion and the corporate good in the present and in future, more simply the good that is sustainable through the ages despite the differences among the public. Affirmative actions then presuppose that such actions should be or should desirably be based on the mutual respect among the individuals, respect that recognises worth of individuals *per se*, not merely as means to our ends. Only then such actions do not harm us or harass us. Such actions should be desirably based on 'trust' because in the lack of it doing well for a section of the population at the cost of some deprivation of others cannot be tolerated. We must keep faith on social institutions that such actions will not take their good and rights away, and make them a class of sufferers. Affirmative actions depend on fair opportunities because most desirably, as we realise value of others as our own being, we trust each other, we do sincerely believe that we all have equal rights to flourish, for our well being, and for all this we have to access to the various opportunities that nature and society have provided us. In short, the values conceived by Hill, that are "cross-time" provide ample ethical justification for actions that aim at public good through public involvement though not forgetting the fact that public's unified involvement asks for some sacrifice. Hill must not be averse to the idea prevailing in democracy advocated by J.B.S. Haldane: "for social good, we must be ready to sacrifice some of our goods".

Well, all these good words by McIntyre, Gilligan, Blum and Hill must be respected for they wanted to stay away from the hackneyed normativism that ruled ethical thinking about crucial matters such as this through the ages. Truly, why should teleology and deontology be the guiding ethical principles in matters such as this? It is difficult to understand that the moral agents on whom depend crucial things like affirmative action involving preferential treatment be left aside for rumblings concerning good, just and right. However, the critiques of the agent based thinking on moral matters such as this have good questions to ask, which turns out to be counter ethical opinion justifying the ethics of abstaining from affirmative action and preferential treatment. At the outset, I confess that I wonder how social beings are unified despite their differences. How do we come to know that respect, trust and so on are needed virtues or values we should possess, which are crucial to social unification? We may say that these intrinsic values are known to us by virtue of our intuition and in that case, Ross' deontic prejudices are hard to avoid. It may be that these are extrinsic values known to us by virtue of our sense experience of the good effects; in that case, consequentialism has not left us. Life-stories not withstanding, we need to have the virtue of getting unified in the milieu of haves and have-nots which is anchored to the idea that either the said virtue is of intrinsic worth (and intuitive) or worthwhile for the several good effects it has. Another important point is that "wishing to unify" and "having that virtue" can never be sufficient on the ground levels of affirmative courses of action or for preferential treatment. Doing something needs careful thinking which certainly one of the virtues is but while doing certain things the computation of consequences are of equal importance. In fact, wishing that while we treat preferentially the persons of different life-stories we should corroborate wilfuly which does not happen on ground reality but we need to push through our programme. It may be that the corroboration imagined by the non-normativists in the main is wishful than actual because actual corroboration in public comes through a *dynamics in and with the public* among tremendous moral and practical heat, traces of which were felt when we considered our earlier issues. Here we are going to face them more so intently. Nevertheless, before that let us see what is in store of ethical justification of non-affirmative actions, such as preferential treatment.

In another seminal paper, John Kekes puts this heading: "The Injustice of Affirmative Action Involving Preferential Treatment"[3]. According to Kekes, "affirmative action is the selection of people for prized, scarce, and competitive jobs, opportunities, or honours. It is customary to distinguish between two forms such a policy may take: *impartiality* and *preferential treatment.* The aim of impartiality is to ensure open areas to the initial pool from which procedural rules that apply to everyone equally. The aim of preferential treatment is to alter the procedural rules to favour some people in order to increase the likelihood that they rather than others will achieve the desired position. One form of affirmative action, therefore, is committed to impartiality and to the rejection of preferential treatment, while the other form is committed to preferential treatment and to the rejection of impartiality. The claim for preferential treatment is that it is morally justified because those favoured by it belong to some group many of whose members have been unjustly excluded from achieving the desired position simply because they were members of the group."[4] Nothing can be clearer and emphatic than this account of preferential treatment, its basic features, its inner contradictions and the moral ground for its justification. We did get some hint as to what is affirmative action in our previous discussion but we now come to know that affirmative action aims at a bundle of benefits to a group of people for the obvious reasons that minimal social welfare should consider the well-being of the deprived groups in the society, deprivations being material in the main but related closely to the deprived group's psychological or emotive and other non-natural deprivations. Clearly, affirmative action is a social tool used by the competent authorities for correcting certain defects in society, which cannot and should not be concealed or neglected because social well-being and strongly united social existence might be at stake. Hence, affirmative action is not another course of action; it is an imperative in our modern states that claims to be civil. However, in reality it *tends to be civil* because there are many gaps in its complete civility. There are widespread disparities and disfavours, wants and deprivations, exploitation and neglect. Hence, affirmative actions are needed as urgent necessities. Last few lines of Kekes' passage reveal that the main moral ground for having affirmative actions is to give what is legitimately due to those who were carefully kept out of getting the due by manipulation or mischief or sheer neglect. Everything sounds perfect as far as meaning, aim and moral justification of affirmative action are concerned but Kekes is apt at unfolding the problematic features of the same while he analyses its nature more clearly.

Thus far, we were harping on the need of "affirmative action" but not clarifying what consists in the affirmative action. Once we start analysing the concept, we find that it amounts to well deliberated acts of impartial treatment to all sections of society in so far as providing equal opportunities are concerned, for instance, we need to be impartial in providing equal opportunities to all the competent applicants for a post of college teacher irrespective of their caste, class, creed and so on. Nevertheless, affirmative action demands certain special favours or reservations or what we call preferred treatment to a particular group of people and should have exceptional rules and regulations framed for specific favours for them because we feel that they are deprived or backward in terms of flourishing or overall development and should come on par with other groups who otherwise enjoyed a better status and privileges since a long time. It appears that we feel a sense of obligation to pay what were due to a section of society to whom historical blunders by our ancestors disallowed the rightful or neglected it, and we have a sense of urgency to correct the said blunder. There must be a feeling of guilt as if on the part of the competent authorities now, to correct the historical blunders and compensate losses of sections of people who are their descendants forming a "class" of their own. The *unethicality* of affirmative action, thinks Kekes (and many others) lies in the glaring contradiction between the two necessary steps in a affirmative actions, that is, to give something to all but at the same time to deny something to some people which were otherwise bequeathed as due to them. Though, the applicants in *general* were free to apply for a college teacher's job for they had the needed basic requirements as per rules which is deemed to be uniform in every case, some handpicked by virtue of the historical blunder and social guilt were favoured for appointment, even for instance, they were five years older than others or have lower marks in their higher degree examination or did not have a research degree and so on. This amounts to the denial of a uniform rule in case of appointment though generally, expectation was a fair treatment by virtue of the bequeathed equality of opportunity, and therefore, in the final run "partial" or "preferential", *not* impartial treatment was meted. How can contradiction in procedural bequeathing by the responsible authorities be touted ethical if it amounts to be a "fake preferential bequeathing"? Can concealed preferences or qualified favouritism be called ethicality just if someone responsible for all this appeared to be impartial, open and just? Can untruth be the basis of social justice? Is deliberate act of openness violated by another act of closeness ethically desirable? Kekes and many others argue in detail that such acts are not only contradictory, it is grossly unethical, and for that matter, there is either nothing such as affirmative action or no moral strength in it if it is the same bundle of contradiction. But the champions of affirmative action who are no less wise to identify the inherent contradiction in the mechanism of social justice, calls for some back up corrective measures such as compensation, redistribution or diversity which are some steps to moral glorification of affirmative action. We have seen that idealists call for an ideal social unity cutting across life stories, the common agreement among the preferred and the privileged for a common good, are some other steps for the moral glorification of affirmative actions. Kekes and others argue that all these glorifications stop as halfway house in overall social justice, they are rather utter failures.

Kekes urges us to rethink whether an undoubted historical injustice to a social group can be corrected practically and ethically by "preferential treatment" (as if that was the only way out), particularly when we inquire whether the trouble-shooter in concern, that is, "impartiality" should be abolished on ethical grounds available to us and just feel comfortable with another part, that is "preferential treatment". Because we cannot be both impartial and preferential and it is easier to abolish the former than the latter provided another fear of historical blunder or guilt for the same does not prevent us in creating new faces in deprivation calling for an endless chain of preferential treatment so that civil societies are left with the holy grail of affirmative action for their proof of nobility. It is equally important for a moral inquiry to find out whether preferential treatment is a normal course in our society or somewhat unnatural because in normal cases we never speak or imagine of taking sides, preferring people because that is against the spirit of social existence and social harmony as well as question the moral strength of any agent or intuition who is bestowed with a social job. We should accept that societies do not necessarily need preferential treatment, but no one doubts that there must be minimal "impartiality" in our society in providing freedom of choice and equal opportunity so that our rights and benefits are well covered. Hence, it will be extremely different for us to abolish "impartiality" as a necessary social tool and continue with the otherwise "unnatural" "preferential treatment". Though no one doubts that being impartial is morally praiseworthy and preferences are allowed only in very special cases when grounds are morally most compelling, it is often argued that preferential treatments are preferred on most morally compelling grounds, but the problem is what to do with our commitment of "impartiality". There is moral debate of great concern here, and it is not easy to take sides that will be correct. It appears that the most avowed champions of preferential treatment would think twice to pooh-pooh impartiality because taken overall, affirmative action (if it exists) must include both and because they run the risk of saying that the social agencies should not be morally bound to be impartial. This must be a blunt unethical call because non-impartial would mean the agency has the privilege to favour the privileged, which is ruled out. Hence, those favouring preferences must favour impartiality, and with it, the value of good of those who are not deemed preferred for many reasons said above. Hence, those toeing the line of pure impartiality are at fault if they do not recognise the moral value of preferences in *exceptional cases* if at all, "affirmative action" makes a sense. In addition, those toeing the line of pure preferences are at fault if they do not recognise the value of impartiality in the society, otherwise they are the worst losers and affirmative action is a meaningless proposition. The contradiction and the uneasiness is clear; there are ways though one is to make sure that despite impartiality we will be exceptionally choosy on moral grounds to be preferential; the other one is to make sure that other than impartiality we will not rule out exceptional preferences, and yet another one is to make sure that affirmative action with its needed component steps should be wholly scrapped because the two alternatives are unacceptable on moral grounds. Only the first among the three alternatives is somewhat sympathetic to affirmative action, but others are not if both aspects are understood properly that constitutes affirmative actions. However, the last alternative is extremely arrogant in banishing the very conception of affirmative action on moral grounds.

To understand the moral grounds we have to concentrate on the touted ethicality of "compensation" of the deprived *individuals* and *groups* because it restores their rights, it is just and obligatory on social agencies. The starting problem is to do justice through compensation with "individuals" and "groups". What should be ethically justifiable end of preferential treatment, to compensate the individuals or the group? The problem is whether it is just to compensate an individual as individual because historical injustice has been suffered by him or her or by his or her predecessors. On the other hand, it is just to compensate a group to which an individual belongs, and thus, some kind of classism for the needed justice. It may well be that an individual of a group did not suffer any injustice, not even in the past by his family, but the group to which he or she belongs taken on the whole is a suffering lot because a number of its members suffered a historical injustice, needing compensation. Hence, there is a tension to compensate any individual of a group and to compensate not an individual but a group overall. Why is there a tension when a group receiving justice automatically provides justice to individuals of the group? Why worry about individuals separately? The point is that as said above, in preferential justice there is hardly any sound way to inquire about the actual state of injustice and the adequate backup need for compensation because that is stupendous task and most interestingly, may be taken as *partiality* within a system of partiality if someone is taken on the "creamy layer" and thus dumped in the group of the historically favoured though the group to which they belong, may be sufferers. On the ethical ground, that compensation cannot and should not be blind to adequate and thorough checks for its legitimate demands such as great material and other losses inhuman to bear by an individual, individualistic compensatory treatment is not prescribed. In fact, if we are blind to individual status at different epochs, compensations are unjust and unethical for they are mere gratis, an act of "appeasement" than compensation. Such things do not constitute to the overall values in the society because the preferred individual gets stronger within a group of the deprived thus stemming out as an island of favoured among bereaved, creating a line of demarcation, a class of its own, which derogates the value of preference as such as the value of compensation of rights of a group. If individualistic compensatory justice is taken too far, it would have a boomerang effect on social agencies because the lack of evaluation of constantly tilting scale of benefit to a person and making him well off calls for serious look at other individuals of the touted historically benefited group or the "general group" which are in the real sense at this epoch deprived materially and otherwise needing urgent compensation for clear injustice in the distribution of benefits. If these things are needed then there can be no linear preferential treatment, it should be given up nevertheless, to a more ethical social justice system that takes care of basic issues in disparities of benefits irrespective of historical considerations and classism, says many.

If compensation and justice cannot be unfair and unjustified whether we speak of an individual or a group, the problem in preferential treatment merely keeping in view a class or a group is no less troublesome. Though it is fairly easy to arbitrarily provide preferential treatment to an individual by counting on his or her colour, creed, caste, handicaps and so on as we said irrespective of the enjoyed beneficial status at the present time by his or her family or by him or her, it is extremely difficult to arbitrarily provide the same treatment to a "group" because the significance of a "preferred group" is highly ambiguous. There are groups demanding for special treatment based on caste, religion, sex, handicaps and many more. The point is why should "belonging to any group" be an automatic choice for preferential treatment when we saw that such automatic choice in case of individuals were fraught with problems? Does affiliation to a group justify ethically that preference is needed? In our times, when we look at "sex based preferences", we do not merely imagine preferences to be given to women, for instance, pressures are from the group of eunuchs and the growing trend shows that serious pressures might be created by the lesbians, and sex workers because for physical and other limits the women have been facing historical injustice; the same may be true of the eunuchs. No sooner, we might bear the pressure to treat the lesbians and the homosexuals differently. Time has come to think whether castes and tribes do not fight each other for preference because those fights would pressurise us doubly. In many cases, religious groups are seriously threatened by virtue of belonging to a majority religion in pockets of a country where they are in fact minority. Can we accommodate them too? Handicaps are various if we go on counting them starting from the physical, even the obese and the ugly may be under social threat needing some care for their honour. Hence, classifying groups and identifying them for preferences do not need a myopic vision of classification, it needs some range and if it is allowed too far, the groups may be wide and weird; soon we will be worried by our richness. Another point is that there are queer variations in income, status, material powers, wisdom, abilities within the groups which calls for a separate compensation than a sweeping overview because in doing so much needed favours do not reach the needy and as usual the advantaged are more preferred, which is injustice and unethical. In such troublesome cases, we finally discover that we should ultimately settle for preference to some groups for their greater demand and as in case of individuals, there is again preferring a few among the preferred, which is to leave others to the "general" group or to a less preferred one, which further contradicts the basic spirit of preferential treatment as well as impartiality and as such affirmative action. "Why should we not be preferred than others in any group?" This can be a nagging moral question as far as impartiality, equality and justice is concerned. There is thus a call for abolition of affirmative action and socio-economic evaluations for justice irrespective of historical blunders and classism.

Then there is an ethical argument for banishing preferential treatment on the ground of intended preferences to "undeserving" people just because they belong to a class deemed for preference. It accepts that redistribution of benefit is possible by encouraging some people who otherwise lack in merit and are not able to compete with other advanced groups. This means that affirmative action as preferential treatment is both partial to meritorious people in our society and even to those belonging to a group of "backwards" because it rules out merit as basis of excellence and of the flourishing of a society by taking sides of unmeritorious on the fictitious ground of the historical deprivation as well as it rules out the separate recognition of excellence of a meritorious belonging to a backward group irrespective of the stigma attached always to the meritorious. Further, taking it for granted that by encouraging people in posts which would have been otherwise taken by meritorious people of advanced classes, a group may be indirectly suggested for their nagging demerit and the pity and gratis most unwantedly provided to them giving them special favours in education, training and throwing them to the arena of cut-throat competition to try to exceed their mental limits by sheer will and effort to excel in the long run. All these things may be thus taking people as defective and standing for pity, which is unethical.

Again, the inherent call is for scrapping affirmative action and opening fields of opportunities to the entire population on merit. In fact, much ethical cry over the systematic suppression of merit of the general mass in the name of unwanted favours to undeserving people, which is nothing but injustice redistributed through a systematic harm to an imagined favour group thus creating new groups of the unsatisfied, oppressed and disfavoured calling for justice or preferential treatment. Preferential treatment thus gives birth to a vicious cycle of favours, endless system of gratis without any benefit. Hence, it should be avoided as unethical practice. There is thus a lot of clamor about making those scapegoats of social justice who by virtue of hereditary misfortune are branded as favoured-lot historically, standing representatives of their ancestral villains, as if history-sheet is testimony to the villainous acts of all of their ancestors. Justice is thus based on an arbitrary conception of persons and groups forgetting completely that the impartial treatment of the masses is possible and justice can be done to those who are backward in socio-economic grounds, where abolition of racism, casteism, classism and the like are most essential. Again, these counter-ethical arguments sound too good, and we are in an ethical imbroglio. However, things are not easy for the con-views we have just seen. It is argued that the upshot of unethicality charge against affirmative action is based on distorted conceptions of equal opportunity and making distinction or discrimination. It can be shown that though there is a needed discrimination, it does not go against or contradicts impartiality or to be impartial in giving equal opportunity to all. Keeping in mind the option before the con-theorists it is equally possible to opt for impartial treatment by providing equal opportunities to all and qualified discrimination for specific redistribution of benefits when moral pressures for the same are irresistible. As humans no one really contests the idea that qualified discrimination is needed in demanding situations because even the favoured ones often feel the heat, particularly when their own people, their kin, family members and themselves are in such need. It is not queer to imagine that a person belonging to higher caste demands reservation on grounds of handicaps physical, mental and sexual. Even the growing importance of identifying the "creamy layer" among the favoured group based on economic grounds and basing economic prowess for social discrimination for jobs and things like that shows the importance and need of qualified discrimination despite equality of opportunity. What thinkers like Kekes and others who wish an abolition of affirmative action for its unacceptable unethical contradiction of impartiality and discrimination misses is that "discrimination" or "preferentiality" by sound logic need not be taken as necessarily and sufficiently contradictory in nature, one is the negation of the other, and that they cannot go together. Whether certain intended voluntary acts of humans are in essence positive or negative takes us to the old debate of intuitive knowledge of intrinsic good *versus* sense empirical knowledge of extrinsic good. The idea of a number of thinkers influenced by intuitionism is that some human acts are intrinsically "positive" and possess moral worth, whereas others are "negative" having moral disvalue. This amounts to say that in essence "killing" is negative, "non-violence" is positive, and they contradict each other. There is no logic in this thinking provided intuitive truths are absolute and sacred. Why should in military ethics "killing" our enemies be negative when its bearings are positive for *us*? The answer may be that it is anti-human and violent against the human race, and therefore, negative, whereas non-violence is positive. Nevertheless, either this idea must be intuitively or sense empirically justified. It is hardly empirically justified that an act of violence of the military to save us is not anti-human, rather for our good whereas non-violence of the militia may be foolish and negative because it is anti-human and thus unethical as well. Even Gandhi did not think that killing rabid dog is negative as violence and Arjuna's participation in the killing in the fields of *Kurūkṣetra* was negative. However, Aristotle, Gandhi and others did believe that some forms of killing are negative; but arguably, not in essence but in what they produce against life, beings, things and humanity. It is possible that acts of violence are negative or positive as per the situations in which they are done by moral agents having different reasons for doing so. This may be true of non-violence as well. Hence, relativism teaches us that though certain human acts are generally or *objectively negative* and unworthy, they are *relatively* positive, and the *vice versa*. In this sense an act of "discrimination" in the society may be *objectively negative* or unworthy in *some* cases irrespective of relative factors, for instance, when we discriminate some castes in our schools for providing free tiffin whereas others are either charged heavily for meeting the subsidy and expenditure or they are supplied with low quality food or no food at all. Whereas discrimination in our society may be in the *relative sense positive* and worthwhile when, for instance, we have a separate section for the unprivileged and backward class students to gear them up providing intensive coaching to meet the challenges of competition. Hence, no one really accepts Kekes' absolutist thesis that *per se* preferential treatment is negative and not morally worthwhile. Similarly, we cannot argue that impartial treatment in opening equal opportunities for job seekers, for instance, irrespective of any qualifications as per caste, creed and so on is *per se* positive and worthwhile because Kekes fails to notice that if it were so, there was no demand for further qualification. We discover very soon that opening of opportunities free from any qualification is dangerous for a balance in our society among the job seekers. Often the mighty section of society licks the cream leaving nothing for the weak, but truth is that there are weak sections, they need empowerment and one way is to provide them suitable jobs for an honest living. There is no intrinsic goodness in equality in opportunities rather it appears like that as a blatant negation of social justice to weaker sections. Hence, the act must be *objectively positive*, that is, irrespective of relativism, the "act of equality" should be taken as worthwhile in many instances. For instance, it is objectively good as far as job seekers if any part of the population of our country is protected for their rights to be informed about a vacancy, details of qualification, specialisation and posts despite the vacancy being open to all. In this sense then, nothing is intrinsic to the act of impartiality, whether good or bad, positive or negative. If this were the case then the two aspects of affirmative action, impartiality in the name of opening equal opportunities and preferential treatment caused by deliberate acts of discrimination have something in them that calls for their objective value and their relative value. In this sense, they never conflict or contradict in essence; they may be complementary to each other though the complementarity of acts for their value depends heavily on the given context, people and time.

What has been said above is strengthened in another way by an excellent counter ethical argument by T.E. Hill. He analyses three arguments provided by those who find contradiction in affirmative actions and demand for their abolition. The first argument is simplistic because it hinges on a non-evaluative sense of the word "discrimination", which is "to make a distinction" and the word is thus in its plain descriptive sense bereft of drawing any sense of good or bad, right or wrong, just or unjust and so on. However, the con-affirmative action argument (henceforth, con-argument) takes an illogical leap from the non-evaluative to the *pejorative evaluative* sense to imply that making distinctions are ethically bad or unjust. The point is, even if discrimination is to make some distinctions among social groups and individuals, it does not logically imply an act of injustice and partiality. Second con-argument is that an act of social discrimination relies on merely fictitious grounds, which are morally irrelevant and undesirable. Therefore, discrimination is bad, unjust and unfair. The argument in reality is based on a predominant sophistical tone to undermine something by whims or arbitrarily than pressing logical arguments. To say that discrimination is merely on fictitious grounds such as sex and colour does not justify the grounds to be truly fictitious and irrelevant. Hence, preferential treatment based on discrimination on several available grounds is morally relevant and strong because there are strong moral reasons behind them. We do not give reservation to women in jobs because they are weaker sex or they are helpless women, but they hold equal rights in society for empowerment, have jobs and strive for their good and social good. It is not whims but reasons in favour of women welfare and empowerment that forces for discrimination despite equal opportunities for all. Third con-argument is that discriminatory acts in affirmative action are generally derogatory to the interests and well-being of the majority and thus partial and unethical. Truly, all ill designed affirmative actions turn out to be generally against the interest of the majority and even for the minority, but in the fear of our mistakes, the act as such cannot be valued as unethical because it does not intend to be wrong doing to a group in lieu of others. Rather, well thought out discriminatory justice often turns out to be extremely fruitful for the majority and the minority. History has shown us that some degree of preferential treatment to the Indian tribes and women have done a lot of good to the society at large in real terms of growth and development though the non-tribes have not faced great troubles in job sectors. However, the point is of balance and constant logical thinking, which is never denied.

Turning now to the aspect of equal opportunity, which the con-arguments could not derogate easily because that amounts to contradict their basic position that abolishing affirmative action will leave us with at least one positive alternative, that is, fairness in opportunities for all sections of the society. The con-argument is thus not con-impartiality-as-equality-in-opportunity. Anyway, we are just brewing the hot pot of controversy now, not filtering the soup. Hence, we will find out what the arguments are in favour of equality in opportunity. There are two arguments that show why equality is ethically viable. One is that openness in merit, ability to perform is best for individual and social good, and the other is freedom in availing chances is intrinsically good. It is found that in many societies both the ethically strong features of equality in opportunity are systematically neglected and thus anti-individual and against social good as well as against freedom of choice. In any case, equal opportunities are good because their *consequences* are good (forward-looking), and they are good because past events are testimony to such an intrinsically valuable freedom (backward looking). To say this is to remind us what was said before, that is, objectively, equality is positive for it recognises the non-relative value of freedom, and it is relatively positive for it recognises the value of the effects of equal treatment in society. Nevertheless, we have seen that equality may assume a negative dimension as well if "elbowing out syndrome" in society prevails with freedom, which is not freedom but freak wish fulfilment. I have said that many people believe that the more negative features are prevented and positives are encouraged, the more equality gains moral face. The point is how to stop "elbowing out" in society. Is it not true that certain discriminations are needed? This is the bone of ethical contention.

I have repeatedly said that intersubjective corroboration, as a method of resolution of social ethical problems should start with an educative programme, that is, to know about pro and con views regarding an issue so that one knows clearly, why ethical perspectives are so important and how they conflict with each other making a mesh of ethical disagreement. Though I have started with more academic and educative programme here, it is not an imperative step because reading a number of newspaper articles, debates, opinions and news items and other journalistic pieces, one knows about the same truth. Most interesting point is that if we keep our senses alert and take some care to talk to common people who have never read Hill or Kekes or Boxill and many more about this issue, one wonders how the same pro and con arguments flow in the society and are contested for respective validity. Let us read some of the interesting passages in Indian newspapers to know about the ethical aspects in "reservation in jobs" as an affirmative action. We will gather some interesting opinions in this regard and careful readers must have noticed that in due course of academic discussion, I have carefully punctuated common perceptions, which I will continue doing now because this information are dear to me which I learnt from public participation and education.

We discussed social justice and in due course, we discussed equal justice or simply equality and said that equality and impartiality remain as great social ideals unless some steps by the social engineers are taken to assure that the most deprived lot got justice by means of equal opportunity and impartiality though some acts of discrimination were needed or preferential treatment was necessary. We also discussed at length that the Indian society is a typical "caste based society" which is difficult to ignore because we never seriously tried to break the jinx rather continued with it. Ardent believers in caste system hold that there is nothing evil in the system but discrimination according to caste, when it comes to reservation of seats in jobs and educational institutions are truly evil in nature. However, there are views that nothing is evil in caste-based reservation of seats in jobs and education though the system itself may be evil for its inhuman face. It is also believed that the system and reservation based on castes are both good and not evil. In fact, equality in opportunity and discriminatory social justice, both needing affirmative action are closely related to the problem of casteism; we cannot avoid these factors in social justice. This is all the more important when we find that castes are numerous, classification of which is a tedious task for social engineers and with it, doing justice to all becomes ominous by any imagination. Not only this, you have to consider other non-caste based discriminations for social justice though they did not produce much of a headache for authorities in India because in jobs and education they stand an infinitesimal percentage for any envious reaction. Interestingly, even reservation of seats for the scheduled tribes did not pose great social threat because sane heads always knew that you cannot help doing some favours to a most backward section of the society, particularly in the remote tribal areas, who are deprived and bereaved by any imagination needing some backup to reach a level of development and human dignity. The problem or rather the great Indian caste based reservation controversy and feud is centred on the preferential treatment to the scheduled castes in a huge number. To add to the woe, are the other backward castes (OBCs), who have a queer ambiguous identity, ever changing, not clear to us who needs what because every other day some party is up with a demand for their favoured status. In the recent times in India, castes fought each other because one was elevated to a more favoured tribal status, whereas the other was left in the caste lurch, though they thought that they should be treated in the capacity of scheduled tribes. The focus of envy, fight and controversy is slowly gripping the otherwise quiet tribal reservation in India. In the recent times some members of higher castes or even backward castes, were marrying tribal girls for a better future though there are growing controversies about extending favours to such male candidates in particular. Controversy shrouds females favouring to marry tribal males. In the midst of all this, as usual, the population and the job scenario in India is grim, they have an inverse relation, the former growing but the latter in its comparison is as ever falling down though on paper there are obvious increase in jobs in India in the 1990s and at present. To add another problematic dimension is that educated and unemployed have risen tremendously, the skilled people are also under serious threat for existence. However, the most interesting feature in India is that everybody assured since independence that good days will come; we have to bear with reservation for some while because everyone has to be uplifted, and socially flourish is not a partial affair. However, the day has not come, the good days when we did not want reservations any more have not come. Our politicians, the social-engineers-in-chief continue with caste-based reservation in jobs and education because they think social justice is not done yet. Therefore, they accept defeat after fifty-nine years of independence though if you tell that, they will be angry with you as a matter of habit. No one really wants the stigma that we are a nation troubled with casteism and caste based reservation and continuing with that in a manner as if nothing will be all right without this system of reservation. Now, the ethical controversy starts here;

some of us have strong ethical reason to believe that the caste based reservation does and will continue doing good to the masses and we must go on with this as a natural course not stigmatised one, whereas others believe that such reservation does a lot of social harm and must not continue any further with this unwanted stigma because all this is ethically undesirable.

A strong proof of our ethical urge to continue with caste based reservation in jobs and education in a non-stigmatised fashion is constitutional guarantee of the practice though some amendments did not suggest serious changes or abolition. Hence, we have a social holy grail for continuing with the practice of affirmative action. It is argued in some circles that constitutional amendments are needed to strengthen affirmative action in India in view of the lingering injustice with the scheduled tribes and castes (the historical blunder being the crux of the injustice). It is important, therefore, to read what our Constitution states. Article 46 states: "The state shall promote with special care the education and economic interests of the weaker sections of the people, and in particular, of the scheduled castes and the scheduled tribes, and shall protect them from social injustice and forms of exploitation." Then Article 335 reads, "The claims of the members of the scheduled castes and the scheduled tribes shall be taken into consideration, consistently with the maintenance of efficiency of administration, in the making of appointments to services and posts in connection with the affairs of the Union or of a State." Without going into the intricacies of amendments and their reasons, let us concentrate on the moral authority derived by the social engineers from these statements. Clearly, the first Article focuses on the facts of "social injustice" and "forms of exploitation" both deemed to be inhuman and unethical in civil states, which have created "weaker sections" slowly, but surely in our society, which the STs and SCs are, and they need "protection" from gross inhuman sufferings. Thus, the moral aim of exploitation free and just society where weaker sections enjoy rights and justice is extremely clear. The next Article is emphatic in the statement of moral authority that administrators ought to enjoy derived from the Constitution, which is the right to discriminate STs and SCs for the guarantee of jobs to them which fall in the domains of the Union and the State. This must be in tune with the demand for affirmative action along with care for moral rights, justice and the creation of exploitation free state. We must then read here that being a welfare state, India enshrines the morality of welfarism, which is beyond economic well-being, holistic flourishing of individuals and society in material and other spheres that is obviously possible in non-exploitative, equitable society where social justice is a desirable utopia. Now let us read what Mr. P.S. Krishnan (former Secretary to the Union Government) states: "Equality is a basic feature of the Constitution, and equality includes social equality. On reservations, the Constitution does not give the state with options to play around with"[5]. It is clear that the moral authority drawn by the social engineers for affirmative action is not a mere decorative item, the "authority" ought to be Kantian mandate, an irresistible, unconditional duty. However, the basic ethic of "equality" he says, is complete only with "reservation" (discrimination) if affirmative action is complete. There is no optional in affirmative action in India, it is an imperative. However, it may be argued, says Krishnan that the expected urge of the mandate is missing to some extent in Article 335, which is true source of the right of SCs and STs to reservation, and therefore, awaits amendments, which he suggests. Without indulging into the nitty-gritty of the same, let us take the message that reservation as a social mandate along with equality is ethically based and constitutionally guaranteed by the Constitution though it is not shifted to Part III that spells out Fundamental Rights or unconditional imperative.

Well, if constitutional assertion and imperatives have moral strength can it be countered on moral grounds and spoken out without fear? Yes, if constitution is to be believed, and Krishnan indirectly suggests that demands and acts of amendments are countering and revising options to mandates and so on. If this were the case, let us take this: "In liberal political thought, 'social justice' is bunk. Nobel laureate Friedrich Hayek, for example, called it a 'weasel word'... the word 'social' sucks out the meaning of 'justice' and leaves an empty shell where once stood a grand idea."[6] Further, "Modern idea of 'social justice' works themselves out not in the market economies but in politics. The process of justice is therefore very different from the process of 'social justice'."[7] Further, "The politician is the social engineer; he is busy targeting groups that he can quickly identify and favour, in exchange for votes.... The wily politician who plays this sinister game knows well that if he can corner the votes of a few small groups, he will have achieved his objective, which is to be re-elected. This is why Indian politicians want to include more and more supposedly disadvantageous groups as beneficiaries of political intervention. This political game of social justice cannot be carried on much longer in India."[8] Finally, "Today's poor have everything to gain in the extension of the market orders, in free trade and liberty with an equal justice. The political process contains nothing of worth for the vast majority of them. Throw out social justice."[9] Can it be more scathing? On the one hand, a government servant (not a politician) urges that based on welfarist ethics affirmative action ought to be mandatory, as imperative for the protection of fundamental rights. The other, an economist argues that it is a trash, should be dumped (and with it the constitutional statements, perhaps!). However, the economist has moral reasons, strangely no less welfarist, but economic welfarism of our age is imported from capitalist societies through the older western legacies of Aristotle, Mill and Adam Smith. Their point is that ethically oriented "justice" is an out and out economic concept and to conceive of social justice which is the handmaid of politicians is to take justice out of the domain because in the hands of politicians in a welfare state, there is nothing but unethical practices of social discrimination in the name of affirmative action because such discrimination does not aim at equality, justice, welfare and the like, rather aims at personal and political gains which are the worst forms of "gross egoism" and not "welfarism". Justice by virtue of wholesome welfare of the Indian society is at hand when there is widespread and effective economic or distributive justice, for which technocrats are needed not social engineers. Hence, in short, social justice as affirmative action in India that assures equality despite reservation is a political gimmick, a public bluff for political gains and thus unethical. Everything sounds iconoclastic but there are counter ethical questions. First is, "what about legal justice?" Is it barren too because it suffices the purpose of the cunning judiciary and its people? Is it not true that though some politicians are gross egoists, the concept of social justice as enshrined and mandated in constitution, the protection of which becomes a legal duty to counter political mischief and constitutional derogation? The ethicality in advocating justice is thus contribution to holistic social welfare, notwithstanding contributions from economic justice, political justice and legal justice, though risks of failure at every point are probable but that does not trash out any of these forms of justice. Second point is that economic justice as stated here in the atmosphere of the great Indian globalisation, free trade and open market economy may be questioned for ethicality or they face serious charges for being gross material egoism of the capitalist *mahagurus* who strives for one proper bloc where all but poor is happy. Of late, the same economists are worried of the slippery slope of globalisation in which welfare without happiness is perceived because economic welfare through distributive justice is struggling under the shadows of capitalism where models of justice are hunted without much success because they have given Indians newer forms of exploitation and a glossy progress for a few though no one party is truly "happy". The more strongly discovered truth is that poor people are still "happy" bereft of the glossy economic or material pleasures.

So where we stand now? After reading about the debates, we now have for us fresh ethical scrutiny. Let us ignite the minds of the readers with more fuel, which I have gathered from the public writings. In his article, "Learning to Speak Caste", sociologist of Delhi University, Mr. Satish Deshpande observes, "1947 was not a revolution but a transfer of power from the British to an Indian elite.... The Dalit challenge was neutralised by the Poona Pact of 1932, an abject surrender—masterminded by a ruthless mahatma of Dalit claims to power-sharing in return for reservations as a sort of welfare programme."[10] In addition, he stresses, "If the Dalit were 'constitutionalised', the Other Backward Classes were 'regionalised' in the Nehru era.... It is only after Mandal that both Dalits and backward classes have begun to speak the language of national power-sharing."[11] Further, "Thus it is that six decades after the abolition of caste we have produced national elite that is overwhelmingly upper caste.... Lately, they have begun to receive partial support from the creamy layer of the backwards and Dalits.... We also have an emergent lower caste mobilisation beginning to address the incompleteness of independence, who insists that caste alone and nothing else must be spoken."[12] Finally, "Once we sincerely recognise caste and begin to track it in the Census, in admission lists, national surveys and every relevant place, we will earn the moral and political right to being contextualising caste in terms of its internal differentiations and specialities. Only then can we truly abolish it. To annihilate caste we must first gather the courage to speak it."[13] After this factual and evaluative statements about caste, caste related talks and caste based reservation, let us continue with an influencing article by another Professor of Sociology Mr. Imtiaj Ahmad, "Caste is Relevant" where he says: "Caste has been a significant determinant of life chances... considerable evidence exists to show that even after having achieved some degree of quality education and having moved up in the occupational hierarchy, life chances for them (backward castes) are not necessarily equalised."[14] Hence, "Poverty and economic backwardness may be distributed across caste lines, but there remains a significant difference in the manner in which economic backwardness affects life chances of individuals belonging to different castes."[15] Further, "Reservations were contemplated not merely to offer economic backwardness, but also to address orientations responsible for rendering caste backwardness.... Caste continues to be significant to the determination of life chances."[16] Finally, "No doubt, the implementation of the reservation policy raises certain questions.... These questions should be debated, but the debate does not have anything to do with the logic of caste-based reservation. It was inherent in the logic of reservation that those who for some reason failed to draw social benefits will wage struggle against those who are able to pocket them."[17]

If we examine these arguments, we may call them, "pro-arguments" or arguments in favour of caste-based preferential treatment and affirmative action in the recent climate of unrest in India. These arguments have moral overtones, which we need to analyse and then try to contrast with what was seen in the con-arguments. It is a unanimous opinion among the pro-people that the historical truth of caste, casteism and caste related backwardness cannot and should not be disregarded because some blunt factual truths cannot be disregarded and some factual truths raising serious questions for moral value should not be disregarded. It has been argued that throughout a long period in India division of the society along caste lines have given us power-lines, some are power-trackers and many are in the making. Among the power-trackers are the so-called upper or privileged castes that have a *lifeline* that is radiant in glory even if economic and educational empowerments have put them in a position of relative disadvantage. However, there are power-trackers among the backward classes who are often touted as members of the "creamy layer" calling for abolition from caste based advantages. However, those, who are getting advantages for their castes for a long time though they do not have the same radiant lifeline, which upper castes enjoy. Hence, caste and caste-based reservation in education, jobs and other positions *should* be enjoyed by a few needy people. The historical injustice is that at the stroke of independence and after that reservation has been largely meek, not a revolutionary step, some kind of a gratis. However, what *should* be done is to have a social revolution in which the very system is abolished only through effective and ultra-dynamic affirmative action, perhaps to evolve equitable "life-line". Hence, the economists' call for a qualified reservation policy irrespective of castes is illogical and unethical because on the one hand, economic uplift does not have quantum improvement in lower caste-life-line overall and it is unethical because social benefits to the historically underpowered classes bereft them of desirable well-being. All in all, taking the same holistic social welfare as the most valuable end for the Indians in general, which was equally valued by the con-thinkers, it is urged that the recognition of the caste-system and affirmative action that counts for systematic discrimination is desirable as means though no one rejects the sensible questions in the methodology of redistribution of benefits because a reversal of the methodology that might consider the "creamy layer" and "economic backwardness" as equally important is viable but not hampering the constitutional provision of caste-based reservation. It appears that though pro and con-views are methodologically contesting with each other as well as contesting to find out the extension of the net of social advantage, both sucks moral strength from "holistic welfare of the people". However, owing to serious differences in methods and targets of affirmative action, the moral evaluation of the means remains vague and undetermined, provided the constitution does not infringe on methodological questions as well, but that is again a matter of stiff moral debate among the masses. Nevertheless, almost every day people come out with suggestions for means or methods in affirmative action that can possibly bring holistic well-being. The suggestions, most of them regarding choice are not arrogant, that is, more often than not they tend to recognise the moral value of respecting the strong points in the contesting views, which is very encouraging. We will find out shortly how people of pro and con views really share concerns about this matter in the real-life moral debate. However, I find it extremely interesting to offer a passage from Kirit Parikh's essay, "A Fair System", which reflects a bright trend among contesting opinions about affirmative action in India. The member of Planning Commission writes, "Reservation for backward communities raise issues of fairness and the constitutional requirement of equal treatment and efficiency. They also fragment society. The Supreme Court has directed that creamy layer should be excluded. Disadvantages of social and economic backwardness may persist over generations. How do we have affirmative action that does not compromise on fairness and merit?"[18]

Now a balanced view, morally based than arrogant would always like to see an end of persistent controversy. Knowing fully well that the controversy will not vanish in a day or two, and that debates are needed for a long period, we can strive best to assure how well we can corroborate our views. This takes us to the *dynamic* aspect of ethics or rather applied ethics where we come to know what is applied and how something is applied in applied ethics. However, a word of caution is needed here. We are already in the domain of applied ethics, because it demands analysis of the value-laden problem in consideration and the statement of the moral controversies, which is heavily *theoretical* in nature. Now, we have enough information for construction of a non-structuralist questionnaire for the moral debate, that is, a set of questions that expectedly brings out moral opinions of participants to the best. As usual, I will provide the Questionnaire used by me to resolve the issue of reservation in jobs in India and provide the list of participants. Further, their ethical perspectives will be put here in their language though the same has been edited by the researcher for bringing out the crucial points leaving out many factual details and controversies, as well as the nitty-gritty of reservation. This is needed without any distortion because an extremely lengthy discussion among six or seven participants cannot be shaped properly. Moreover, there are common points, repetitions and loose ends in debates, which should be put in order. After having read the opinions in the said debate, my final task as said before, will be "post-corroboration analysis of moral dialogue" to discover which normative theses were effectively involved in such dialogue though none of the participants are trained ethicists. However, for our readers, even if they were ethics trained, theoretical work thus far provides us to evaluate independently what moral perspectives amount to and what if anything they have to share.

QUESTIONNAIRE

What is the Moral Basis of Reservation in Jobs?

1. Why do you think that human beings are valuable to the society? Is it important at times to make distinction among individuals in a society? What should be the ethical basis of making such distinctions?
2. What in your opinion is social justice? What is the basis of doing such justice?

3. What in your opinion is the basis of doing justice to a professional in either public or private sector?
4. Do you think that caste/class/language/physical handicap/ gender etc. should be the bases for selecting professionals in private and public sectors?
5. Do you think that caste/class/language/physical handicap/ gender etc. should be the bases for promoting professionals in private and public sectors?
6. Do you think that reservation in jobs is intrinsically bad because it divides the society?
7. What in your opinion should be the mode of selection and/or promotion in private and public sectors?

An analysis of the questionnaire reveals that the first question tries to evaluate the value perception of the debaters about human beings, society and the intended act of discrimination among individuals in a society so that it becomes easier to judge whether further replies about the preferential act of reservations on different grounds are logically consistent with the general value-perception of the debater. Moreover, the participants have an opportunity to ethically evaluate why an act of discrimination among individuals is desirable, which is again expected to be logically consistent with his or her replies to the ethical validity of reservations on different grounds which is an act of discrimination. The second question was needed to evaluate the broad ethical perspective of the participant regarding social justice and then try to find how well the reply fits with his or her replies to the ethical value of professional justice. These evaluations are needed to judge what a participant feels about the value of social justice, justice done to professionals of a society and try to find out how logical he or she is in replying to the following questions asked particularly to evaluate their ethical judgements about selection, appointment and promotion of professionals all of them expected to contribute to the well-being of the professionals and of the society at large. To make a final dig at the participants' ethical opinions about reservations in jobs that affect professionals and the society, and to find out whether the final reply contradicts his or her earlier ethical positions, an enticing question with the introduction of the negative concepts of "evil" and "the attitude of divisiveness" in the context of reservations in jobs has been asked. The last question becomes a natural one provided ethical corroboration has enabled us to construct decision-making rules.

Let us now find out the selection of the participants in the debate and the reasons for such selection. The following participated in the dialogue:

1. Sri S.K. Chand, Retired IAS, Ranchi.
2. Dr. R.K. Jha, Professor of Political Science, Ranchi College, Ranchi.
3. Dr. A. Sajjad, Former Head of University Department of Urdu, Ranchi University.
4. Dr. P.C. Oraon, Director, Tribal Research & Welfare Department, Ranchi.
5. Dr. B.K. Sinha, Lecturer in Political Science, St. Xavier's College, Ranchi.
6. Mr. Ratnakar Bhengra, Advocate, Convenor of "Johar", a Tribal Welfare Institution, Ranchi.

The selection of the participants reveal that there is more or less adequate blend of representatives of the pro and con views mentioned before. Though the selection is here restricted to some of the most forceful thinkers about this matter in a small city, what they argue may not be wholly satisfactory. India is a vast country, in applying ethics we have to start somewhere with some people who are concerned about value issues rather than waiting for large city population to participate. However, applying ethics is a huge task for a number of ethics corroborators who are spread over the country to arrange more and more debates and inform us about moral consensus and decision-making rules. The question is "How do we select the participants from the vast population of a city?" This is a tough problem for all social scientists and empirical ethicists who by virtue of models like intersubjective corroboration are closer to a social scientific vocation where data interpretation is relatively subdued by logical analysis of strengths and weaknesses of moral perspectives of common men about value-laden issues. Anyway, only a de-classed ethicist or those having ethical training and willing to act moral corroborators should be ever alert and inquisitive about what the public is speaking around him or her, and what they are writing and debating. The person must be by virtue of an urgency trying to find out from as many people who takes interest in particular value-crisis or have training in a discipline that makes him or her automatic choice for the debate. The most important point is to choose the right person and to have a nice balance of opinions in the panel for a debate. This is again a matter of visiting people who should be personally interviewed first to gauge his or her interests and ethical opinions, which is not difficult if the art of inspiring and inciting a person about well-debated moral matters is known. The best way is to talk less and let people talk more, only giving a direction to the talk to evaluate moral positions and ability to put things logically. Again, this is done when one intermittently quotes or refers to contrary opinions. Requesting people for a dialogue with a probable set of questions to give him an idea about what is required in the debate is the next stage. The debate might go for a long time. It is important to moderate it well along the ethical path as laid in the questionnaire, not giving much heed to lengthy factual reports and nitty-gritty. Following these ways, the author in the year 1999 selected the above-mentioned people because they constitute a panel that is a fine balance of views from the tribal scholars, scheduled castes, upper castes, political scientists, person having good sociology background, social activist and NGO.

Now let us read the replies of the participants (edited as I have said), in their own words arranged as far as practicable according to pro-con pattern. The points of corroboration and normative analysis of views comes last. The views are as follows:

First, let us go through what Mr. Ratnakar Bhengra has to say.

Q. 1. Why do you think that human beings are valuable to the society? Is it important at times to make distinction among individuals in a society? What should be the ethical basis of making such distinction?

Ans: It could be said that all things, inanimate or animate, have some use or value in society. The same statement may appear more applicable to all animate creatures—in the case of human beings, there is the feeling or reasoning that human beings are valuable to the society is self-evident. In human beings the characteristics of cognition, contemplation, planning, action, and reaction are considerable, and his/her ability to influence, regulate, subdue, control, manipulate, annihilate, preserve, conserve, manufacture, create or recreate is considerable, and therefore, he/she is valuable. At the same time because of these characteristics and abilities in him and her, he/she need care and caution in their thoughts and deeds.

Distinctions are necessary; this also could be considered self-evident. Particularly in the case of children, differently able (disabled), aged or very aged. In world where every thing is equal, it is not necessary to make distinctions, but we function not in the abstract, but in the fallen or unequal world and hence distinctions are more of a manoeuvre to balance.

In India or South Asia, this is more particularly true where the notion of hierarchy has resulted in such a complex and festering scenario in both the immaterial and material dimensions to the detriment and degradation of every one that making distinctions is the only way to some relief. Distinctions may at times not be notionally feasible for various reasons but these are hard, practical and political decisions governments must make. Distinctions, however, can be of different kinds and could be varied in time and circumstances.

Q. 2. What in your opinion is social justice? What is the basis of doing such justice?

Ans: Human beings are many faceted or multi-dimensional creatures, so the justice that is or can accrue to him/her will of necessity also consist of others like economic, political etc. and not only the social. Moreover, they are also inter-related.

Nevertheless, to answer the question, social issues have to do primarily with things like health, and education and hence, matters like child-care, mother-care, the family, primary and middle school education, high school, higher education and employment, housing, environment and care for the aged. In a broader sense, it would include the well-being of the community.

The basis of doing social justice, individual or group wise, would be the presumption that everyone is created equal and has equal dues.

Q. 3. What in your opinion is the basis of doing justice to a professional in either public or private sector?

Ans: My first answer has relevance to this question. Succinctly put, we can say that because there has been an age-old and historical hierarchy that has denied individual and groups social dues, to rectify this imbalance, a preferential treatment becomes necessary.

Q. 4. Do you think that caste/class/language/physical handicap/ gender should be the basis of selecting professionals in private and public sectors? and

Q. 5. Do you think that caste/class/language/physical handicap/ gender should be the basis of promoting professionals in private and public sectors?

Ans: My answer to question nos. 4 & 5 would necessarily borrow from what I have already said in my first two answers.

In the instance of differently able people, it is not a problem, in the case of gender the issue of caste and minorities do raise plausible questions.

Sometimes the distinctions proposed may be better for job/ professional selections. For instance, there are constitutional provisions and state/or Government of Bihar directives for instance for having bilingual teachers (also knowing Khurukh, Santhal, Ho and Mundari) and that primary education should be in the Adivasi mother tongues, then teachers should naturally and commonly be Adivasi or those who know these Adivasi languages proficiently. Nevertheless, teachers not having knowledge of these Adivasi languages have made a mess of Adivasi culture and identities, particularly as far as languages go.

Q. 6. Do you think that reservation in jobs is intrinsically bad because it divides the society?

Ans: The answer to question 6 briefly is—Reservation is not the cause, it is an answer. Society that is Indian or South Asian societies have been divided for millenniums. Could be said that division is intrinsic to majority Indian populace—reservation is to ameliorate or rectify or lessen these divisions and their consequences. In equal societies, the need for reservation should not arise, except in the case of the differently able.

Next, we have a brief reply from Mr. S.K. Chand; the view is edited leaving out as many common things as possible, which he shares with Mr. Bhengra.

Q. 1. Why do you think that human beings are valuable to the society? Is it important at times to make distinction among individuals in a society? What should be the ethical basis of making such distinction?

Ans: Every human being is valuable to society because given empowerments and opportunities he can make contribution to social good and advancement. Men are born equal, therefore, there is no ethical basis for making distinctions. Distinctions are made because man made institutions impose a system of ranking according to prevalent social norms and values.

Q. 2. What in your opinion is social justice? What is the basis of doing such justice?

Ans: The engineering of social justice is to create conditions in which every individual has uniform and full opportunity for realising the fullest potential of his personality.

Q. 3. What in your opinion is the basis of doing justice to a professional in either public or private sector?

Ans: Distinction between public and private sector is artificial. In either sector, professionals should get what is due to them according to the social value of his contribution.

Q. 4. Do you think that caste/class/language/physical handicap/ gender should be the basis of selecting professionals in private and public sectors?

Ans: Selection should be made purely based on merit. However, the society should give necessary opportunity to the disadvantaged groups to turn preferential.

Q. 5. Do you think that caste/class/language/physical handicap/ gender should be the basis of promoting professionals in private and public sectors?

Ans: No, promotion should be based on merit and performance.

Q. 6. Do you think that reservation in jobs is intrinsically bad because it divides the society?

Ans: Reservation is not intrinsically bad. It was one of the methods, which constitution-makers thought of for ushering in an equal society. It is its politicisation and scramble for reservation for non-deserving groups, which is bad. Supreme Court judgements on reservation give us the right to express my views on the subject. Creamy layer should be excluded from reservation.

Q. 7. What in your opinion should be the mode of selection and/ or promotion in private and public sectors?

Ans: In selection/promotions, instead of a general mode, categorisation should be made. Reservation cover should be given in types of job not requiring high intellectual and educational attainments but in high-tech areas selection should be on merit. However, if other things were equal between a general candidate and a reserved quota candidate, the selection should favour the reserved category candidate.

Further, we have a thorough reply from Dr. P.C. Oraon, which goes as this.

Q. 1. Why do you think that human beings are valuable to the society? Is it important at times to make distinction among individuals in a society? What should be the ethical basis of making such distinction?

Ans: Human beings are valuable to the society as they are the basic components of society, who work for the uplift of it. Sometimes, it becomes eminent to make distinction among individuals in the society to judge the right criteria for further development. The ethical basis of such distinctions should be standard of living, economy and education.

Q. 2. What in your opinion is social justice? What is the basis of doing such justice?

Ans: Social justice is a compound word made up of the adjective 'social' and the noun 'justice'. Social means relating to society, society is a group of men with a common organisation. Justice is the quality of becoming just and fair to all the individuals in the group. The basis of doing justice is to give everyone what is due to him.

Q. 3. What in your opinion is the basis of doing justice to a professional in either public or private sector?

Ans: The basis of doing justice to professional in either public or private sector is to give the necessary adventitious aids to the deserving professionals, so that they may have the equal opportunity with the more advanced in the race of life.

Q. 4. Do you think that caste/class/language/physical handicap/ gender should be the basis of selecting professionals in private and public sectors?

Ans: Each individual has divinity, dignity and the equal legal title to unfold his/her full potential; this is inscribed in and underwritten by our Constitution.

Every man must be able to manifest his/her capabilities despite the disabilities through the dynamic discovery of himself/herself assisted in the process by society in the field of education, employment, cultural exercises and the pursuit of happiness. Hence, the basis of selecting professionals in private and public sector should be based on capable and skilled persons belonging to class/physical handicap/ gender. It should totally be economically based.

Q. 5. Do you think that caste/class/language/physical handicap/ gender should be the basis of promoting professionals in private and public sectors?

Ans: One per cent of the vacancies shall be reserved each for the blind, deaf and the orthopaedically handicapped with an overall ceiling of three per cent in group 'C' and 'D' posts in Central services and in comparable posts in government of India and public sector undertakings (O.M. No. 39016/6/77, dated 04/11/77). Hence, only the capable and deserving persons belonging to class/gender/physical handicap should be basis of promoting professionals in the public and private sector.

Q. 6. Do you think that reservation in jobs is intrinsically bad because it divides the society?

Ans: The question is baseless.

Q. 7. What in your opinion should be the mode of selection and/ or promotion in private and public sectors?

Ans: In my opinion, there should be one and only one mode of selection and/or promotion in private and public sectors and that is merit.

Next, we read brief replies from Dr. R.K. Jha and Dr. B.K. Sinha respectively.

Q. 1. Why do you think that human beings are valuable to the society? Is it important at times to make distinction among individuals in a society? What should be the ethical basis of making such distinction?

Ans: As the society is composed of human beings, they are the core of society. If there is no distinction between the members of a society, the very purpose of society, the social well-being will be defeated. The distinction should, however, be based on achievements of the individual, not on caste, religions, sex or lineage.

Q. 2. What in your opinion is social justice? What is the basis of doing such justice?

Ans: Social justice has many facets. Primarily, it is absence of privileges based on birth and lineage. However, as some members of the society lag much behind others in many fields, distributive justice may help the underprivileged and deprived classes. If through distributive justice social engineering is not done, not only the deprived classes will be alienated from society, but also the structure of the society shall grow more asymmetrical, which will not be conducive to the healthy growth of society.

Q. 3. What in your opinion is the basis of doing justice to a professional in either public or private sector?

Ans: Giving each employee, not only a professional, an opportunity for self-actualisation and recognising the work done by him/her and his/her merit should be basis of justice.

Q. 4. Do you think that caste/class/language/physical handicap/ gender should be the basis of selecting professionals in private and public sectors?

Ans: While every opportunity should be afforded to individuals to earn his/her livelihood, no criteria other than merit should be the basis of recruitment.

Q. 5. Do you think that caste/class/language/physical handicap/ gender should be the basis of promoting professionals in private and public sectors?

Ans: Promotion should be made strictly on merit.

Q. 6. Do you think that reservation in jobs is intrinsically bad because it divides the society?

Ans: Yes, reservation of any form is injurious to the health of society in general and organisations in particular. I do not share the view that it divides society, the society is already divided; but it hampers the fulfilment of the purpose of society.

Q. 7. What in your opinion should be the mode of selection and/ or promotion in private and public sectors?

Ans: The mode of recruitment and promotion should be examination, and selection and promotion should be based only on merit.

Q. 1. Why do you think that human beings are valuable to the society? Is it important at times to make distinction among individuals in a society? What should be the ethical basis of making such distinction?

Ans: Human beings are invaluable to the society as human relationship stands at the centre of it. At times, it is not only desirable but also imperative to make distinctions in view of the socio-economic disparities in the society. However, this should be accomplished only by enabling the deprived to have access to the necessary means to the desired goals.

Q. 2. What in your opinion is social justice? What is the basis of doing such justice?

Ans: To me, social justice is ensuring equality of status and opportunity irrespective of sex, caste, creed and religion individuals may belong.

Q. 3. What in your opinion is the basis of doing justice to a professional in either public or private sector?

Ans: The only basis of doing justice to a professional in either public or private sector should be honouring his or her merit, and devotion and honesty to work.

Q. 4. Do you think that caste/class/language/physical handicap/ gender should be the basis of selecting professionals in private and public sectors? and

Q. 5. Do you think that caste/class/language/physical handicap/

gender should be the basis of promoting professionals in private and public sectors?

Ans: Caste/class/language/religion/physical handicaps/gender should make neither basis of selecting professionals nor basis of promotion.

Q. 6. Do you think that reservation in jobs is intrinsically bad because it divides the society?

Ans: Reservation in jobs is intrinsically bad because it divides the society.

Q. 7. What in your opinion should be the mode of selection and/or promotion in private and public sectors?

Ans: Merit and merit alone should make the mode of selection and/or promotion in private and public sectors.

Finally, we come to the specific task allotted to the ethicist having an academic value to analyse the moral perspectives and find out which moral theory or theories have been dynamic in the resolution of the said value-laden issue so that we come to know at least three things that: (a) a training in moral theories is not necessary to express our views on crucial moral matters; (b) moral theories which we know might or might not find a place in real life moral debates and moral resolution; in case they do not figure, we might find a new theory for further analysis, and if they do figure, we are enriched with the knowledge that moral theories are not static, nor do they drop from the blue or are creations of intellectuals; and (c) application of moral theories in and with the public is a good way to know that normative theories are well supported in cases of their real life involvement for value resolution. To teach theories first to people and then make it act artificially is unacceptable. These points in turn enable us to know that normative theories of ethics are not handmaids of intellectuals and they are active when intellectuals apply them. The value of "post-corroboration analysis" in applied ethics now comes out to be clear, and with it is clear that applied ethics as a whole consists of parts, theoretical-descriptive, empirical/social-scientific activism and normative analysis. It demands involvement of the public and those trained in wholesome ethics.

The analysis of the ethical opinions of the six participants reveal a startling feature, which is to my mind, unique. The truth is that not all scheduled castes and tribe are pro-reservation in jobs, if that means mere *caste based reservation*. Similarly, it is an obsession to think that all upper caste Hindus are con-reservation because it favours certain castes; the truth is stranger; some of them believe that reservation *as such* is a desirable course of action. However, there are participants who are out and out con-reservation if that is *mere caste based*. What do we find then? We find that reservation in jobs, though it is ethically desirable in India in very special cases, it should *not* be "merely caste based". Hence, reservation, if it is at all desirable in the qualified sense, should at least have an extended net, that is, should cover broader grounds for discrimination; the most important ones are already in practice in India. Another feature of the dialogue is that perhaps none of the participants (pro or con) could justify the abolition of the case of *merit* in selections and promotions in jobs. Hence, caste based reservation perhaps cannot completely ignore the call for "merit" to be protected in selection and promotion. Similarly, the debate reveals that no one is perhaps ethically able to reject calls for reserving seats in jobs for the different handicaps prevalent in our society, whether it is, gender, physical, mental and so on. Almost all con-views hinges mainly on selection by virtue of merit and nothing else, which is an idea, based on the main ethical norm that justice as fairness in selection is possible in this way and that "fairness" is basic to social justice. Further, "equality" of humans in terms of their natural and social existence calls for just treatment and enjoyment of claim rights they have, and equality and enjoyment of the due is basic to social justice. These points stress the fact that "social justice" is a valuable concept as far as human dignity and social existence has to be restored; these are crucial because together they contribute to the *well-being* of humans and society. In the final run, the basic ethical thesis is "well being" of the human race and society on earth that calls for the contribution of *"some forms of qualified reservation notwithstanding merit as a main factor in selection and promotion in India"*. The participants in different ways have advocated the well-known normative thesis of "well-being" or "flourishing". In case of Mr. Bhengra the thesis emerges as, "In a broader sense it (social justice) would include the *well-being* of the community" (Though he advocates qualified caste based reservation). In case of Mr. Chand, "to create conditions in which every individual has the free and fair opportunity for reaching the *fullest potential of his personality*" (though he is a proponent of qualified caste based reservation as well). However, for Dr. Oraon, "to give everyone what is due to him" and *"to unfold his/*

her full potential" (though he is a qualified pro-reservationist, that is not caste-based). According to Dr. Jha, "the very purpose of reservation is social *well-being*" (though he is a qualified con-reservationist, that is, does not favour caste-based reservation but has some sympathy to positive social engineering that cares for the underprivileged). For Dr. Sinha, "ensuring *equality* of status and opportunity" is basic to reservation. In any case, even though the phrases differ, their thinking as I heard from them, hinge on the well-known "welfarism" that cover social, political, economic and metaphysical/religious flourishing of the individuals and society. It is again interesting to find that the welfarism becomes the holy grail for both the pro and con reservationists. The reason is that "reservation" is well understood as a mere means to a higher ethical end, that is, "well being" or "flourishing", and despite the uniformity in views about normative first principle, there may be stiff difference in obtaining means for attaining the said end because value perceptions about means are different owing to other than ethical reasons, reasons which are by far practical or factual in nature. Hence, the participants differed a lot about "caste based reservation" as means to human well-being for various reasons, which we have found in their replies, the cause of disagreement being the factual truth of neglect of merit and subsequent worries related to it versus historical neglect of rights of a large chunk of the population based on caste hierarchy. The point is where is an agreement? The agreement is noticed on two points: first, qualified reservation is needed and second, merit based selection cannot be dumped as situation now demands thus strengthening the case of qualified reservations in India.

Notes

1. Hill, T.E., "The Message of Affirmative Action" in Cahn, S.M. and Markie, S. (ed.), *Ethics: History, Theory and Contemporary Issues*, O.U.P., Oxford, 1998, pp. 860-61.
2. *Ibid*, p. 872.
3. Kekes, John, "The Injustice of Affirmative Action Involving Preferential Treatment" in Cahn, S.M. and Markie, S. (ed.), *Ethics: History, Theory and Contemporary Issues*, O.U.P., Oxford, 1998, pp. 878-887.
4. *Ibid*, p. 879.
5. Krishnan, P.S., "Rights Reserved" in *The Times of India*, Patna, Ranchi, National, 12-12-2006.

6. Chakraborty, Sauvik, "For an Equal Justice", *The Times of India*, Patna, Ranchi, National, 17-01-2007.
7. *Ibid.*
8. *Ibid.*
9. *Ibid.*
10. Deshpande, Satish, "Learning to Speak Caste" in *The Times of India*, Patna, Ranchi, National, 03-05-2007.
11. *Ibid.*
12. *Ibid.*
13. *Ibid.*
14. Ahmad, Imtiaj, "Caste is Relevant" in *The Times of India*, Patna, Ranchi, National, 11-06-2007.
15. *Ibid.*
16. *Ibid.*
17. *Ibid.*
18. Parikh, K.S., "A Fair System" in *The Times of India*, Patna, Ranchi, National, 10-02-2007.

3

Nature and Justification of Political Ethics

In an interesting dialogue with the two elder brothers of Plato, Glaucon and Adaemantus in the *The Republic*, Socrates was trying to explain what was the most popular but unsatisfactory way of knowing "justice". He was of the opinion that to know what "justice" is, it is required to know the sense in which a state and an individual are just. Hence, the ethical concept of *dikaiosyne* or just action needs to be explained in terms of a justly intending and acting states and individuals, the former overreaching as far as Socratic-Platonic "organic theory" holds good. The interesting part in the dialogue is that Socrates first explains what is a just state because when the state is itself rogue, wherein rulers and ruled follow a rogue form of life—each one ought to maximize self-benefits without concern for quality of the beneficial means and ends most suitable to them. This, Plato's brothers said was "a city of pigs" about which they are not at all interested because "city states" ought to be the one wherein rulers and ruled follow an ethical way of life, certainly not the egoistic way. Then much to our pride, Socrates satisfies the brothers with his excellent explanation of a "city state" or simply a "state" in the proper sense, much like our "modern states" as uniquely identifiable "political bodies", flourishing within a definite boundary, having a population and obtaining mechanisms desirable for the said flourish. Our states are thus political entities, governed ably by a Philosopher King. Plato's Autocracy does not prevent us from conceiving a state as a political body ruled methodically and nicely (though in a centralised method of power tracking by wise Kings). However, in a modern state, political mechanisms are integral parts pursued more or less ably by a battery of "politicians" if the more harsh use of "rulers" is not preferred. Politicians, politics and governance of the states are extremely important in our times though we are now more enthusiastic about an interference of ethical scrutiny of what politicians decide and do, what routes politics takes in a state (the methods and means of social governance, so to say), and what are the desirable ways to govern the society of discrete individuals. Truly, we are more enthusiastic now about ethical talk in politics, but that is hardly a contemporary or modern phenomenon, it is Socratic-Platonic and Aristotelian in the West if we do not want to excavate the remote past. In the days of Socrates, Plato and Aristotle in the West, and in the epic periods and in the period of Kautilya (if we do not go far back) in India, we have been always enthusiastic about ethics-talk in politics because some mechanisms by a handful of experts in society that influence and affect individuals and society greatly needs serious scrutiny regarding what were the desirable decisions, actions, duties, obligations and so on of these experts, the politicians. Hence, the preceding ethics-talk relating to "society" should ethics be backed up by ethical talks about its polity.

As usual, "political ethics" first demands "nature analysis" in terms of analysis of meaning and significance of "political", "ethics" and "political ethics", which is one of the major concerns in this chapter, the other concern being the "justification" of ethics-talk in politics or what is the sense of having "political ethics". At the outset of the said analysis it should be clarified that "political ethics" is where "politics" and "politicians" are, it is perhaps equally active where we conceive of "statelessness", an utopia of a state devoid of polity and politics as affairs of the "herd" or "groups" or "institutions" because in "statelessness" individuals are free *ethical anarchists*, their own *moral* kings, so to say, needing no herd for governance. Hence, in a queer utopia, there may be a state devoid of politicians, politics and political institutions though it is difficult to imagine that state which is bereft of at least "free ethical anarchists" (refer to the political philosophy of Mahatma Gandhi). Of course, we can endlessly debate on the *ethic of* statelessness and the *ethics as force of* statelessness. For us, in this work though, political ethics taking centre stage, ethics of statelessness do not matter much. So let us take up analysis of meaning of "politics" and "political ethics", skipping largely the analysis of "ethics" because we have done that in the previous chapters.

The root of "politics" is the Greek term "polis", meaning "a city" or a "state" or more simply, a "society", man as its building block is thus a "social animal" or a "political animal", says, Aristotle. According to Socrates, Plato and Aristotle, humans are in essence social or political beings who live in city-states or states self-sufficient and free in many respects, particularly in governance. In the capacity of social or political beings, it is thus obligatory on individuals as just course of action to serve for the humans' welfare of a state. It is thus an ethical mandate on civil citizens to work towards political goals of a city-state, the main being "human well being". "Politics" as we get it from the root, amounts to a course of action on our part (on the part of political beings), to achieve human good, which is "welfare". However, of late, we have effectively changed our conception of humans as *mere* social and/or political animals, who have a defined goal as said above. Moreover, politics is often seen under the scope of the "social" as is the case of "economics". Hence, speaking of humans as "social" would not necessarily and sufficiently amount to the speaking of humans as "political", it is much broader. The social functions of humans that testify their social character does not only amount to political functions or politics as means to human welfare because human welfare is obtainable in many ways, many social functions of humans, the political, the economic and so on. In this sense, we now hesitate to say that social ethics and social studies are the same as political ethics and political science because ethical inquiries in social matters is very broad, which needs no mention now. We had clear idea of this broadness. Most interesting is that political ethics may be an aspect of social ethics, but not the whole of it and political science may be an aspect of social studies but not the whole of it. Broadly, when we consider ethically relevant sociological talks, we might consider ethically relevant political talks as well, and therefore, as we said before, the two are closely related, which most probably the wise Greeks might have in mind when they were rhetorically ambiguous in speaking about "political humans as social". However, as we reach this chapter, we find that when we consider ethically relevant social talks *narrowly*, one such talk is "ethical talk in politics" or "political ethics". Hence, social and political ethics are different though closely related much like social and political sciences and social and political philosophies, which are related though different. Interestingly both social and political philosophies fall under "philosophy" much like social and political sciences are under "social science", and social and political ethics are under "ethics". It is a grave mistake to imagine that social and political ethics are branches or scopes of sociology or political science, rather they are under ethical studies for here we are not doing anything related to the social sciences as such but doing something that *relates* both the social sciences and the *normative discipline* called "ethics", though the said relation stands its ground on ethical cues or *ethical reflections about* social scientific talks. In this sense, we are not studying about democracy or governance or voting or constitution, we are studying about many ethically relevant questions pertaining to democracy or governance or voting or constitution.

Turning to the analysis of "politics" and "political" now, it would be too simplistic to follow the same Greek line. More often than not, we take (wrongly) politics as government, but these notions are not the same. Government in the common parlance governs the state; it lays down the rules and methods for the effective functioning of the state by means of its three important organs, the legislative, the executive and the judiciary. Politics on the other hand, is an important activity in our states, which is effective in the well-deliberated acts of individuals and groups that forms, reforms, affects and influences government and governance of states. Politics, for instance, is responsible towards forming a government or toppling it by means of franchise or revolt or both and is thus the most responsible intended act on our part to influence a social life we have, the kind of economy and welfare we have. Government and governance are thus heavily dependent on the polity we have. However, there is always a tension when the judiciary as an organ of the government as far as it assures the violation of enacted laws by the legislative, which the executive strives to enforce, to be fittingly met to see that the state is in order and governance is fine. The tension is that the judiciary as an independent organ wants to remain out of the interventions of the "government in power", "politics" that gives the needed "power" to the government by virtue of soft or hard politics, the former being not power-politics, the latter is power-politics, wherein the needed power is grabbed or encroached by use of powers of money, muscle, mischief and so on. The point is that the sacrosanct laws of the constitution and the enactments of the legislative need free and fair custodians, which the judiciary is by virtue of the constitutional provisions. Hence, it will be very distasteful for the judiciary to see that the government in power does not abide by the laws that they enacted or which they had for them to follow demanding no makeover or amendments. The same may be the case when the executive, including the bodies of local governance demand freedom and non-encroachment provided everything they do abide by the sacred laws. This means though government is a responsible institution for governance, its organs must work in tandem as per law without unnecessary hitches and interventions. Nevertheless, politics being heavily responsible in forming a "government in power", and those in power does not wish to lose it in any case, but some forces tends to see the loss of one with the gain of others by means of counter-politics either hard or soft. In this tension maze of politics and the running of government, more often than not politics-in-power breaches laws because forces of politics pushes to power tracking or power saving. Naturally, we have conflicts among the organs of government. Again, we find that "politics" though related to but different from 'government' might result into several intricate tensions arising mainly out of "power-tracking", "power-saving", "breaches in laws" and "conflicts with the judiciary" (and even the executive). All these explanations are good enough to show why toeing the Greek line in the explanation of "politics" is not sound. We have an important reflection that what belongs to the "realm of politics" or what is "political" cannot be the same as what belongs to the "realm of social" or what is "social" because *pertaining to politics* or "political" is just an aspect or an important dimension of what pertains to sociological or simply, "social". When we speak of something pertaining to politics or political, we speak of unique thoughts, decisions and acts of individuals, groups and institutions, all belonging to society that affects government and governance, but in society, individuals, groups and institutions think, decide and act, and come into numerous forms of relations which are *non-political*, that is, not related to the shaping and functioning of government and the workings of *state*. Humans as social beings are not necessarily and sufficiently "political" beings because even if a large number of them are engaged in political activities and governance, they do many things, which are other than these activities, though in essence well deliberated, intended and decided. In this sense, we can say that "politics" is complex form of thoughts, decision-makings and acts that pertain to the state. Many among us think that this is a safe way to explain what is "politics" and "political". D.D. Raphael, for instance, writes, "The political is whatever concerns the state, and on the whole this way of delimiting the sphere of the political still seems to me the clearest"[1]. This explanation, which we have followed in the preceding paragraphs invite some changes for being a "too narrow" explanation of "political", says Raphael because "In the first place, it seems to cover only 'government'... but not the political behaviour of individuals and groups in voting, political parties etc. Secondly, there are societies which are not States but which contain activities that we are bound to call political"[2]. Raphael refutes both the charges by saying that the first charge is myopic in so far as it overlooks the truth that our political thinking, decisions and actions amounting to form or reform government are complete sets of individual and group thoughts, decisions and acts covering the necessary political dynamics such as voting, party based political actions and so on. It is expected of us that in isolation and association we deliberate well about which party to come to power and whether their agenda are approvable and desirable. What we call "political behaviour" covers all these things are not merely functions of government. About the other charge, Raphael says that "politics" in the sense of an activity bereft of the conception of a State and government of the state is true either in case of "primitive societies" or in case of unique "social units" because in the former we do not have organised forms of political behaviour patterns with correlative governmental functions because everything in such societies are determined unilaterally by a person in power, an authority so to say; whereas in the second case, we speak of politics in schools, colleges, unions, church and many other social institutions and organisations which is not the same politics related to shaping and running a government or a State. Raphael replies that here we are speaking in the major about modern States and politics that comfortably sidesteps primitive societies and politics therein, though even in an authoritative rule as this, there are choice of people of clan or group or individuals requiring authority or else, if authority comes to power by the use of power-politics, there are still rules, laws, executing them, some form of governance and conceptions of prize and punishment. In the second case, we are equally narrow in considering patterns of individuals and groups within a small society and not of complex patterns of behaviour in the society or in the State. However, here we are dealing in wider political behaviour in States and not tiny societies, though even then we speak of well-intended decisions of individuals or groups to authorise some people to the use of powers unique to them for shaping rules and executing them. In fact, when we speak of college or university politics we are using term "politics" more or less *metaphysically* than normally. Raphael thus clarifies many narrow uses of the terms "politics" and "political" to mean thereby behaviour of individuals and groups, which appears to be in essence beyond the conceptions of government and governance. These conceptions (metaphysical) in the main are influenced by the idea that "politics" must in essence be involved with individual and group dynamics concerning power tracking or conflicts for power. Power-seeking and power conflicts must be then defining essence of "politics", which is for us (and Raphael), tragically mistaken. Readers are aware of the fact that in an earlier paragraph I wrote about politics as "power-tracking", mild and hard. Raphael says that the idea may not be wholly misleading because organised politics leading to forming and running government can toe the line of power-tracking, but the misleading part lies in the idea that this is the defining essence of "politics". In fact, much confusion is owing to the unnecessary and ambiguous use of "power" in this context because we are not clear what kind of a "power" is tracked in politics. Certainly, it is not mechanical power or willpower or authoritarian power because not necessarily and sufficiently politics involves physical, or authoritarian power or both of them taken together. One way is to say that here "power" is "political power" but the use of "power" in this case too is ambiguous. Hence, there are some ambiguities in "political" and thus "political power". It may be wholly misleading therefore, to say that 'politics is power'. Politics may be defined simply as "individual or group dynamics related to government running turning and functioning". This is good enough to show why "politics" cannot be defined in terms of "conflict" because even though there are conflicts among utopias and opinions, all these makes sense in a unique "political" context. Hence, it amounts to a circularity to say that "politics" amount to "political conflicts". Hence, says Raphael, "Power and conflict are indeed key ideas for the understanding of political activity, but they cannot be used as defining terms in order to distinguish political from other social relationships."[3] Having said this, we must take "politics" and "political" as dynamics related to State functioning and to be clearer, not the functioning of a household or neighbourhood or society or social organisations or even communities. It is crucial that politics must be understood in relation to State functioning, wherein "the State is differentiated from other associations by its universal jurisdiction, its negative function, and the special character of law in being backed by force and having sovereign authority. The compulsory nature of State jurisdiction, and the State's positive function, differ in degree but not in kind from similar features of some other associations. We may therefore, define the State as an association designed primarily to maintain order and security, exercising universal jurisdiction within territorial boundaries by means of law backed by force and recognized as having sovereign authority"[4]. Hence, it will be good enough to say that "political" in "political ethics" is what "pertains to politics", and things pertaining to politics concerns the affairs of State, the affairs no less clear at this point. Any civil State in our times then goes along with political dynamics; it cannot be freed from the dynamics.

This is not the right place to jump on an analysis of "ethics" and then "political ethics" because we have to clarify further that what pertains to politics and which political matters should be studied under the branch called, "political science", but neither under philosophy nor ethics. Moreover, "science" of politics has a distinct air of gravity unlike philosophy or its branches, as if it is improper to relate the scientific and the non-scientific (philosophy etc.). Surely, philosophy is not a science, it does not claim to have that nature of "science" in dealing with factual matters and have empirical methods for study. However, does that prevent philosophy or any of its branches like ethics and logic to be "scientific", even if they are "non-scientific" in essence, that is, does not take interest in studying facts and phenomena? No one has really prevented philosophy from being scientific in spirit if that means having pertinent ways or methods of doing things under its purview, things essentially non-factual in nature. Hence, philosophy and its branches as ethics or moral philosophy primarily does not even aim at any factual study such as study of the politics of the State. Still, it remains scientific or methodical in its selection of tasks or subject matter, methods to approach them and perform with all meticulousness reaching definite conclusions so far that is possible. We may say that though the "first order task" of philosophy or its branch called ethics might not be factual study such as political study, some of their "second order tasks" might be related to the said first order tasks of the science of politics. The science of politics in this sense is then a study of a "first order scientific tasks" of the complex dynamics of politics in matters of States. The science of politics stands on the edifice of hypothesis, observations, experiments, theories, analysis, laws, rules and so on regarding matters pertaining to individual and group dynamics that affects the dynamics of States. In this sense, philosophy and ethics is hardly a first-order scientific study of politics, but it can be seen as a second-order study of politics, which is extremely scientific in spirit if the study has a definite method and correlative justification.

It was believed not too long ago that philosophy is where science ends, and it is the mother of all disciplines, meaning thereby that sciences like politics and physics are based for their essential reflections on philosophy and that whenever these sciences are at sea in order to excavate essential truths, they refer to nothing but philosophy. Hence, the natural conclusion was that "political philosophy" is a philosophical study of political matters wherein reflections basic to the science of political matters have failed or went "sick". This is a horrible idea that political philosophy starts when political science goes on long leave. The saviour status of philosophy has led many brilliant minds to argue that therefore, moral philosophy or ethics is where politics is sick and have failed to do its much needed but lacklustre "scientific" grinding. The boastful ethical thinkers find comfort in thinking that the failure of the first order scientific inquiry is inevitable because man and social organisations often turn out to be rogues without philosophy and ethics, and soon find that the science of individual and group political activities affecting State have not only run out of ideas, they have failed miserably. We often hear that politics of individuals and groups of any part of the world has become valueless; they are degraded in the lack of philosophical and ethical vision. All this may be literally true but to derive a conclusion from this that therefore, political science has failed, that philosophy and ethics has won, and that political philosophy and political ethics rises from the ashes of the science are tragic, most illogical and unphilosophical. Then what are the needs of political philosophy and political ethics? Why are they so important though science of politics has not failed? Coming to political philosophy first will be better in this regard because reasons in favour of having ethical reflections in politics are not the same as those given in favour of political philosophy or philosophical reflections in this regard are parts of philosophical reflections taken overall. Hence, justifying political philosophy, which is not based on the hackneyed emotional thinking about this matter, relies mainly on the second-order task of philosophy, which is the task of logical analysis of basic concepts and language of political discourses. There are reasons for taking the linguistic concern so seriously. In fact, if we go by the history of evolution of such an analytic enterprise, which is touted fundamental to philosophy, it has evolved out of a sceptical line of thought. It has evolved out of scepticism about the "synthetic interests" in philosophy, such as inquiring about the nature and structure of world and worldly phenomena, to prescribe courses of actions in politics or economics and so on and to obtain methods not amenable to philosophical queries, such as the methods of observation, experiments and intuitive subsumption. If this is the case then philosophy *per se* should take little or no interest in factual political affairs of the state, recommend decisions and actions and follow unphilosophical scientific methods of factual inquiries. Such scepticism, however, failed to be nihilistic though in an early era of sceptical analysis it amounted to some nihilistic conclusions, which were extreme reactions refuting and possibility of philosophical reflections about non-philosophical matters. Soon it was found by many revisionist minds that it would be too myopic a vision to rule out a second-order linguistic inquiry, which analysts thought, is the heart of philosophy. No one has really prevented the philosophers to enter into the task of *conceptual clarity* or to inquire into the conceptual forms of our thinking about the world and its phenomena, whether that take us to politics or economics or physics. Such a philosophical interest gives us no new knowledge about the world of facts, but it does give us important visions about the structure, meaning and truth of language much different from the way of the grammarians in linguistic inquiry. Philosophy thus enters political discourses through a new route to dispel several conceptual confusions in thought. It does not enter into the debate of forms of government as the best or more suited given political reasons or on pragmatic grounds, rather it tries to throw light on concepts like "government", "governance", "democracy", "autocracy" and so on and of course analyses the strengths and weaknesses of debates about good governance based on the formal rules that are available to them. It does not enter into politics rather into the word "politics". Largely, political philosophy takes us to language of politics or the linguistic discourse of politics for analysing its nature, structure, meaning and truth. Political philosophy is thus "politically neutral" because without having no practical interest in real politicking, as we are now poised in this discussion, we can be philosophically honest on political matters. To take a cue from the famous work of C.L. Stevenson's *Ethics and Language* (1944), in analysing the truth and meaning of "Democracy is good", though it is extremely important to discuss about the descriptive account of or meaning of "democracy", without taking practical interest in democracy or participating in patterns and behaviour or forms of life adequate to democracy, we can analyse the way the descriptive and the evaluative meaning of "democracy" are related, and what is the meaning of "good" in this assertion. We can analyse the truth and meaning of the assertion taken on the whole and in parts, to see whether it is cognitively or non-cognitively meaningful, that is, whether the assertion is known to be true and sensible as a matter of fact through our sense experience and/or intuitive experience, or whether the assertion is true and sensible as it exhorts speaker's emotions, attitudes, commands and so on. Such second-order inquiry regarding the "language of politics" constitutes in the main philosophical politics or political philosophy. Hence, philosophical inquiries about the language of politics or the evaluation of justifications of political theories, methods, principles are in no way dependent on "real politics", that is "doing or partaking in politics", but philosophical politics for its needed inquiries are inseparably *related to* "real politics" in so far as complete ignorance of matter of facts or political facts does not help us in second-order inquiry, though *knowing about* intricacies in real politics does not compel us to participate in a form of real politics. A philosophical interest in language analysis helps the political thinkers and political philosophers immensely. More often than not in "constitutional interpretation" (an important aspect in political affairs), clarification of concepts and language becomes extremely important. It is also helpful in evaluating the avowals of the participants in political discourses, particularly those pertaining to political theories, methods and principles, which have far-reaching effects on real life political decision-making and courses of political activism. However, it will be too narrow to say that philosophical inquiries regarding political matters are merely logico-linguistic inquiries. Despite debate, many philosophers argue that even if we keep off political activism for political inquiry, philosophically relevant inquiries should not be narrowed down to logico-linguistic analysis of political discourses. The reason is that philosophers take serious *metaphysical* and ethical interests, which transcends the limit of logico-linguistic inquiries. This is important to understand before taking on the case of political ethics for its justification because political ethics need not be understood as a narrowed down language analysis of political assertions which carries a distinct evaluative overtone. For instance, it will be too narrow to understand that political ethics is all about logical analysis of value-laden political assertions such as "Democracy is good", "Communists belong to the axis of evil", or "Democracy is worse than autocracy" and so on. What other things constitute political ethics is awaited for explanation. For the time being, we can conclude that political philosophy though in the main takes logico-linguistic interests, it takes other interests such as metaphysical and ethical, the former sub-branch of political philosophy may be called, "political metaphysics" (if we prefer that expression), the latter may be called, "political ethics" (we have chosen this expression without much fuss in contemporary writings, and shall continue with it here).

Some philosophers argue that metaphysics, if it is true to its basic spirit which is philosophical, it must relate itself to analysis of language of metaphysics and nothing else. This must be true of political metaphysics if there are discourses truly about metaphysical matters in politics. However, as we have just seen, metaphysical interests in philosophy and politics may not be narrowed down to the analysis of language. The squabble about the subject matter of metaphysics and political metaphysics owes much to the basic debate in fixing a linguistic task for metaphysics and political metaphysics. Hence, we have to show the ways in which metaphysics and political metaphysics dwindle past the task of language analysis. It is believed that metaphysics as a branch of philosophy has to answer some basic questions about the nature and number of "ultimate reality". The ontological priority of matter, mind, Self and so on are furiously debated in philosophy along with the care for the body of language that emerges from such debate for analysis of truth and meaning, and of course the conceptual clarity of "matter", "mind", "Self" and so on. It is also important to evaluate the logical strengths and weaknesses of the contesting theories about realities and ultimate reality or realities. No one prevented philosophers of metaphysical interest to argue until date whether matter is over mind or whether our world is material or divine. One wonders, if metaphysics concerns with such things and about creation, evaluation and so on and so forth, where is political metaphysics? The sceptical question arises when one goes by the subject matter of the science of politics stated in some preceding paragraphs. Even if politics relates itself to the matters of State (as we have said), the most important non-political though related to political question is, "What is basic to or ontologically prior to State? In what sense do we claim State as an existential, is it an entity that is identifiable in space and time? Do humans constitute the existential? Alternatively, is it an ideal, a form of rules and institutions? Is State an embodiment of authority? Do we say that State can be explained in terms of either matter-in-motion or ideally or spiritually or in other ways? Answering these questions takes us to the metaphysical realm. A number of interesting questions takes us to the realm though they hover around the field of politics. Hence, philosophy as metaphysics entering the field of politics, gives us "political metaphysics". It will be interesting here to remind our readers about Plato's interest as a philosopher of metaphysics to deal with matters such as the nature of State and the ontological priority of State over individuals by virtue of an "organic theory", and the ontological priority of the "philosophical wisdom" in the governance of the State, which is found in the discussion of the Philosopher King. The political theorists of "social contract" *gharana*, Hobbes, Locke and Rousseau found something else as basic to State though they had traces of organic theory in political metaphysics. In fact, they found a basic purpose or *teleos* of the State. On the other hand, the Hegelians had another thesis to offer by virtue of their metaphysics of absolutism. There are numerous theses, metaphysical ones about the relation of individual and the State, which makes political metaphysics an interesting study in philosophy and politics; it is difficult to see why philosophy *qua* philosophy should not take such interests. We thus conclude that political metaphysics is an adequate philosophical inquiry being metaphysically oriented though entering a field other than the philosophical, that is, the political, and this inquiry is something more than what is analysis of language of metaphysics, politics and metaphysical politics. We are closing on to the basic contention, that is, political ethics is equally adequate philosophical study though it is more than philosophical, if that is the only analysis of language of ethics or politics or political ethics. However, we have to wait for some time before drawing such conclusions because traces of scepticism are still demanding a wipeout because sceptics are hard nuts.

Philosophical sceptics argue that even if it is shown that metaphysical inquiries in philosophy might transcend linguistic interests in some sense, and that political metaphysics or political philosophy as transcending linguistic discourses in some ways are still justifiable within the broad field of philosophy, what we have shown thus far is that philosophy and metaphysics (as branch of philosophy) takes political interests in so far as the interests are predominantly "theoretical" and not practical because philosophy and its branches like metaphysics, ethics or whatever even if they enter politics in the ways in which we have seen does not offer anything to a "life of practice", that is, what things are in practice in politics. Hence, though politics is heavily a practical affair in real life, where theories and theses are not merely analysed and churned, something should be "done" or "practiced"; philosophy *qua* philosophy has no practical side, there is no "philosophy of practice" or what is fashionably called "practical philosophy". Hence, metaphysics and political metaphysics, we have seen are merely theoretical enterprises, there is hardly any practical political metaphysics. This must be true of ethics as another branch of philosophy. It is predominantly theoretical and not practical. There is no practical ethics and no practical political ethics.

Some people are very worried listening to these sceptical challenges because they find that it is intolerably disturbing to be cursed as "non-practical" philosophers, metaphysicians, political metaphysicians, ethicists and political ethicists. However, they should not be so anxious about being called "non-practical" because they are not abused as "impractical" or "hopeless" or "saprophytic theorists". In fact, a large number of sceptics, who argue philosophy to be "non-practical", argue equally forcefully that it is not an impracticable enterprise because philosophers have other relevant things to do. For sure, they need to do, and they "do" in fact things extremely important socially not egoistically, they are not subjectively arrogant either. Philosophers, in "doing", logic, metaphysics, ethics and language analysis contributes to the field of study, the philosophical fraternity and philosophers help many people who await a philosophical scrutiny of different issues tremendously. In this sense, philosophy and its branches are in practice and of pragmatic value. But the doubt is that as other practices like medicine and politics, philosophy and its branches does not take up any "other than theoretical, practical tasks" like teaching the art of logical argument (sophistry), teaching the art of ethical behaviour and ethical resolutions (casuistry), teaching the art of knowing the ultimate realities or reality and teaching the art of becoming a Philosopher King or a Politician of status having known the ultimate political truths. Alternatively, philosophy and any of its branches have nothing in store in method and theory that is pressed in practice in real life; philosophy is then not practical. The argument goes to conclude that though politics has in store in method and inquiry that are pressed in practice in real life, and there are *practicing* politicians, there are no practicing philosophers or practicing ethicists, or no practical philosophy or practical ethics. To press it hard now, political philosophy and political ethics are theoretical enterprises, do not confuse them having any "practical" side, they are "non-practical" in nature. We need to face these extremely important and interesting observations before coming to justification of "political ethics" because we might find that the "practical" interests in ethics and political ethics are far too clear, and they are not "non-practical" in nature, if by "practical" here we do not confuse to the least that like medicine and politics, there are physicians and politicians who practice as based on theories and methods available to them to eke out a living. Well, for sure, there are no practicing philosophers and ethicists in this sense, but there is practical philosophy and ethics in yet another sense. Before reaching practical ethics and political ethics as practical ethics, let us deal with philosophy and philosophers of practice though something has been hinted in this regard when I was clarifying about the pragmatic aspects of philosophical enterprises, even if the enterprise of language analysis is considered most important. As we said before, philosophy have a sound method for conceptual and linguistic clarity, and there are different other methods when we take up metaphysical, empirical, logical and ethical inquiries, each having specific subject matter and aims. The fact that all philosophical inquiries obtain a method, propound theories, come to distinct theoretical conclusions and reach the most desired aims fixed by them, they are pragmatic or practical inquiries in one sense. In the eastern wisdom, particularly in India, philosophy has been thoroughly a teleological enterprise, a practical one, not the kind of armchair theoretical churning of wise people about intricate concepts, theories, facts and judgements. In this wisdom, philosophy is practical in finding the essence of or essential truths of life and world. There are debates (we have seen) whether philosophy can and should be involved in search for such truths. Still, the search for truth and meaning of the language of morals, science, politics, and religion and so on cannot be completely detached from our concerns about life and world because language itself is an aspect of our practical life lived in this world, a life of discourses, exhortations, descriptions, agreements, disagreements, and many such acts. The language concerns in philosophy is thus closely related to our life forms and our speech acts are the ways in which we perceive, imagine, think, decide and do in this corporeal life. The inquiry has a *teleos*; it is surely practical in being deconstructing the structure of our conceptual and speech world. This is true when we are involved in the conceptual and speech worlds of politics, ethics, and religion and so on. Hence, political, moral and religious philosophies are practical as far as they are involved in the deconstruction of their conceptual and speech worlds. A philosopher of politics and ethics is thus a philosopher of practice of having a practical attitude for he or she aims at doing meaningful things about concepts and speech-acts. This is no less useful and social than medical practice with a difference that in the latter the methods, theoretical bases and objectives of practice are those we find in any positivistic inquiry, which is the "world itself". Philosophers of practice are not concerned about the world itself, that is, to deconstruct the world and its affairs, rather they have a practical concern about what things are *said about* the world and life therein, that gives us a body of discourse or language. In this sense, a philosopher of morality or ethical philosopher of practice is not concerned about the good and evil nature of man, the reasons for becoming good and evil and aids to overcome evil; they are concerned about the use of "good" and "evil" in the judgements of evaluation of human intentions or character. Ethical philosopher thus do not take any anthropological, sociological and psychological interests and thus they do not have such practical interests, they are practical in being contributing to our understanding of the ways in which we talk about human intentions, decisions, characters, virtues, vices and actions. This must be good enough to understand that though a politician has a practical interest about the world of politics about what goes on in individual and group dynamics relating to the State, a political philosopher and a political ethicist does not have such practical interest but are nevertheless practical in being clarifying the concepts and language in which we speak about the said dynamics relating to the State. All this is fine if we take philosophical concern in the main as language concern, but there is something more in store.

The practical features of philosophy, political philosophy, ethics and political ethics have taken a different turn since the debate of limiting "practicability" of philosophical ventures. This has sharpened particularly after the early twentieth century. Die-hard practical philosophers were hell bent to see that first philosophy is not limited to the said language concern and the said practical attitude, which is heavily theoretical because in that case where is practice if everything is theoretical and academic? Even if philosophers are not equipped to speak about the nature and structure of world, life and facts, they are never allowed to remain scot-free in the practical turmoil of world and life that invites their participation to face and find ways out of turmoil in the most adequate fitting and sensible ways open for them. No one really demands that a practical philosopher or a political ethicist takes head on to the challenge of the politics of aggression and colonisation in our times, as in the case of "politics for oil". The real politics of parleys, debates, and pressure tactics are all fine but no one really presses on practical ethicist to do them or else they will be impractical or at least non-practical in approach. However, a political philosopher and a political ethicist cannot and should not quit easily in the face of such grave political issues as sensible and conscious civil citizen of the world remain impractical. The problem is that they can take two courses of civil approach as civil citizens and these courses need to be scrutinised for being called ethically (and thus philosophically) appropriate though transcending the linguistic tasks we have seen before. One course is to participate in a social scientific vocation to collect data through systemic field work, analyse them and find out what are the ethical opinions of the sections of people of the countries entangled in political tension, draw wide spectrum ethical conclusions perhaps reflecting what is more or less desirable to smother the conflict and find out the theoretical ethical bases to diffuse the crises. Much like this is done in "empirical ethics", and political ethics may be thought as a practical enterprise of the philosopher who takes this empirical vocation though not acting a politician or a head of a State. The other course of action open to political philosophers and political ethicists is to widen and heighten the social scientific vocation. Its widening covers sections of world citizens not merely to collect their ethical opinions but to cover what are their major ethical arguments in the ethical debates to resolve the said crises. It is heightening covers corroboration of ethical views for resolution of crises, framing decision-making rules and finally, analysing the debate and closure of debates to find out the real dynamics of ethical first and secondary principles in cases of political imbroglios that are value-laden. The readers of this volume already have an idea of these vocations of practical ethicists, but we will not be so scrappy here. Yet, we will wait for the elaborations as we have reached a climax with regard to the debate of practical aspect of philosophy, ethics and political ethics. We come to know that philosophy and some of its branches can be "practical" without being merely analytic and positivistic, that is, without being pragmatic as language analysis and useful as social scientific vocation. However, having said all these things about the possibility of practical philosophy and practical ethics, sceptics can still ask, what if philosophers (and philosophy) and ethicists did not partake in any such non-analytic pragmatic enterprises? Will it not be sufficient to leave social scientists, the political scientists, the politicians and partly the anthropologists, military scientists and psychologists to take on such pragmatic tasks? Where is philosophy or ethics in all that has been said in the assumed pragmatic enterprises? Well, this must be too good challenge it appears, but in reality the loose ends of sceptical challenge appears clearly. This takes us to the justification of practical ethics and with it, political ethics.

Most importantly, we have reached the climax to understand what is "political", "philosophical", "practical", "practical philosophy" and to some extent "ethical", "practical ethics" and "political ethics". Put in a simple manner now, what pertains to matters of State are "political". Those pertaining to conceptual clarity, metaphysics, epistemology, logic and ethics (to name some tasks), is "philosophical". "Philosophy" when "practical" is either valuable for clarity of ideas for philosophers and others or valuable for practical inquiries, discussions and resolutions, which are grounded philosophically. "Ethical" is something that pertains to philosophical study of moral issues, which we have seen in the earlier chapters as metaethical, normative, practical or virtue related issues. "Practical Ethics" is our common ethical experience and knowledge pressed to discuss and resolve value-laden practical issues and to analyse real dynamics of ethical theories or principles in practical cases and their resolution. Finally, as we now come to know, "political ethics" is ethical or moral philosophical inquiries into matters that pertain to politics or matters pertaining to individual and groups of individuals in matters of States. We now come to elaborate what exactly we mean by (a) moral philosophical inquiries in the field of politics, and (b) the sceptics' loose ends that is, nothing is practical in ethics because there is no ethics and everything is merely positivistic practice. Both these points will take us to *justification* of political ethics after having completed analyses of nature of the same. In an earlier chapter and in this chapter we have spoken about ethics as philosophically relevant discussions on ethical or moral issues such as metaethical, normative, practical and virtue-related issues, but we have refrained from calling sophistry and casuistry as philosophical by relevant approaches towards moral matters, and we have avoided calling a purely scientific vocation found in empirical ethics as philosophically relevant approach in matters of morality. Then political ethics must be philosophically relevant approach towards issues that crops up in the field of politics. In addition, we know that such relevance could be traced in the main in metaethical, normative, practical and virtue related tasks of ethics or moral philosophy. Hence, political ethics is a non-starter if ethical tasks mentioned above do not find any relevance in the field of politics. Clearly, one way to justify political ethics is to show that metaethical and other task performances of ethics finds place in issue of political relevance. As such, the nature of political ethics is clearer when the above justification backs up our analytic effort to clarify what we mean by the concept called, "political ethics". This is supported when we are able to show that different issues in politics does not merely invite scientific or positivistic inquiries for an understanding rather, they open up for ethical inquiries because the issues are *value-laden* or that they raise distinct questions of value to be analysed taking a unique ethical prospective. The nature analysis covered by justification of political ethics is further backed up when we are able to show that in political ethics there is no drab practical nitty-gritty of political science rather, there is academic ethical involvement, particularly those of ethical theories and principles in a climate of practice. Hence, in political ethics, philosophers are not deprived of their theoretical work and they are not static. It will be noticed while we move on to these justifications now that the first set of justifications are wider and more general in nature, whereas the second set of justifications is more specific in showing that the normative and virtue ethical theories and principles are not handmaids of academic churnings but they act in a climate of political problems. This in turn clarifies the sense in which "political ethics" is neither purely theoretical nor purely positivistic but concerns theoretical analytic and social scientific vocation, showing why *lasseiz faire* and empirical position all by themselves fail to justify practical ethics and political ethics. In this chapter, I will prefer taking a different course, much different from what was preferred in an earlier chapter while discussing justification of social ethics. Rather than taking one after another the justification that the tasks of ethics extends to the field of politics and that political matters opens up for ethics, I would like to deconstruct the dynamics of ethics in the proper sense to show that it coagulates all the previously explained ways to justify political ethics.

One way (not foolproof) to show that politics and ethics go hand-in-hand together is that many political thinkers and ethicists claim that either ethics is a branch of politics or politics is a branch of ethics or ethics and politics needs to be equated. An exception may be noted when it is said that ethic and politics are completely unrelated as they are non-relatable. Interesting point is that there are either justification in a "weak sense" to show that ethics and politics are related in so far as one of the two is the ground of the other, that is, one is based on the other or, to show that ethics and politics are completely unrelated and any talk about one being the ground of the other is wayward. To justify that ethics and politics are related in some way is "weak" justification because "political ethics" cannot be strongly justified as a sensible ethical inquiry by merely showing that politics and ethics are in some way related because one is the ground of the other. The *stronger justification* according to some is to show that ethical tasks find relevance even, when we come to an alien field of political issues, and when political issues are found to be value-laden awaiting ethical scrutiny and resolution. Whether showing the said "relevance" and "scrutiny and resolution" amounts to show that one is "based" on the other is seriously doubted because "basing" one thing on the other carries a distinct sense of "logical basing"; we may call it a kind of "necessity" or "implication" amounting to justify that in any case any reference to politics implies a reference to ethics or *vice versa*, which is poor logic because we can show several instances of political discourses needing no necessary reference to ethics or the *vice versa*. For instance, not all talks in metaethics need be necessarily based on politics, and not all talks in State governance need be necessarily based on metaethics, though some metaethical talks involve politics and some political talks of governance involve metaethics. If this be the case then neither ethics nor politics can be shown to be necessarily (and sufficiently) based on one another though in "some cases", the involvement of the one in another may be justified, which as I have said, are involvements of ethical tasks in politics and political issues inviting ethical scrutiny and resolution, thus showing the relevance of the field called "political ethics". Political ethics is thus not fortuitous relation of politics and ethics, nor is it a necessary and sufficient grounding of one on the other. Political ethics does not become a sensible study by just juxtaposing politics and ethics or implying one from the other. Two juxtaposed things may be shown to be related in some ways but that does not justify a study called "political ethics". Emotional ways to show that ethics is the mother of politics or the other way round, which has been poor ideas in philosophy and political science, does not serve the purpose of justification of "political ethics". Among other defects, how can politics as a positivistic study be logically derived solely from a normative study or, how can ethics as a normative study be logically derived solely from a positivistic study? It may be argued that calling politics "positivistic" and ethics "normative" studies is misconceived, both are complex studies, politics bearing positivistic and normative elements. Thus, one can be logically derived from the other. However, the point is that political studies "involve" normative inquiries in some cases, though it is a positive study; and ethical studies "involve" positive inquiries in some cases though it is a study that is normative in nature. Hence, politics and ethics are not naturally alloyed studies, they are characteristically predominantly positive and normative respectively but that does not prevent them from getting "involved" in non-positive and non-normative studies, where "involvement" as we said, is *not* fortuitous relation. Neither there is a necessary or logical relation between the two. It may be objected that though politics is by nature predominantly "positive", ethics is not by nature predominantly "normative" because it possesses metaethical and practical elements. It needs to be understood here that to call ethics as basically "normative" is not to say that it is a body of ethical norms and nothing else, rather it is a study wherein metaethical and practical ventures or tasks are "normative" in character, that is, wherein certain discussions concerning the theories, principles, models or methods or in short, *norms or ideals or paradigms* relating to language, moral evaluation and character (virtuous) are discussed. In this sense, it is the study, which is *predominantly* "normative" in character, which however, does not prevent it from 'entering into' or getting 'involved in' non-normative or positive studies. This is why it has become old fashioned to harp on philosophy as the mother of all sciences or to say that where science ends, philosophy begins though hardly anyone doubts philosophy and science are characteristically different studies but one gets "involved" in matters of another in "some" cases but not in all cases, and that their mutual involvement is neither fortuitous nor logical. Hence, politics and ethics are mutually involved in some or in many cases but *not in all cases.* This is enough to show that they are not equivalent or equatable. In addition, they are *not* logical grounds of one another; one is not the prior to the other and one does not include the other. Hence, it may be good enough to say that Aristotle's conception that ethics is wholly based on politics (as in *Nicomachean Ethics*), Hobbes' idea of equivalence of both (in *Leviathan*), Kant's conception of politics as based on morals (as in *Perpetual Peace*) and Hegel's idea that politics is ultimate to morals (as in *Philosophy of Right*) are misconceived and old-fashioned. Tragically, even if they were true, they hardly justify "political ethics". Hence, we will refrain from justifying political ethics in these ways though it may be true in many cases that ethical thesis *needed* political reflections or *vice versa.* This fact of "need" has led many thinkers to believe that one is based on or dependant on the other though the truth is that the "need" of something shows the likelihood of an "involvement" of two different things and not the fortuitous or the logical relation we normally think about. Hence, even if Kant thought that politics is seriously in "need" of ethics, it is based on ethics, must be weak logic though he may be successful in arguing that ethics is in some cases seriously involved in political matters. Nevertheless, what about Machiavelli (in *The Prince*), who argued that politics is *divorced* from morality? This question must be answered because it is a serious sceptical question amounting to the disjunction of politics and morality. Well, why are we so worried about "divorce" or '"disjunction"? It is literally true that "politics" and "morality" and different. Another point of caution is we need not suddenly shift our stance and start discussing about "morality" and not "moral philosophy" or "ethics". Machiavelli must have taken things colloquially to mean that ethics is largely dealing in moral affair or simply morality, that is, intending and doing good or virtuous, and thought that such issues make no great sense in politics. However, he must be cautious that this way he might not be proving ethics disjoint from politics because ethics, apart from other things is *philosophical scrutiny of moral matters* or of morality. Even if politics in many ways, by many people like Hitler and Idi Amin were taken "indifferent" to morality of our political thinking and action, because the emotional fools drag such nuisance in politics, that does not amount to show that politics should be "indifferent" to ethical reflections of such morality of Hitler and Amin. Even this fails to show that politics and ethics are unrelated and are non-relatable because an *attitude* of indifference and having a relation or no relation of the two are different issues. If we are serious about showing that ethics and politics are unrelated as they are non-relatable categories, we must show that why they are "non-relatable". Machiavelli argued that it was a "category confusion" to say that ethics and politics are related because these categories *per se* are "non-relatable"; it is a good sceptical challenge. In that case, we reply that though ethics and politics belong to different categories of inquiry the one, as we said before, is normative inquiry and the other positive, we are not arguing in favour of their equivalence or equation because that surely is committing category mistake. We should never draw a political conclusion from an ethical premise or the other way round thinking that for such conclusion no intervening premises are needed. In addition, we said that in no case was Hobbes correct in equating ethics and politics. Neither did we agree that Aristotle, Kant and Hegel were correct in logically deriving one truth from the other taken to be true. It is therefore, futile to hold that the sceptical challenge of Machiavelli is strong on the ground that he meant to show disjunction of ethics and politics. More or less, he had in mind that politics involves some such thinking and doing that amounts to talks of moral good, bad, right, wrong which are all futile; politics is a different game that should keep off hopeless things, which sentimental fools do. In this way, he was nowhere close to disjoint the sciences of politics and ethics; he was rather an emotional person (!) thinking it was so foolish to be morally sensitive in political matter. This is how even today many among us urge that looking at today's politics which is certainly so poor and nasty that morality is very different. Alternatively, that politics should do away with morality if one wants to succeed as a politician. However, these people are not ethical sceptics, they are "psychological sceptics" suffering from a mental disease so to say. In fact, it is not even "ethically" (or philosophically) relevant to take up such sceptical challenge, but let us assume that Machiavelli was arguing that politics involves morals in no case. What do we find? Simply stated, the Machiavellian urge is to show that politics involves and invites thoughts and actions which as "necessary evils" must be adored if politics has to sustain and with it the authority ("The Prince"), and for that matter politics demands "necessary immorality" on the part of the authority or authorities. Hence, going against social codes, standard fixed in societies as dogmas, the authority or the politician must be doing a greater good than evil. This issue is called the necessity of a "dirty hand" in politics thereby giving us a fresh look at political morality, which transcends the barrier of psychological scepticism to ensue a challenging ethical scepticism if and only if one needs to have a *philosophical scrutiny* of the issues of *private morality vis-à-vis public morality* with regard to politics. Only in this way can we say that even the call for a "necessary immorality" of the dirty hand in political game asks for ethically relevant inquiry. First, we need to inquire into the *conceptual clarity* of "morality", "immorality", "public and private morality", "necessary immorality", "moral dogmas", "moral codes" and so on which are *metaethical* inquiries. Further, we need to have a *normative inquiry* into the suggested "value of a disvalue", that is, the good of a necessary political evil for the public though that may be individually bad. Or, to find out based on which norms do we say that dogmatic social or public moral conceptions, codes, rules and so on needs to be disregarded by authoritative political actions which are deemed to be expedient in the larger interest (in many cases expedient in personal interest) and thus comes to be good as a "strategic evil". This might take us to the normative evaluation of personal and social moral dogmas on overreaching ethical standards as well as evaluation of obtaining *means* for political ends which are either immoral on social standards or on overreaching ethical standards or on personal standards. The inquiry further takes us to *practical ethical* scrutiny of the desirability of dirty hands in politics to find out in association the *reasons* for either having or not having such a course of activism, and to see what limits if any could be or could not be set to dirty hands in politics. This is to *resolve* the *value-laden case* of real politics in association through moral debates amounting to a consensus and formulation of decision-making rules. Further, the issue invites us to have *virtue ethical inquiry* into the *aretaic* or *deontic virtue* if any of the said course of action, and to suggest which virtues awaits such real politicking. It is interesting to see that in case the issue is taken for a crisis resolution, there is still a *theoretical analysis* left in ethics that reveals the dynamics of normative theses in moral debates and consensus. As I said before, political ethics need justification like this, to show that an issue of "dirty hand" of the Machiavellian obsession opens out involving political and ethical scrutiny. Equally true is that ethical inquiries such as metaethical, normative and so on makes perfect sense when they are involved in non-ethical, political matters such as this one. This is for me one-way to see what political ethics is and why it is a justified inquiry.

The necessity of "dirty hand" in politics since the support of

Machiavelli has raised many value-laden political problems, which finds place in the writings of Stuart Hampshire (*Public and Private Morality*, 1978), Michael Walzer (*Political Action: The Politics of Dirty Hands*, 1973), T. Nagel (in the edited work of Hampshire, 1978) and many others. It has been a pet issue in Platonic political writings and in the political writings in India, where the concept of necessity of "dirty hands" and moral evaluation has been explained in different ways. What interests us most here is that the problem is "value-laden" or it raises questions of ethical value, particularly those about the ethical desirability of such necessary evil in public life, for public good though at some risk of private immorality, or in another way, an evil for the public though good for a person (a politician). Our point is that in political ethics we initiate sensible ethical discussion about such issues, which appears to be positivistic in nature needing political explanations and nothing else, but a careful examination reveals that the core issue of public *vis-à-vis* private morality in dirty hand politics raises distinct ethical questions of desirability, good, right, duty, obligation and so on. Deliberate choice of speaking a blunt falsity or bluffing the public or plotting elimination of a person or a group or war in the name of politics always awaits moral evaluation. It awaits evaluation of why such decisions and subsequent actions are desirable means. Are they ends in themselves? In addition, if they are, why are they ethically just? We ask whether such outrageous political actions are ethically good for a person or persons. Are they obligatory on our politicians? Are they duties of politicians? Here the focused questions do not inquire why such outrageous actions are practically or non-morally good or bad; they inquire on what unique ethical reasons we value such actions as good or bad. A close scrutiny reveals that such *ethical reasons* often transcend reasons like, "they are beneficial politically, to politician or politicians, to the party in power and so on", because the lingering ethical questions search ethical reason for calling what is politically beneficial to be good and just. In that case, we finally take recourse to answers like, "what is politically beneficial does a lot of public good than evil", or "such political benefits are obligatory on politicians *qua* politicians", or "such benefits are good *per se*". As such, we finally come to ethical grounds such as utilitarianism or deontology. Hence, "value-laden" political issues such as dirty hands are so-called because it moves beyond the realm of political inquiries and ask for ethical scanning of the political decisions and acts. It is in this sense we speak of "political ethics" as a sensible study that covers ethics to enter into politics with the important tasks it has to perform. Coady remarks: "The necessity to manipulate, lie, betray, steal or kill may arise in private life occasionally it is much more *frequent* in politics. The political arena involves choices and consequences of much greater weight than private life. Actors in political life are *representatives* and so need to be morally assessed in a different way."[5] It is important to note that Coady draws our attention to the truth that politics is extremely complex phenomena, the ethical evaluation of which asks our visions to be more catholic than absolute because in many cases political decisions and actions do not demand the same degree of ethical scanning which is demanded in many other cases. The absolutists would never agree to such a view, they prefer a strict moral scanning in all cases of political decision-making and actions. Again, in political ethics, without being involved in anyway of politics, we can examine the soundness of the logic of the relativist and absolutist ethical opinions. This further takes us to the scrutiny of the logical grounds available to the relativists and absolutists for the justification of their opinions. In the capacity of philosophical moralist who enters into questions of such political questions, we perform an important *metaethical task*. Coady analyses the relativist and absolutist arguments regarding political dirty hands to find that they are in the main referring to the logic of *consequentialism* and *deontology*. Hence, we are dragged to explain and evaluate these normative theses, and for that matter enter into both *normative* and *metaethical* tasks.

An influential argument regarding the relative worth of dirty hands comes from T. Nagel, which takes us to the evaluation of the logic of consequential value or worth of political *impartiality*. It takes us to inquire whether the role of politician to be "impartial" in the face of resorting to an act of violence because that may be as a consequence of greatest value, is pertinent to political ethics. This may be good enough to argue why spoken falsity, bluffs, mischief and violence in politics may be ethically so relevant for an inquiry. We need to see whether it is proper to argue that bluffs and violence are political obligations having ethical viability and whether the theses of impartial and consequentialist approach is viable. In our times, the issue of *political corruption* as an aspect of dirty hands opens for ethical inquiry, and ethics in turn with its said tasks analyses the said concept, scrutinises the pro and con normative arguments, allows us to freely debate and resolve such issues and find out the normative dynamics and the required virtues on the part of the political agents with regard to corruption. It is interesting to note that the use of the term "corruption" with "political" do not necessarily and sufficiently allow us to dump the notion as "immoral", and therefore, no discussion about its moral or immoral value in ethics should be needed. The point is that though we speak of "dirty hands" and "corruption", we also speak of it "necessity" (a political necessity, something like a political game-plan, an important aspect of real-politics), and for that matter it invites absolutists to come up with their ethically cogent reasons to show that no such necessity exists or it invites relativists to come up with their ethical reasons to show that such things are needed. As political ethicist we are not deemed to belong to any of the two groups, we are invited to find out the logic of the arguments and thus evaluate the worth and disvalue of these contesting thesis in politics, "corruption" being one issue in it. Still better, we do not stop here; we are invited to arrange for resolution of such problems and to inquire normative involvement, which has been already mentioned. In fact, political ethics allows ethicists to see what is otherwise avoided by fashionable philosophers and absolutists that there are a few "moral circumstances" demanding close evaluation for the ethical worth of dirty hands in politics, whether that amounts to falsity or corruption. Coady says, "Philosophers and other theorists have in fact been too complacent in their acceptance of the neutrality and immutability of the background circumstances which generate 'dirty hands' choices."[6] He further goes on to show that political ethicists needs to reflect on at least three "moral situations" to evaluate the ethical worth of political decisions and actions which are called "dirty", which he thinks are those of *compromise*, *extrication* and *moral isolation*."[7] What is more interesting is to see that a political ethicist remains neutral to any of these commitments and must not go through any of these situations before taking on the tasks of evaluation of moral situation. Scrutiny of the arguments in favour of our moral compulsions to obtain a dirty hand is equally important in political ethics. Once we enter into this realm, we will come to know, for instance, whether it is logically correct in arguing that often our cooperative *compromises* for greater benefits that adopt dirty courses in politics, which Machiavelli was trying to say, is going against the normative first principles or constitutes an unprincipled character. The same ethically relevant scrutiny may be opted for when we argue that *political compulsions* enable us to take a course in dirty hands though the agent personally wants to *extricate* from the course. On the other hand, the argument that the urge for *moral isolation or individualism* for the sake of politicians' survival and good justifies dirty hands. In any case, political ethicists are not here to act moralists and moral saints to tell us "final things" about dirty hands in politics because political ethics is not about telling the "final" truths because there may be none.

Machiavelli has been an interesting and important thinker of political philosophy but we now find that his reflections in this regard are extremely useful for political ethicists. Machiavelli contributes to the justification of political ethics in another way. His conceptions of "State" and "power" which is linked to what we have just seen, that is the conception of dirty political game plan as necessary contributes to an understanding of the necessity of political ethics. The conceptions of "State" and "power" came from the notion of "sovereignty" of the State (and of the nation), meaning thereby the "function of political control" on the part of agents and agencies in "power", whether that amounts to power of monarchs or those of the government agencies but represented in decisions and deeds of any responsible person or groups of persons, the politicians, law-makers, executives and the judiciary. With the shift of "power" from monarchs to people in democracy, particularly in large areas of the globe, it became important to see whether "power" changed its basic significance, with the "political control" over population, and with this entered inquiry whether the conception of political state power is or should be bereft of ethical judgements. Here, we need to be careful that we are not worried about "moral interceptions" of groups, races and communities because these interceptions on their turn are subjected to ethical scrutiny. Such an inquiry into the role and significance of state power some way or the other takes us to the ethical evaluation of *forms* of state power employed in the status having different forms of government and governance. Ethically speaking, there are two conceptions of state power and ethical adequacy, one is the *totalitarian* conception and the other is the conception of *statelessness or nihilism of state power.* (Refer to our discussion about "statelessness"). As far as Machiavellian contribution to political ethics is concerned, he initiates us to discuss whether state power as absolute or totalitarian is ethically justifiable. The nihilistic view is no less provocative provided we do not take it on the face value and find out what thinkers, as Gandhi has to say in this regard. The totalitarian view awaiting ethical scrutiny is that the State is an embodiment of power and holding on to power is an end-in-itself because without that, there is no State, and then there is political catastrophe. It is said that even at the cost of the so-called "dirty game plans" politicians and others "in-power" should refrain from being guided by or moved by moral influences because such sentimentalism takes the State nowhere, it loses power. In fact, power as an end-in-itself and the good that does to the State overall has its own ethics, that is, "power is for the glory of the state and its people, and therefore, ethically good". Hence, it may be useless harping that the theory of totalitarianism has avoided ethicality because it has its own ethical justifications. This takes us to the ethical evaluation of Fascist States and its governmental formations. Similarly, it is immensely challenging to explain, compare, contrast and evaluate ethically the role and significance of "power" of state in democracy and socialism and other forms of government, which truly cannot be said as having no power or no use of power. The point is to evaluate in what ways the need and use of power in democratic, socialist and communist states are ethically justifiable than the autocratic or the totalitarian need and use of power. This is an extremely old question, as old as Plato's *The Republic*, which is in a major way ethical critique of state power though as we normally expected from him, he was scathing in the attack of democratic state power than the totalitarian one seen just now. This is well portrayed in Socrates' bitter arguments with Thrasymachus, wherein Socrates (also Plato) opened up with ethical support to the totalitarian state power aided with the available "organic theory" of State. Plato's analysts say that it was this theory that is responsible in the Frankensteinian (or Leviathanian) conception of State that went against a nobler democratic state power. It appears that an ethically noble way to avoid any talk of the state power in any form is to shun power in any form or in any degree. We have said before and we stick to the point that the conception of "statelessness" and thus lack of power tracking in states is not altogether useless or unjustifiable. It is not ethically irrelevant either because it is not an arbitrary or illogical call for dissolution of state and its power rather it is based on its own ethicality and logic that any "compulsion" and bondages of authorities on free individuals or moral agents hinders their moral evolution and thus the evolution of the human community as such. Hence, in place of state and power enforcing external authorities, free individuals should themselves seek authoritative stature for them and for the community. Whether the ethicality of freedom of political self and evolution of a mere political state to a moral existence is viable, is certainly a good exercise in political ethics.

Even if we stick to our old conception that rather than having no state power we must have some state power, there is no common agreement in abiding by the idea that therefore, democratic state power is most ethical. Still, if we win by virtue of strong ethical and practical reasons in favour of democratic power in modern states, it remains to be seen whether it is ethically more desirable and just to have democratic state power to do a lot of welfaristic duties or it is ethically desirable and just to curb such power of the state to allow a lot of individual liberties in matters of personal and public good. This takes us to another ethically stirring venture into the political matter of *limits* of state power in democracies. The issue is all about limiting the welfaristic duties of the state as well as its social and economic tasks as means to the fulfilment of welfaristic duties and encourage more and more participation of private parties in the fulfilment of these duties by means of social and economic ventures. The heated ethical debate about *laissez faire* in democratic use of power in welfare obligations in states *vis-à-vis* the dynamics of individualism and private powers in our times have gained momentum in the debate of globalism, privatisation and liberalism (see Vol. 5).

In the climate of role of states in public and private good and ethicality therein, even in the age of globalism we speak of welfaristic obligations of the government and find ethical inquiries relevant therein; particularly when we try to find out whether public office servants need to be seen as scapegoats in the state sponsored welfare and lose private morality to do some good for themselves. Public and private ethics comes to the fore in welfaristic tasks of public officers, therefore, most of the time private profits in public office are judged ethically unjust. We need to go into the ethical grounds for such conclusion before hasty generalisation. The point has grown all the more important when private benefits in the private sectors are soaring high, and more often than not private morality of maximisation of justifiable private good in any office influences public morality of the same. It is not a point of examining the ethicality of bribes and private benefits extended to government officers. It is deeper than that because we are poised to examine whether in a democratic set up welfaristic duties should be given up and whether welfarism, if it must stay, should give up all forms of maximisation of private good of public servants. This must then crop up in the areas of administration, legislation, defence and even judiciary. It is important to see whether legislators need special favours, which are ethically justifiable. It is in this regard that the ethical scrutiny of *political sponsorship* becomes necessary along with the private role, particularly the role of private business houses in state politics, sponsosing political parties and extending monetary and other favours for gains. It may be argued that in democracies legislators belonging to political parties (or even if they are independent) are not supposed to be wealthy people spending a lot of money to come to power, though there are some people who come to power in this way, at times with a benevolent motive. The point is that the prospective legislators need some sponsors who are generous in funding for political activities. The ethical question is whether political sponsoring is just as far as it is social and political obligation of private parties to see that there is social good in the land in which they thrive and extract benefits. Or, whether the participation of the private in such matters are susceptible to either extortion, pressure tactics and exploitation or allowing subsequent reverse extortion, pressure tactics and exploitation of the legislators and the public.

In a seminal paper on "Morality and Politics" in an edited work of R.T. De George (1968), Brand Blanshard observes: "I submit that all political problems are in the end ethical problems. And by political problems I mean here both the day-to-day problems faced by the legislator, and the problems of political theory of how government itself is to be organised or justified."[8] It appears that Blanshard takes deep interest in political ethics, particularly its justification because in the opening lines he declares: "I should like to advance three theses; first, that political thought depends on ethics; second, that the kind of ethics that provides its firmest basis is an ethics of consequences; and third, that conformity to this ethics would make a large difference in our political theory and practice."[9] These passages are extremely important for the readers of political ethics who think the study must have some justification at least. These passages are extremely important for me in two ways—first, I will now end up in examining an unfinished thesis that political ethics is justified in so far as politics is wholly *based on* ethics, and second, whether political problems as problems of legislators and government wholly *depending on* ethics is narrowed down to the consequentialist normative ethics of utilitarianism. However, I want to sum up the points of justification of political ethics concluded just now. We have seen that political ethics is justified inquiry in the field of ethics in so far as certain value-laden issues in politics such as "state power" and its use, the forms of use of such power in a totalitarian or democratic states, the notion of statelessness and lack of power-tracking and the role of the state power in propagating the good of the public in *laissez faire* or dynamic fashions open up for ethical reflection in so far as it demands evaluation or judgement of ethical value or disvalue of these political dynamism. Ethics attempts to inquire into these issues by virtue of its metaethical, normative, practical and virtue ethical tasks. These issues are best treated metaethically when we analyse the nature and meaning of important concepts such as "state", "power", "and state-power" and the "ethic of state power" and "ethic of welfare" and so on. Further, the normative inquiry is to see whether standard normative theories are effective in the evaluation of and resolution of these issues. This in turn involves metaethical scrutiny of contesting logic of different theories. Practical task of ethics is to find out ways in which these issues may be resolved and then analyse the outcomes of resolution, and finally, the virtue ethical task to analyse the agent based or agent focused or agent prior virtues as well as aretaic and deontic virtues which may be vital in the context of political decision-making and actions when it comes to questions of power, enforcing power, welfare and so on.

Let us turn to Blanshard now, as the discussion below will throw more light on the way ethics opens for politics and *vice versa* for justification of political ethics. We will continue using above instances for our discussion. In what sense does Blanshard conclude so strongly that political thought depends on ethics? Though he does not throw much light on "depends", we normally expect in the philosophical writings as this to mean "logical dependence", some sort of "implication", that is, the body of political thoughts imply that they are truly a body of ethical thoughts. In this sense, "depends" carries with it the sense that political issues of "power tracking of the state and the dirty game plans" imply that they are in essence ethical issues. However, owing to some ambiguities in explanation, Blanshard's use of "depends" may be taken as either "political issues are in essence value-laden" or "political issues call for ethics for solutions of its value-laden problems". There are some doubts on whether all political issues are at all logically contingent on ethical issues because that amounts to urge in favour of logical necessity that positivistic issues of politics are all necessarily and sufficiently evaluative issues. In this sense, all political problems are ethical problems, which is however not the case. There is a great deal of controversy whether electoral colleges are necessary at all for the presidential election in India. However, this is largely a factual or positivistic question in the science of politics, which calls for our pragmatic reasons to resolve the problem. Hence, the issue is in essence non-ethical, not to the least value-laden *depending* on ethics, if that means the problem of Indian presidential election is truly an ethical or value related problem. Thus, Blanshard's idea that all political problems are in the end ethical problems must be a loose one. Nevertheless, if we urge that in India presidential election should be scrapped because president is here a mere decorative authority enjoying tax payers' money in lavish, we are not simply challenging a scientific issue of model of election, we are challenging an issue that is value-laden or ethical. However, does that amount to say that the said value-laden issue is logically contingent on ethics rather than on scientific thoughts? Blanshard's problem lies elsewhere, like many ethicists he imagines that when political problems assume the status of "value-laden" or "ethical" problems, it is our ethical reflections or thoughts which are superimposed on political thoughts or the one overrides the other or the one includes the other like cause of an effect. Take this: "A non-moral question becomes moral the instant values are introduced."[10] But this must be palpably false because the non-moral or factual question, which is a political question of the justification of an Indian President for he or she is needlessly expensive decorum does *not assume* the status of value-question or ethical question by inputs of our ethical thoughts. We have seen in the earlier chapter that such questions are not value-laden inherently or by nature either. What we have urged before, and repeat the same here is that such political questions are *scientific* as far as they are related to questions of methodologies of how governments need to run in reality given the present position of India. Nevertheless, such questions are "value-laden" or "ethical" as well because analysis of these factual problems reveal that they not only challenge our rationality to decide how something needs to be done rather, why something that needs to be done, *should* nevertheless be done or *ought* to be done. The point is here not of blunt political science but political ethics because it asks us why at all in India *should* we go for a President of a lavish stature who is a mere statutory head? Another point is that the analysis of our ethical reasons for desirability of having such an Indian President though banks on *scientific answers* such as why President in India is not a statutory head, a decorum but enjoys enormous political powers and obligations, and on *ethical answers* found mostly in standard primary and secondary norms of morality such as welfarism, deontology and so on. Hence, a political problem is an ethical problem as well, that is, at the same time they are anchored on both scientific and normative or evaluative analyses, not on any one. We can at best say that resolving the ethical standoff about "desirability" of something that needs to be done is *primary*; the methodological questions of science should come next. Similarly, having an electoral college and so on are questions of the science, the resolution of which is primary and most desirable in political science but not in political ethics. In this sense then, Blanshard should agree that certain things could be both methodological or scientific and value-related or ethical; none really "depends" on other logically speaking. However, it may be largely true that "some (not all) political issues are ethical" and that they demand ethical reflections for resolution. The most interesting part is that Blanshard finally comes to see this truth in [p. 3] when he says that he is not speaking of all practical or scientific issues in political science that are contingent on ethics rather he is speaking about political theories that concerns with what ought to be done in politic, for instance, whether "governments have a right to limit freedom of speech. Then Blanshard switches gear to conclude abruptly that questions of political "ought" have impact or should have impact on political practice, and therefore, "political theory as well as political practice *ends* in ethics."[11] However, strangely, as usual most loosely he asserts, "If *all* political questions are in the *end* ethical questions... how it will affect one's convictions in politics?"[12] Even if it is true that by "political" in these contexts he is not speaking of political science but thoughts, how can thoughts and practice "end" in ethics? We have just seen that the *practical questions* of having a lavish President and curbing freedom of speech should better give way to primary questions of the "ought" of political practice, for which we enter into political theories and find out their ethical justifications, which is entering into ethical theories, normative in the main. However, does this prove that we "end up" in ethics? The truth is that we do not end up at any particular point rather, we find that political decision making and practice, though largely a methodological matter in real life, is closely related to or it should be related to inquiries about political theories and this inquiry is descriptive. However, knowing why the grounds of such practices should themselves be called desirable on ethical grounds, that is, based on evaluative bases of ethics is different though related to the said descriptive science. What we found is that the *relatedness* of these inquiries is not logical in character because we find instances of political practices without logical begging of their ethical status. We can say that in civil states, this should not be the case because this is unethical on such and such grounds, but does that mean that practical and theoretical politics ends up (logically speaking) on ethics? Certainly not. What we urge is that in civil states, questions of politics that takes us to theories and practice, those having wide and deep impacts on society and population, ethically speaking, should not be left aside on the science alone, they should be inquired thoroughly for ethical good, just, right, and so on. If this is done, political practices are based on theories, which are ethical.

Now it is exactly due to this that Blanshard was in search of *ethical* justification of political thoughts and actions, but he thought this is proof for ethics as the "end" of political inquiries, to which we disagree. Ethics is not the end of politics, politics has its own aims or ends, though its ends, means and acts should have some ethical justification, at least this is desirable for us in the modern world. Ethics as *one of the grounds* to justify some political thoughts and practices is thus in itself not an end of politics and is not the logical basis of politics. In fact, the end of politics is what pertains to politics and the end of ethics is what pertains to ethics; thought pertaining to politics may pertain to ethical reflections as well, and this is when we have "political ethics". "Political ethics" is thus justified when we inquire into the *metaethical* question why political thoughts and actions are "based" on or "dependent" on ethics. The justification of "political ethics" as we have just seen drags us to the talk about ethical norms, to which Blanshard is dragged as a natural course perhaps because if political thoughts have been ethically justified, we know that those justifications must have come from the body of *academic ethics*, which is normative ethics. Blanshard picks up the *consequentialist* normative theory and after intriguing explanation of how the theory justifies one ethical thought over others in the resolution of practical issue of freedom of speech or any other, he comes to see that "one ethical theory does make a difference then, to the principles of our politics, it supplies them as ultimate ground. If it does this, it is bound to affect our thinking about particular cases too."[13] Now this is another important finding of Blanshard to which I disagree because consequentialism may not be the only basis that justifies democracy or autocracy and thus basic to freedom of speech or curbing such freedom. That consequentialism s not the only theory available to us comes from the truth that ethical justifications are not necessarily and sufficiently "academically" dependant. In ethics, particularly in normative and practical ethics we fiercely debate in our times whether justifying democracy for freedom of speech should be an exclusive "academic affair" left to politicians and theorists or ethicists or political ethicists. In fact, we debate whether ethical justifications of grounds of practical decisions and actions *should* be at all predominantly "academic" needing normative ethics as tools in the hands of ethical engineers or in the hands of political ethical engineers (see Volume 1). Many ordinary people might reach to an option of consequentialism or even deontology or another normative theory not finding a place in our academics when we come to *ethical debates* about what is just in a political theory and action. Further, political ethicists themselves cross swords in such matters of justification though in both cases "corroboration" of views is possible amounting to transversality of theories coming to a point of closure. Hence, in political ethics, we need to discuss normative ethical justifications of political theories and courses of action, the ethics of monopolistic application of norms and following one course of action deemed to be ethical. In the next chapters, we will find many interesting things in this regard. For the present purpose, political ethics deals with many metaethical, normative and practical ethical questions in the field of politics as thoughts and practice. Our discussion has revealed how political issues of thoughts and practice open for ethics, and ethical tasks are performed when we take them to inquiries about political thoughts and practice.

It is exactly in this sense that we discuss about the moral bases of *political obligations* of governments and in due course find ethical critiques of theories of political obligation. We discuss the ethical validity of *State Authority*, *Liberty* and *Freedom*. We discuss about the ethical strengths of *forms of government* and *political ideologies*. Political ethics is thus an extremely wide field that inquires into a number of politically relevant issues based on ethical reflections available to us. Overall most political ethicists believe in the truth that the focus of ethical inquiries into matters of State is basic to political ethics and the central justification of normative study of the non-normative field ensues from State matters. If this were the case, one cannot resist a brief analysis of what Robert Nozick has propounded in *Anarchy*, *State* and *Utopia* (1986), which is an excellent work on political ethics, particularly when he puts matter of State and moral constraints for a thorough inquiry that extends to a critique of moral obligations of *minimal* and *ultraminimal* states. The minimal state is a "night watchman state" for Nozick which takes on the burdensome task of protecting all its citizens against "violence, theft and fraud, and to the enforcement of contracts and so on."[14] This "appears to be redistributive."[15] However, the minimal state differs for its approach from "private protective associations", but there lies between the minimal and the private protective associations, the *ultraminimal state*, which "maintains a monopoly over all use of force except that necessary in immediate self-defence, and so excludes private (or agency) retaliation for wrong and exaction of compensation; but it provides protection and enforcement services *only* to those who purchase its protection and enforcement policies."[16] The minimal state in the main is thus redistributive because it "compels some people to pay for the protection of others"[17]. More clearly minimal state as an extensive form of state is redistributive for having *types of reasons* for an arrangement—"whether we say an institution that takes money from some and gives it to others is redistributive will depend upon *why* we think it does so"[18]. However, despite the *appearance* of minimal state as merely redistributive, the *paternalistic* or *protective* functions of the state may be justified on distinct *non-distributive reasons*, thinks Nozick. The point is that the protective functions of the state apart from other things must have certain "reasons" which are well-deliberated in the institutions by moral agents having moral ends or goals. As such, the paternalistic functions of the state as *means* to the moral goals may be seen as *moral constraints* of the state, which must be justified for ethical validity based on the welfarist normative ground available to us. Hence, the moral constraints should be ethically justifiable if the *end* of *enforcing* the constraints on agents are morally justifiable or are normatively justifiable. Hence, the protective function of the state to *punish* a person or a group for rioting and thus disparaging the rights of many people need to be morally justified on normative grounds such that punishment as means is justified by an end that is itself morally justified. More often than not, this overriding moral norm or end of protective function of state is maximization of human good through minimum violation of human rights. In another opinion, our moral goals need some *side constraints* in the form of "non-violation of human rights", which "forbids" us to violate the moral constraints in our goal-directed pursuits. The "side constraint" view thus does not favour incorporating the conception of "rights" into the end state (of maximization of good) rather holds that the view of having an objective to minimize violation of rights allows violation of rights to minimize total rights violation in society. The greatest problem with a paternalistic conception of function of state is that it's assumed moral value rests on the touted moral value of non-violation of human rights or minimization of the violation of human rights, which is fraught with a threat that things like punishment should be justified though it violates the said rights. Then do we say that for the state it is ideal to refrain from any side constraints or from the ideal of maximization of human welfare? One reply from the side constraint view is that the paternalistic means of welfare, which is a moral constraint on the agents' selfish decision and acts, should be better replaced by side constraints like non-violation of human rights upon our actions rather than conceiving it as an end state for realisation. In this sense, the view suggests that though the side constraint of non-violation of rights "forces" us to protect rights of others, it does not imply that others have protected or are protecting our rights. However, the point is the side constraint view cannot be free from ethical evaluation either even if it is not included as an end state theory. The Kantian deontologists would morally justify non-violation of rights as desirable side constraint towards the realization of human good because humans should not be treated as "means towards our ends", they should be treated as our person and thus conceiving an ideal of members of "Kingdom of ends". Though this deontic support to the side constraint view attempts at justifying constraint as ethically desirable though not itself an ethical end state, there is (as we believe), a clear deontological conception of moral goal as "realizing the intrinsically valuable end of non-violation of human rights" if not "maximization of happiness". Nozick thinks that the basic conflict between paternalism and deontology is that for the former, "*minimization of use* of persons as means towards realizing welfare" is ethically justifiable whereas for the latter, "*never use* humanity as means towards any extrinsically valuable end such as welfare" because "non-violable human worth is intrinsically valuable and non-violation of the worth is itself an intrinsic value". If we go strictly by the Kantian deontology, though "non-violation" as a side constraint might take us to "welfare" but "non-violation" is an *end unto itself*, not means to human welfare and thus valuable. Hence, the moot issue is whether "welfare" being an ethically justifiable overreaching end state for institutions (and agents), some humans at times, should be used as means or whose rights may be severely curbed for "greater human good". The issue is whether the state should act in paternalistic fashion for welfare using agents as means for greater balance of good over evil in the state though for that assurance of minimum violation of rights is required. It is exactly this issue that is basic to political ethics that deals with matters of state as primary, should be answered; once we enter into it, we come to know easily that evaluative discourses about end state of welfare, non-violation of rights as part of end state, side constraint of right as deontically justifiable, the status of individual as a moral agent who ought to be or not to be free from constraints, the liberal, the anarchist and the orthodox—everything comes to the fore for serious evaluation. We believe all evaluations are extremely challenging in political ethics, which as we can now see takes us to intriguing discourses in metaethics, normative ethics, practical ethics and virtue ethics. We have thus for us a number of issues relating to the tasks of the states that invites ethical criticisms and justifying what we call "political ethics". I will like to end this chapter with a note that though at many places we found that normative theories tend to overwhelm in ethical resolutions of political matters, it may be a misconception because that amounts to an academic pursuit in ethical engineering. Further, note that in "political ethics", neither "politics" nor "ethics" are logically based on each other meaning thereby that their close relation and interdependence cannot amount to the logical deduction of politics from ethics or the vice versa, and that politics in the end is not all ethics; it possesses many things which are non-evaluative, which is not in the purview of political ethics. Finally, we may not have found final answers in political imbroglios as in the cases of the functions of the state mentioned just now though Nozick thinks that he has found one in "liberalism" or Rawls found others in the combination of consequentialism, contractualism and Kantianism. It may be extremely dangerous in resolution of political imbroglios if any absolutist stance is encouraged by a finalistic inquiry. This may be dealt now in the next chapter when we discuss some major value crises in Indian political scenario and their resolution.

Notes

1. Raphael, D.D., *Problems of Political Philosophy*, The Macmillan Press Ltd., London, 1976, p. 27.

2. *Ibid*, p. 28.
3. *Ibid*, p. 32.
4. *Ibid*, p. 53.
5. Coady, C.A.J., "Politics and the Problem of Dirty Hands" in Singer, Peter (ed.), *A Companion to Ethics*, O.U.P., Oxford, 1991, p. 376.
6. *Ibid*, p. 379.
7. *Ibid*, pp. 379-81.
8. Blanshard, Brand, "Morality and Politics" in De George, R.T., (ed.), *Ethics and Society*, Macmillan, London, 1968, p. 1.
9. *Ibid.*
10. *Ibid*, p. 2.
11. *Ibid*, p. 3.
12. *Ibid*, p. 16.
13. *Ibid*, p. 21.
14. Nozick, Robert, *Anarchy, State and Utopia*, Basil Blackwell, Oxford, 1986, p. 26.
15. *Ibid.*
16. *Ibid.*
17. *Ibid*, p. 27.
18. *Ibid.*

4

Two Value-Laden Political Issues and Intersubjective Corroboration

Thus far, I was dealing with the nature and justification of political ethics, and in doing so I have shown how a number of political problems invite ethical probing and the ways in which ethical tasks relates to the field of politics to remain emphatic and sensible. I have tried to justify that political problems are not merely practical problems with which only politicians and legal experts are concerned because these practical problems have a distinct ethical side, they raise questions of ethical desirability, right, just, duty, obligation and so on. Hence, more often than not, in the present civil states, political problems that are value-laden or those having ethical side are probed carefully for what should be done or what is ethically more desirable before deciding on what practically needs to be done by the politicians, the lawmakers and the legal experts. Though it sounds very simple that ethical queries should better go along with political queries, it is fraught with a serious problem; the problem of public disagreements about what is ethically more "desirable" and thus what needs to be done in practice. The reasons for disagreements are many but stated simply, in most of the civil societies today, we enjoy a few political rights, backed up by constitution and protected by law, and for that matter, they are "claim rights", not to be breached or left out in the lurch without inviting legal problems. One of these "claim-rights" we enjoy in most of the civil states (including India), is the right to express our agreements and disagreements (that is our pro-con views) about political issues, particularly if the issues ask for value judgements before practical decision-making and political actions. We are supposed to enjoy freedom in expressing our pro-con views about what "should" be done at the political level. In addition, "we", is for sure the collective, irrespective of class, creed, colour, caste and any discrimination for sex and faith, provided "we" have a level of maturity at an age and in a healthy state of mind. Any value-laden political issue thus demands social scrutiny for value of political decision-making, and it will be a breach of freedom of the people if some agencies in society force us to either shelve our views, or manipulate them to fall along a fixed line of thought. The participation of the public freely in our societies to disagree and agree on moral matters in the field of politics is but natural, justified, civil and legal. Such participation on the one hand widens the net of social discourses on key value-laden issues, thus assures better coverage of pro-con arguments on such issues leading to a widely acceptable resolution, and on the other hand heightens the status of the collective for its moral evolution and pragmatic wisdom. It is due to this that we justified "intersubjective corroboration" as application of our ethical knowledge and experience to resolve value crises in politics. We said that practical ethics as application of our knowledge of the right, good and just in a non-theoretically oriented way in the collective shows how value crises may be successfully resolved through our enjoyment of freedom to express on such matters and how de-classed, non-chauvinist ethicist or those trained in ethics can lead and participate in ethical discourses and resolution, as well as in unique theoretical analytic work to unfold the normative character of public opinions and the points of resolution leading to decision-making norms. It is time now that the readers are supplied with some value-laden political problems and to show how "intersubjective corroboration" as practical ethical enterprise in value-resolution is useful. I have said elsewhere that not all value issues make urgent cases for inquiry and resolution in our societies. In India, for instance, the value-crisis in "sponsoring politics by the corporate" is of some worth but it may not be an urgent case. However, in India the crisis owing to the secession of states and uprisings for autonomy surely make a case for urgent discussion and resolution. Similarly, in India the value crisis owing to the adoption of varied modes of civil disobedience and protests, particularly those of violent nature calls for urgent inquiry and resolution. Surely, one can add in this list the case of dirty hand in politics, criminalisation of politics and many more but I take the cases of "secession of states" and "political protests" as two value-laden political issues for their nature analysis, framing questionnaires, arranging debates and analysis of views as steps of "intersubjective corroboration". However, in this work I will refrain from detailing the debate about political protests in full-length because this may be a good exercise for our readers interested in people's ethics after they have read a full length discussion on the issue of secession of states. Let us then start with the case of "Secession of States in India and moral hunches".

First, the matter of concern or the matter of fact that has grown into a problem practical and ethical is alarming discontent seen in many states, the voice that calls for secession, for being dissatisfied with part of a diaspora. Whether it is Kashmir that wants autonomy or Kamtapuri in North Bengal or the turbulent lower parts of Assam, voices of discontent is loud and clear. The voice is of violence and rage—some people just do not want to be called a part of a particular state for ethnic, religious, or other social and political reasons. Hence, the contentment is sought in the secession of states, carving out smaller states for the grumbling and protesting masses. Moreover, the Indian government has been obliging such people with membership of smaller states since independence though for taming an ominous tempest, most of the time that is glossed with a pragmatic cover of tactical or effective governance. Being a citizen of the state of Jharkhand, which along with Uttarakhand and Chhattisgarh were carved out of Bihar, Uttar Pradesh and Madhya Pradesh respectively, I am aware of the secession movement, its pathos, fall-outs, benefits and tragedies. There is no regret in saying that the aspirations of the most common people remain betrayed, there are no distinct mass benefits, no clear signs of effective governance after seven years of creation of Jharkhand. Most tragic is that the ethnic tribes are the worst sufferers, there is perhaps little they can boast about except for the matter that they are now in a new state, but they are ethnic minorities surrounded by people who never embrace them for uplift and welfare, their own people in power not different because they have become creamy layer *dikus* (the trouble shooters). Then the point is, what is right and just, and good and desirable in secession of states on ethnic or other grounds, when the moot issue is a shift in the nature and stature of exploiters? The whole issue appears to be politically grounded backed by economic milching of a *Kamdhenu*, which many states are or to milk the bleeding cow to the brink because that is a way of life, a matter of habit so to say. No one is pleased if we go on imposing the unethical charges of those who fight for secession or who have succeeded in it because they have their own ethicality arguments. They have to say that if the social, political, cultural, ethnic and economic aspirations of erstwhile-deprived masses are fulfilled to some extent and if governance is much easier, despite no visible changes at a quantum proportion, there are slow but steady changes for the good of the masses, which counts to be ethically just, right and good.

It is believed by many people that the secession of states draws the ethical impetus from the common people's urge to break out of the monolithic structure of globalism, the structure of a dominant unification touted to be so great. This "break away" zeal is so ethical because with the fall of the monolithic superstructure, awakes the assertion of pluralism, diversity and identification of the discrete monads of social existence, the rise of the nameless, faceless, powerless masses which is so good to happen. So the ethical tension is between a dominant conception of the State Superstructure backed by the conception of the globalism which places a central or pivotal political power at the helm of affairs so that people are bound to fall in line of unity and a liberal conception of the decentralisation of political power so that people enjoy more freedom and liberty though not falling out of a greater unity. Hence, the ethicality of secession lies not in disharmony and anti-nationalism, it is a conception of harmony and nationality in the climate of enjoyment of autonomy and liberty. The ethical tension is thus between holistic good through stringent power structure and the same through liberal power sharing. The ethical tension is the tension between good means and ends; for some of us secession is a good means towards the ethical end of nation's holistic well-being, whereas for others non-secession is a good means for the ethical goal of nation's holistic well-being. Then, the moot issue is whether the secession of states is an ethically desirable means towards and end called nation's well-being? Question is why "secession" is in itself or intrinsically an ethical conception? Because intrinsically "secession" is a negative, derogatory, chauvinist and disparaging conception, the point of its desirability does not arise at all. It may be countered by saying that secession in itself is not a negative or derogatory conception because the point is the use of the idea in relative contexts when it come to secession of states, the political concept carries with it an idea of an urge to "liberate" within an Union, which is in no sense a "negative" or "derogatory" conception. However, it may turn out to be "negative" when such "secession" of states inherently amounts to "separate" than "liberation" within a Union, thus amounting to become an "islander State" or a "parallel State or Union or an absolute autonomy". In a sense, the wrongly conceived conception of "secession of states" as "tendency to separate or to become an islander State" creates the illusion of unethicality, when the truth is that it is liberating in a Union for many reasons for the good of the state and the Union at large. Hence, "secession" is *not* an intrinsically unethical notion.

Equally true is that "secession of states" is charged with unethicality owing to the conception of "ethnicity" or better said, "ethnically backed separation". The unethicality lies in the anti-people and anti-nation fervours in a "separatist" psyche, more so when it is ethnically charged because as such separation breaks us from within, it does not bind us whereas we know that strength is in a binding not breaking. Ethnic affairs are thus not seen favourably in the ethical scanner because of its non-coherencies, more likely to be "partisan" at the cost of communality, narrowness, selfishness and hatred. All in all its ethnicity is more often than not taken as grossly egoistic and thus unethical on the part of sections of people who are otherwise integrated in a nation, looked upon equally and treated likewise at least on paper, because that is a constitutional prerogative. Ethnicity cannot be divisive even if it has its own reasons to be assertive of rights and benefits of sections of people on social, economic, cultural, linguistic, and religious grounds. It is unethical for being partisan, communal and separatist because of justified grounds mentioned above, particularly if by that a small group, a minority, or even a sizeable group enjoys equal rights and benefits being parts of a greater nation. Truly, these groups demand legitimately for their uplift, benefits and aspirations, and for all these they press on a manageable territory for effective governance by those who realise the grassroots issues. It is thus a matter of social, political, and economic justice for the otherwise deprived or less cared groups or territories that secession is not "negative" or "derogatory" in essence, not unethical so to say. To this is added the strategic value of a territory, mainly in terms of territorial sovereignty and safeguards, which is the just or rightful ground for secession and thus ethical. The just grounds for secession are thus varied. Hence, there is no monistic pattern in ethical justification of secession. It is due to this that the secession of Jharkhand, Uttaranchal (now Uttarakhand) and Chhattisgarh, all tribal areas having distinctive geographical, demographical and cultural recognitions should be evaluated for ethically differently *vis-à-vis* the call for secession of Kashmir valley in totality from the Union itself, and *vis-à-vis* the secession of the areas of North Bengal and Assam.

What can be the ethicality of the secessionist call for an independent Kashmir? This is the bitter question we need to face, but not right now. We will continue with the ethical bases for secession a little farther.

Ideology and utopia are two factors inciting a call for secession of states, which is true in case of India as well. The utopia of forming an ideal government for the deprived people, by the deprived people of states where all are treated equally, is an old conception. This utopia of the "ideal", the flawless form of governance for the mass have swept the erstwhile Eurasian region armed with the communist utopia but in the garbs of *glasnost* and *perestroika* a number of States seceded from the Soviet Union. Hence, the Marxist Utopia for human good was replaced with the capitalist utopia for the same. Most interestingly, this is the replacement of the pluralist-world-order-utopia with a mono-polar-world-order-utopia though it appears a contradiction in terms because the underlying ethos of secession, I have said, is monopolism. The reason is that such secession of States appearing to be as pluralist stands on the ground of the monopolist Great American Capitalist Utopia. In any case the Eurasian secession heavily backed by the American and the pro-American trumpeters as ethical because the older utopias were unethical in being anti-human and anti-welfarist whereas democracy and capitalist utopias are pro-human and pro-welfare. Closely related to this is the factor of ideology that counts for the ethical evaluation of secession, which is visible in the conflict between ideological differences between the Islamic Chechneyans and the Russian democrats and the Kashmiri separatists and the Indian State. The democrats that the Chechneyans and Kashmiris are, have ideological differences about "people's good" because one party visualises a particular *religious thesis* basic to people's good, the other party visualises *secular theories* basic to people's good. In India, for instance, the ethicality of seceding Khalistan, the areas of the state of Punjab some time back was spurred by the Utopia of the "capitalist conception of regional good" which owed mostly to the well-being of those who produces the beneficial things for the masses at large or which is simply egoistic hedonism, taken as the ethical *mantra*, though things were not so simple, as the ethical gloss was lost in the unethical practices of anti-sovereignty of the Union of India which was largely a military strategic game plan across the border cashing on the said egoism and provocative religious biases. Hence, the utopias of "regional good" conflicted with "natural good", "egotism" clashed with "altruism". On the other hand, in case of the creation of the three tribal states in the recent past in India, ideologies conflicted, those of the Hindutva and the secular, one trying to cash the minority cultural plurality to unify them under a Hindu clout because only such "cultural unification" was ethically good for the greater well-being, whereas the other trying to cash the minority cultural diversity to pacify them under a secular safety-valve politics that did greater good for the minority. Things may not be as simple as this because there may be deeper economic and political grounds for letting secession or not letting secession of the areas rich in resources, natural and human. In any case, the ethical ground of "human welfare" was relentlessly projected whether that was camouflaged by ideologies or utopias.

Despite social, cultural, emotional, ethnic, ideological and utopian bases to secession of states (particularly in India), the basic factors and economic and political, ethical justification of secession should take note of these factors. The economic basis for secession remains the milking of natural resources and benefits out of it for the people of a region, which was otherwise bereft of benefits owing to siphoning the same in the name of the larger good of the nation or the State. The secessionist call in Jharkhand when it was part of the state of Bihar was this economic ground. It was thought that the mineral rich tribal state was deprived of economic or physical benefits though the area has been systematically milked for benefits. The ethical ground in favour of such secessionist call is that altruism cannot be at the cost of egoistic benefits because depriving one for benefits of 'all', is but inconsistent as well as unethical. The bluff to reach benefits to urban Indians or to those having enough needs and capacity to spend for their needs, whereas the needy ones of tribal or neglected mineral rich or agriculturally rich regions are malicious and unethical. Hence, the ethical course of action should be secession of these regions and giving people the needed power to control the resource utilisation, production and distribution, and to earn and distribute profits or benefits equitably to its people, to develop the region in many ways and to give reasonable share of benefits for altruistic goods. Whereas the charge of unethicality in such thinking is that federating states of the Indian Union needs to remain united and strong despite having large territories or diverse population because only in that way states remain economically well off and contributes to the Union's economic good. It cuts the unnecessary expenditure on creation of states, their infrastructure, governance and elections. Hence, the ethics of general good that underlines federating states overwhelms the regional good underlying seceding states.

This debate takes us finally to the political basis for secession or no secession and correlative ethical evaluation. The moot question is whether we want a culturally strong democracy in India or a decentralised form of the same. Hence, the question is about centre-state relation when it comes to the decisions of carving new and smaller states for effective governance or whatever. The question is about the ethic of democratised polity in India. The unethicality charge against decentralisation of political power in the form of secession of states is that the act diminishes the basic spirit of the federating states and the glory of unification in diversities. Once this political main theme is uncared for, the union should be willing to grant the secessionist demands on any extra-political emotive and/or ethnic grounds. There will be then really little or no ground not to grant statehood to any big or small uprisings because each of them has legitimate extra-political reasons for secession, which are touted to be ethically just mainly on egoistic grounds. Whereas the ethicality of secession on political grounds is that democracy needs pluralism, it needs unification in diversity. Indian union shall remain strong only when unique needs and aspirations of even small regions are recognised though they come into a perfect discourse and harmony with the union for greater good. Hence, secession of states remains merely an effective means towards the nobler and higher goal of holistic good of nation.

Let us now come to the touchy and delicate issue of secession of Jammu and Kashmir (J&K) from the Union of India. The blunt question is why should it not secede if there are enough reasons, and if the reasons are ethically anchored? To start with the debate, we need to fall in line with the view that in India, states need to be federating than separating if the spirit of unity in diversity is ethical for being pro-altruism. Whereas, we may follow another line, that is, some states for reasons well known to us enjoy a different status, not in essence federating and for that matter, for reasons of the speciality of states, they might secede for the obvious ethicality of a non-violent order for recognising the well-being of a region and its autonomy. If we follow any of these lines in debate, we must first find out whether Jammu and Kashmir is a part of India and follow the federating course despite enjoying some unique advantages of autonomy but not complete autonomy or self-rule or independence or a merger with a State of choice. The cause of disagreement is thus the "special status" as spelt in the Article 370 of the Constitution of India which many argues, gives J&K a separatist status, whereas others argue that the article in essence is an instrument to federate J&K in India despite approval of its unique place in the Union. It is due to this Article that since independence a group argued that without repealing the Article, J&K shall ever remain a separate islander state, not federating with the mainstream and thus an unethical ground to artificially integrating a region. Whereas others argue that, the Article cannot and should not be abrogated because it is only through this instrument that politically and legally speaking, J&K acceded to the Union of India, and the arrangement does give it the advantages in defence, foreign affairs and communications. Hence, the instrument cannot be repealed; J&K does exist as separate or seceded state owing to negotiated advantages during 1949 and any attempt to overlook it will be both morally and practically unjust. In fact, it may be true that without parting with J&K as state of the Union forever, constitutionally Article 370 cannot be repealed, and most absurd is to think that the repealing act cannot be at all conducted by authorities of the state of J&K and the Union in connivance or agreement or any of them solely or unitarily. Hence, rather than doing good to the nation on the whole, quashing the said Article would finally secede the state wholly forever and give it freedom to choose its fate of governance outside the Constitution of India. Whereas the historical fact is that through the arduous parleys in 1949 as the state acceded to the Union on 25 November 1949, the then rulers *accepted the Constitution of India*. This "acceptance" is basic to the Article 370. Hence, whatever status of a separate identity and advantages the state enjoys, it remains *a part of the Union of India* by a legal arrangement. As such the main ethical line of accepting the seceding nature of J&K despite acceding to the Union is the Article I of the Constitution of India setting up the Union of India with effect from Order of 1950 (26 January), applying to J&K, which guarantees "equality, justice and rights" to the people of J&K for their good and for the good of the whole. Nevertheless, the unethicality charge is that the 1949 arrangement itself is concerted and forced by a handful of people and thus the wholesome accession status of an otherwise touted part and parcel of the Union, which leaves the separatist state with a room to gamble and blackmail the nation whenever that is needed, and allows threats to the integrity and sovereignty of the nation, is unethical. The point is why should an exception be there in the Union that constitutionally recognises integrity basic to its existence and uniformity of status, rights, and advantages as valuable? There is perhaps no ethic in the principle of policy of regional appeasement on ethnic, religious and strategic grounds that give the region an islander status in Union. The policy itself is unethical in being partisan and unjust to people of the nation overall. It is due to the unethical arrangement of a forced accession, in essence contradictory in nature that forces are now plundering the state with all might of terrorism and separatism, calling it a freedom fight. The violence, loss of life and property, the threat to integrity, peace and sovereignty of the land, and the abject poverty and misery of masses of the state are all ethically repugnant as they break us from within, are anti-people and anti-poor. In the name of a freedom fight that is religiously intoxicated, the secular nature and structure of the nation overall is threatened, it is thus anti-national and unethical.

In the light of the ethical opinions, considering secession of states in general and the same in the context of India, it is now important to frame a questionnaire and arrange a debate with some concerned parties who are ready to resolve the ethical problem resulting out of secessionist decisions.

QUESTIONNAIRE

1. What in your opinion ought to be the primary duty of a citizen, regional welfare or welfare of the nation? Is it possible to harmonise the regional and the national welfare?
2. Do you think that regionalism is "sectarianism" and is immoral as well or do you think that without regional feeling, one cannot be a nationalist?
3. Do you think that it is just to give a separate status to a state and to give it a package of benefit for obvious reasons? What are these reasons or do you think that it is essentially divisive to do so, and therefore, immoral?
4. Do you think that it is just to support a movement aiming at secession of a region from an Indian state or from the State itself? Give reasons.
5. If secession of a region from a state is considered separately, which political actions do you think are morally permissible?
6. Do you think that secession has some practical value, and therefore, justifiable?

7. How would you like to tackle the problems of giving separate status to states and secession of states in India?

These questions were put to the following participants:

1. Sri Tej Bahadur Sinha, Advocate, Ranchi High Court, Ranchi.
2. Sri M.C. Subarno, Retired IAS, Ranchi.
3. Sri Y.B. Prasad, Retired IAS, Ranchi.
4. Fr. Benni Ekka, Director, XISS, Ranchi.
5. Sri Sudhir Prasad, Secretary, CPI (M), Ranchi Unit.
6. Sri J.P. Chaudhary, Senior Member, Congress Party, Ranchi Unit.

There are reasons for the selection of the parties in intersubjective corroboration debate. To start with, we need to have participants well versed in constitutional affairs, particularly those pertaining to secession of states, which most of the participants have by training or virtue of their academic interest. Fr. Benni Ekka was selected particularly for his expertise in political affairs and constitutional matters. The two experts with administrative background were selected for having good experience in the governance of tribal areas in the atmosphere of the secessionist movements. Among the participants, we have those inclined to different political ideologies and utopias. As I have said before, I will present here the edited versions of the participants trying to resolve the ethical crisis owing to secession, but here I will refrain from the post-corroboration analysis of the moral opinions. Let us now turn to the moral arguments of the participants.

Replies of Sri Tej Bahadur Sinha

1. Let us not define the nationhood any more rather realise the nationhood enshrined within us itself. The territorial, geographical and utilitarian nationalism cannot solve the problem of our nation.
2. State cultures etc. are the necessary ingredients of a nation. State provides some laws and code of conduct for a citizen. Too many regions inspired by the sense of integral nationalism constitute a nation. If this view is properly injected in the minds of the citizen of a region only then regionalism can be merged or annihilated with nationalism and I believe there

would be no confrontation of regionalism with nationalism, then. In my view, regionalism is not synonymous of sectarianism. Citizen of a region is a national of a nation too. For paltry political gains some play fraud with it and only then the regionalism is converted into Sectarianism otherwise it is innocent expression of regionalism in itself. Regionalism is a part connotation of nationalism.

3. Those who cry for special package for a state only in dire necessity are not wrong unless and until it has no vicious aspirations hidden beneath. Things in its naked self are not wrong; it becomes wrong as soon as it is clad with evil design. If interpreted in right perspective, question of its being immoral does not arise.
4. Yes, I do think so only, when its (secessionist movement's), narrow connotation is not preached and persisted in practice, by a vested interest group of the national secessionist gang.
5. In such condition, only the administrative wing of a nation-state is competent to deal with.
6. Secessionist of a nation in no case should be adorned with having practical value. The history bears witness that such secession is based on intense hatred. Therefore, the secessionists if let loose, will certainly destroy every fibre of humanity. It will be to appease the vanity of secessionist if we adore them. We should try our best for the sublimation of the secessionist instinct first, failing which suppression too should follow of those who play with or do away with the dignity and solidarity of a nation.
7. The states have separate status for all practical purposes, i.e., administrative, economic (concurrent list), despite that an errant secessionist can be declared outcast of a nation and agents of disruptive forces such as fifth columnists, if they tie up with our enemy nation. Hence, such secession should be meted out with punishment otherwise mushroom growth of secessionists may prove grave danger for a nation. No slogan of socialism, secularism or pseudo humanism is allowed to vitiate the sanctity and integrity of a nation. An obstinate, ill designed or a fanatic race or clan on lame excuses must not be allowed to flirt with the spiritual sanctity and integrity of our nation.

Replies of Sri M.C. Suborno

1. Obviously, welfare of the nation is followed by regional welfare. There is no inherent conflict between the two as welfare of different regions eventually adds up to national welfare.
2. Emergence of regionalism is not surprising in the today's context and is not necessarily sectarian in nature if it does not affect adversely the national interest.
3. Regional feeling is not a necessary qualification for being a nationalist. On the contrary, a true nationalist is one who has the same feelings for the nation and the region where he hails from.
4. In the absence of the context in which the question has been framed, it is difficult to give a categorical answer. However, in a multi-cultural and multi-racial society such a move is justified to protect the certain ethnic people from the onslaught of the larger races, which have a tendency to devour them in the guise of national integration. Similarly, the package of benefits should not be treated as largesse but as "a socio-economic balancing action" hitherto denied to them for historical or other reasons.
5. Such an action cannot be called divisive for reasons stated above and these actions are morally justified.
6. There are two parts of this question. The first part relates to perhaps formation of a separate state while the second part refers to secession from a country. The first part could be justified on socio-economic grounds. For the second part, the answer is an emphatic 'no'.
7. If the demand is justified the party in power ought to respect the aspirations of the people and pave the way for statehood. Formation of a new state within the Indian Union should not be termed as secession because its justification will depend on the merit of each case. In the present context formation of some new states are justifiable.

   It would be too simplistic to lay down a set of rules. Granting special status will again depend on each individual case and so the formation of a new state. However, there would be some guiding principles, such as ethnicity, age-old socio-political structure, traditions and customs, the level of socio-economic development besides historical and geographical factors.

I firmly believe that there could be more than one pattern of socio-economic development. Further, real development of certain regions is possible with the formation of new states. It is necessary that the decision-making power should rest with the people of the region concerned thereby eliminating possibilities of remote control by the people of the majority party/community.

Replies of Sri Y.B. Prasad

1. The Constitution of India by an amendment made in 1976 has led down the fundamental duties of a citizen. Regional welfare and national welfare do not necessarily clash with each other. Both are complimentary and over half a decade old national polity has exemplified that benefiting Regional Welfare does reinforce national welfare. The Andhra Pradesh state polity headed by Chandra Babu Naidu proves that regional welfare is of utmost important which goes long way to cement the national forces.
2. The fifth and sixth Schedules and the 11th and 12th Schedules to the Constitution of India have provided constitutional sanctity to the regional aspirations of the nation. Many state governments have already a detail legislation to bring their loss in conformity with the constitutional mandate. A healthy regionalism is a *sine qua non* for a healthy nationalism.
3. The State Reorganisation Commission appointed by the Government of India has definitely dealt with the matter in detail. Separate states and package of benefits to them are not mutually disparate nor do they substitute each other. What is important is to take into account that even larger states have done better and provided better governance than the smaller states. Equally true is the fact that even smaller states have fared miserably bad in delivering public goods especially to the sections most deprived. Neither corruption has been checked nor could efficiency be brought in. Therefore, the prime question is not of being divisive and immoral. The real question is whether the governance is true and honest. Whether it reflects the aspirations of the deprived sections

and how it has been able to provide hassle free and sensitive governance responding to the spirit of the Constitution and the content of the state laws.

4. The Constitution of India does not provide for secession of a region from the country. This is an article of faith, which no Indian should tamper. As the population grows and the cultural, linguistic and national formations emerged, the resultant polity dimensions have to be assessed and evaluated not in the way Jharkhand or Uttarakhand or Chhattisgarh are being allowed to be formulated. The basic cause of action resulting in the movement in the areas have been the corruption, inefficiency, maladministration overtaking the state government and their neglect and incapability of making meaningful efforts towards solution of the underlined problems which has apparently given rise to the movement. None of the provisions made in the Constitution under Article 244 or the 5th Schedule were ever given due regard, for instance, in Bihar State. The State Tribal Committee as a constitutional entity remained very largely a defunct body. No assessment was made to reorient the administration to show the regional issues and the result have been that most of the scandals erupted in Chhotanagpur and Santhal Pargana, like fodder scam, mineral scam, education scam, land scam and many others. Even today, there has been no effort to implement the newly enacted central legislation provisions of Panchayat Act, 1996. However, this is just a part of the hollow scenario of state government wherein Panchayat elections are held up for over two decades; all the co-operatives are defunct and superseded. Even the funds provided for the implementation of poverty alleviation programme are being siphoned off even though none other than the secretary to the government of India brought those faults to the notice of the state Government for proper corrective measures. Nevertheless, no action has been taken until now.
5. Referendum as provided in the German Constitution.
6. Secession is a measure of desperation. In the context of the federal polity of India, secession is constitutional. Secession may have practical value but this generally is dictated by individual, egoistic aspirations. In Indian polity spurt of

secession have come to the fore in south as well as in the eastern regions but largely they failed to consolidate and consequently could not fructify.

7. The Constitution of Soviet Union made provisions for secession of states but the provision did not prove good enough either to hold or to let go the federating states and eventually the Union itself collapsed. In the Indian federal system even though the federal powers vested in the Union, the states have considerable flexibility, means, and resources to cater to the regional and grassroots demands. The 73rd and 74th Amendments to the Constitution have come in a long way to obviate the problems of the separation and secession but unfortunately the general experience have been that the States are reluctant to part away with their power and resources to the grassroots institutions of local self-government even though they ask for more and more from the Union list (7th Schedule). The 11th Finance Commission and the subsequent deliberations have opened up avenues for greater fiscal devaluation from the Union to the States, which should reflect in corresponding percolation from the States to the Panchayats and Municipalities. With these precautionary measures and further improving them with police, judicial and legislative powers within the framework of 11th and 12th Schedule will surely go a long way to tackle these problems.

Replies of Fr. Beni Ekka

Introductory Note

The context against which we would like to discuss the questions is:

(a) In India, States have been organised after the principles of Federation at the normal times and Unitary at emergencies.
(b) Federation recognises the different interests of constituting State units. In this organisation, there always is a tension between the interests of the States and Constitutional provisions.
(c) All the State units are placed on the equal footing. Sharing on the common good of the Federation does not depend on the principle of equal sharing which is presided over by the

Head of the Federation but on the principle of bargaining capacity of each State unit.

(d) Constitution of India has clearly classified the subjects as focus points for both the Federation and the State units, i.e. (i) Central List, (ii) State List, and (iii) Concurrent List. In this process, a point of order has been made, that is, if the Federation and the States make laws on the same subject and if the two laws are contradictory, the laws of the Federation prevail. Against the mentioned principles of the democratic system of governance, I would like to answer the questions.

1. Nation takes up the first place in the priority of all the citizens hence the welfare of the nation definitely demands the primary duty of each citizen. Regions are within the Nation. The welfare of the regions is subordinate to the interest of the nation. If there is contradiction in the interest of the region to that of the nation, the former has to sacrifice its interest for the sake of the greater good and for greater number of people. Nation stands for the good of all the citizens spreading overall the regional units within the nation.

   At the normal times, regions have their fundamental right to bargain for the benefits of the people of its region but at emergencies, the regions have to sacrifice all its conflicting interests and join hands with the Centre/Federation.

   It is possible to harmonise the interests of the regions with the Federation.

2. In democratic system of governance, there is no place for privilege. Place is only for Merit. Bargaining for one's regional interest should not be interpreted as a process of "Sectarianism". Methodology is constitutional.

   Democracy is the rule of the majority in practice. Hence, if the minority is tired of using the constitutional means because the majority does not heed to the demand of the regional units— the minority, takes up to the unconstitutional means, as in the North-East region. It is a point of reflection for both the Centre and the State units.

   There is a rule of games in the interaction. There is also a provision of Umpire to settle the problems. Hence, the violation or rules can be settled within the framework of the Constitution and both the parties should be ready to give and take.

Hence, my opinion is that first, the process of bargaining should not be interpreted immediately as a process of sectarianism. Second, any overstepping should be solved as per the guidance of the Constitution. Third, regional feeling is within the national feeling. Again, I say that at normal times, as per the rule of the games, I will have to bargain for the interest of my region, my immediate interest. Fourth, the regional feelings should not be steered as detrimental to the Constitution. At this point of time, the Federation has ample provisions to deal with such development.

3. Federation is a proof that the constituting units have divergent characteristics and divergent felt needs, and if the characteristics and needs were to be the same or similar, Unitary Form of organisation of the country would be advisable. In India, we accept that there is great diversity between States and in the diversity, effort has been made to bring about unity. Politically, it is the Federation of divergent states.

   Therefore, if we recognise the divergent character and needs of the states, there is no problem in giving either separate status or special package to some States. Example, the tribal concentrated Panchayat Units asked for an exception. Tribal concentrated in Northeast regions also asked for a special provision to govern itself based on the special situation of the people.

   Move for secession begins when the people of a particular region feel that the majority does not recognise them duly. Hence, in my opinion there is no fear to Federation in giving special package or giving a special status provided they are for the betterment of the people. Strength of the Units should be the strength of the Federation and not weakness.

4. No, because
   (a) India has been forged into a Federation in spite of great divergences of its constituting units. There is so much uncertainty regarding security and viability in relation to the nations of the world. There is cutthroat competition in all spheres.
   (b) If the small regions are allowed to secede, they will in no time, become the stooge of other nations who will give them material benefits but will work against the nation.

(c) It is the interest of the greater number of people, a small number of people should not be allowed to secede from the Federation.

(d) Several times, out of despair, the regions begin the process of secession. Hence, the Ruling party should pay attention to the demands of the regions and settle the problem at their earliest.

5. First is the Presidential Rule and second is the Emergency. These two steps are the temporary solutions. Primary solution has to be within the principles of governance in a democratic system, i.e., election. Electoral has to be educated. Constitution has given the freedom of opinion as one of the fundamental rights, yet the opinion or ideology or methodology working against the Unity of the Federation is considered outside the Constitution because freedom cannot be granted for suicide.
6. Late American President Woodrow Wilson has promulgated the principle of "Self-determination". On this basis, all the colonised nationalities called for the movement for independence and seceded from the colonising nations. This action is considered justified. So also, if there is a viable sub-nation within a nationalism, in principle, their process of secession can be considered justifiable.
7. I am not in favour of secession of states but in favour of promoting every state so that people in every state is above the poverty line and become better and better with the passage of time. In other words, package of development should be justifiably distributed. It should be duty and responsibility of Federation. This holds good in Kashmir, North-East regions, Jharkhand, Mumbai, old Madras state, etc. It is the normal story with the states in India.

Hindi Cow belt wants to impose several things upon the Southern States. Hence, came the thinking of secession of the southern states from the north. In my opinion, the root cause for secession lies with the ruling class, the majority, their selfish and the feudal attitude.

The ideology of secession was not at the beginning of the organisation of states. It started later on. In other words, something went wrong somewhere. Minority was disenchanted with the majority. If there is dictatorship of the majority, there will be reactions against it. Hence, if every citizen is equal before the state, the later should take of the former equally. In spite of it absolute contentment may not be possible but the process of secession will not arise.

Replies of Sri Sudhir Prasad

1. It is possible to harmonise the regional and the national welfare. Regional Welfare is very important as well, which is a part of the national policy. Caste, class, religion has to be cared but not at the cost of class struggle and freedom, economic condition and cultural identity.
2. Those who do not look into regional interest in the context of a national interest (protection of the interest of the people of the same type in other region) are certainly sectarian. Feeling of regionalism in isolation is immoral.
3. Separate states and package to states is immoral if it is overlooked that statehood is essential for maintaining a separate socio-linguistic and cultural identity. For a democratic setup to serve the purpose of the needy and the aspirations of a region (according to variation), separate statehood is needed.
4. No, not in case of a country. Within a state, criteria should be formed; Linguistic basis is one for the formation of a state and for ethnic minorities and tribals within the state; regional autonomy should be given by amending the constitution if required. However, this is not enough; a movement is still needed to ensure the economic progress of that area. Communism believes in integration and unity as well as internationalism; as such, the political liberation of a state within India is not desirable. Internationalism not at the cost of national interest at the present juncture.
5. People's movement aiming at the true economic and other types of liberation. Armed movement—not presently suitable. Chalk out such programmes that makes people conscious of their rights, oppressions and liberty. Armed revolution is not ruled out, however.
6. No such things.
7. (i) People's interest should be cared, and they should be educated that secessionist movements are misuse of people's power and which does not serve their basic interest.

(ii) Formation of states should not to be guided by petty emotions.
(iii) Decentralisation of power in the democratic setup.
(iv) Democratic centralisation.
(v) Educating the people.

Replies of Sri J.P. Chaudhary

1. Primary duty of a citizen should be to *harmonise* the regional and the national welfare in India, which has a Federal structure as enshrined by the Constitution.
2. Regionalism is not sectarian and immoral because local aspiration, traditions, culture, way of living and long should be maintained. In addition, keeping all these factors in mind, one can be a good nationalist. Hence, regionalism and nationalism do not conflict.
3. So far different types of divisions are concerned, which the government has taken up, there is nothing immoral or unjust in certain regions, areas or states which are underdeveloped, those areas should be given special status for their development by constituting different development authorities, and if needed, creation of separate state so that a situation will emerge of self-determination and self-development of the region.
4. Indian Union ought to be kept intact and any secession should be looked upon as anti-national and immoral. However, to prevent unnecessary secession of states, a proper centre-state relation should be maintained. A democratic framework of agreement is proper in this regard.

5, 6, & 7. Regional dominance causes great social loss to the inhabitants and for better management secession may be permissible. Armed revolution should be stopped and persuasion and timely negotiation is much better. When political consensus has emerged, regions should be given a proper status by timely intervention of the government. National consensus is most important.

Participation of regions and state service motives should emerge among rulers. Democracy should be strengthened. Criminalisation of politics should be stopped. Nationalism should be encouraged.

After having the full length ethical debate packed with a number of ethical arguments, mostly in the final run in favour of regional secession in special cases, it is our task as ethicists to analyse the arguments for their ethical nature, logical strengths and points of corroboration and most importantly for unfolding the normative dynamics in the corroboration debates. It is important to note that the first question tries to evaluate the ethical perception of the participants regarding duties of moral beings of civil societies who are nevertheless, faced with the dilemmas of regional and national duties. Further, the second question tries to gauge the opinions of participants regarding moral commitment of agents towards his or her own region (or state) and the nation on the whole. This question tries to find out whether the conception of moral duties and commitments *vis-à-vis* state and nation are logically coherent or contradictory. To unravel any concealment in this regard, the third question concentrates on the reasons for providing special status and benefits to states in the broader context of national well-being. This question is followed by a more searching question about the ethnicity of ultra-secessionist movements, that is, separatist movements aiming at autonomy and self-rule (some sort of independence), much like what is happening in Kashmir. This is also to find whether the participant has any ambiguity about state secessionist movement which are ethically grounded and others which are not so if they are movements for secession from the nation. Further questions (three in all) tries to find out what exactly the participants think are the just courses of actions when it comes to secession of states and their values.

A close look at the replies of Sri Tej Bahadur Sinha (Mr. Sinha henceforth), reveal that his conceptions of a nation and duties towards a nation is not limited by so-called, political and welfarist definitions, he prefers the realisation of the self (from within), the organic unity that moral agents have with the holistic Being, that the nation is. This is much like the idealist Hegelian conception of a Supreme Being that the nation is and the moral agent merging in the Being for a complete realisation of the holistic good. This is followed by his conception of the organic unity of the meso-entities that the states or regions are and the macro-existence that the nation is. Following his main idea stated before, he argues that the micro-existence, which the moral agents are, should then realise that the good lies in the perfect harmony at the micro, meso and macro levels of social existence, and then individualism, regionalism and nationalism are coherent aspects in a whole that is of supreme value. In this sense then regionalism is not equivalent to a negative idea of sectarianism or separatism, and for that matter regional aspirations and identity should be well recognised, there should be no crisis in their identity. This is clarified in his emphatic assertion of legitimate demands of regions for esteem, respect, justice and so on within the larger interests of the nation as good or desirable. For that matter, he has no hesitation in giving special benefits to some regions if they urgently and legitimately need them provided that is the only intrinsic end of the regions, not to the least a means to petty separation for extrinsic gains. It is due to this conception of organic unity and coherentism in justice and good that Mr. Sinha favours stern political and administrative activism to weed off anti-national secessionism or a "secessionism of vanity", a kind of unethical, undignified adventure of political hooligans. He concludes to say that such hooliganism in our times is witnessed in pseudo-humanist movements and be meted with stern legal punishments and a step towards the ideal of the sacred (spiritual) integrity of nation where the micro and the meso-existential mingle in harmony should be taken effectively. It must be said that Mr. Sinha's logical ingenuity to start from a spiritual conception of a nation, coming to spiritualisation of existential therein and ending up with the just and right of the spiritual meso-level existential which is the state to secede for holistic good is worth commending. However, it remains to be seen whether his *Absolutist ethical* conception of the nation as spiritual Being finds any ethical support. In any case, though Mr. Sinha clearly does not refer to ethical absolutism as a norm in an academic fashion, his ethical experience and knowledge enables him to apply the said norm in the resolution of secession of states as intrinsically good. This must be a fitting education for those who think that academic ethicist knows and applies ethical theories.

An inquiry into the moral replies of Sri M.C. Subarno (Mr. Subarno henceforth), reveal that much like what Mr. Sinha said, there is no antagonism between regional and national interests of moral agents of regional interests to serve the higher interest of the nation thus harmonizing the micro, the meso and the macro. Nevertheless, there is distinct welfarist fervour in Mr. Subarno's reply, which was noticed in Mr. Sinha's reply that nationalism is supreme and intrinsically valuable, and nation is a sacred Being. It is expected of Mr. Subarno that without falling into the Hegelian line or the spiritual line, he harmonises regionalism and nationalism by virtue of the goals of welfare, the meso-welfare being means to the macro-welfare. This reply is further strengthened without any logical discrepancy by saying that for socio-economic holistic good (or welfare), it is important to realise that a means towards the higher end needs to be good as well, and if the means of regional or micro-meso welfare is good-itself, the higher good is assured. However, any hindrance, or onslaught on the use of the means for reasons ranging from cultural, racial and economic should be treated as equally unethical. In fact, in the fabric of multi-cultural and multi-racial Indian diaspora, the complete welfare of the nation is achieved by means of individual's welfare, which is again not petty individualism or partisan unethicality. There is not much antagonism between the two participants because they reach the same place with a difference that Mr. Sinha does not approve of welfare as the higher ethical principle, though Mr. Subarno's opinions amount to welfaristic teleology. Teleology is a suspected thesis that Mr. Sinha supports as well because his Hegelian absolutism and nationalism cannot be anti-teleological. The realisation of the sacred nationalism is for him an idealist teleos. It appears that Mr. Sinha comes closer to deontology in advocating the intrinsic value of nationalism as supreme and thus it is our duty to serve the goal for its value, but his call for *realisation* of nationhood (enshrined within us, *sic.*) is far from being deontological. Then following his logical course, Mr. Subarno supports the secession of small states for the greater good he visualises though emphatically rejects secession of states from the nation, which is a negation of integrity and welfare of nation, and is thus unethical. Again, our teleologists on different normative grounds come to agree a similar conclusion and clarifies the two senses of "secession", the positive and the negative, the latter unethical in being isolative, partisan, chauvinist and divisive. Mr. Subarno shows some apathy in using the term "secession" when carving out new and smaller states are justifiable on welfarist grounds, perhaps he fears that the term is inherently "negative" or tends to be so, but Mr. Sinha does not hesitate using the term while he supports state secession in India because the negative connotation goes only with a state assuming the status of a "nation state". Much like Mr. Sinha, Mr. Subarno accepts the value of formation of smaller states on *extrinsic merits* such as ethnicity, customs, culture, and so on, and finally does so on the *intrinsic merit* of the overreaching principle of total welfare. He completes his arguments in favour of secession of Indian states on merit by suggesting that the procedure should be left to the aspiring population of the region and should not be "remote controlled" (*sic.*). Hence, it should not be centrally dictated, controlled, or even suppressed.

It is interesting to note that the first reply of Mr. Y.B. Prasad (Mr. Prasad henceforth) is well in the line of what earlier participants said, with a difference that he does not agree or disagree emphatically to a normative principle like welfare or any other at the first instance. Rather fortifies the means-ends harmony thesis of well-being by citing the Fundamental Duties of citizens (who constitutes the society, the state and the government) to strive for a balanced regional and national welfare. This is further exemplified in his second reply where he cites the fifth and the sixth schedules and the eleventh and the twelfth schedules to the Constitution of India to justify what has been said by other participants, that is, fulfilment of regional aspirations and good that fulfils the national good or welfare, the former being the (*sine qua non, sic*) of the latter. It is now that Mr. Prasad's adherence to the end principle of ethical welfarism comes to the fore. However, there is a reluctance in the ethical opinion of Mr. Prasad accepting in an abrupt, emotional and adventurous separation of small states from larger ones and to give them unique status and package of benefits. The reason is that some large states in India are doing perfectly well in so far as welfare and socio-economic goods are concerned. Hence, secession of states for merely trimming large states for advantages of governance may be misconceived. On the contrary, seceding small states resulted into poor governance and ill-being in many cases. Hence, for him the problem of ethicality is not in secession and divisiveness rather in misgovernance, whether that is of a large or a small state. This is not well in agreement with our two speakers who thought governance aside; the moot point is secession of states on specific merits. Nevertheless, there is a logical shift in Mr. Prasad's view, that is, from coherence in regional and national well-being to coherence in governance subduing regional aspirations and demands of secession and largesse. However, in replying to the fourth question in details Mr. Prasad agrees that though the Constitution of India does not allow independence of a region from the Union because that is divisiveness and anti-national act, it would not be completely out of the way if regions for their misgovernance, exploitation and neglect demand separation. As governance being the key to state control and welfare, any act that disparages it needs to be rectified, and only then, regions might be allowed for secession. Hence, unlike the two participants Mr. Prasad thinks that the evaluation of secession as a needed step does not necessarily and sufficiently beg extrinsic factors such as the cultural, social, and so on, we need to keep in mind the political, economic and governmental malfunctions, rampant malpractices and so on for the aspiration of states such as Jharkhand. Hence, it is the alleviation of poverty, exploitationless society and good governance, which are ethical grounds for good governance and which are ethical grounds for carving out smaller states. If we expect that these ethical grounds be in fact, *means* to the greater well-being of people the Welfarist agenda is here clear again. Any case, Mr. Prasad is not averse to secession on merit, but secession is essentially negative in import if that means desperate movement to separate from the Indian Union. This is unethical for Mr. Prasad in being grossly egoistic and anti-national.

Father Beni Ekka's replies are based on the idea that secession of states is a matter to be discussed in the context of the truism that in India, states are federating in essence and as such, it cannot and should not decide and act in discordance with the federation. Hence, as we have seen thus far, the federating states and the federation are in perfect harmony, which is ethically desirable as well. The point is why the same is ethically good. This comes up in Fr. Ekka's first reply where he says that it is the "total welfare of the nation that is the primary duty" (*sic*) of each citizen. Similarly, it is the duty of each states (meso level) to contribute (as means) to the good of the nation (macro level), and it is the duty of the federation to care for the good of individuals (micro level) and the states. Hence, in normal situation states enjoy rights to strive for their betterment, demands, for the same, whereas in cases of national emergency the same rights are clipped for greater good. It is interesting to note that though in Fr. Ekka's reply the conception of "welfare" as normative principle is well projected, he has something specific to say about rights and duties of individual, state and federation. This does not amount to the support of ethical deontology because performance of state or other duties are not the intrinsic ends of the agents and agencies; they are rather means to the higher ethical goal of overall well-being of individuals, states and federation. However, mention of duties here clarifies that there are specific duties, the welfaristic ones, that is, only those conducive to general welfare and not any subjectively determined or arbitrarily fixed egocentric duties. This is backed up by the idea that though individuals and states enjoy rights correlative to welfare related duties, they are nevertheless, clearly not omnipotent rights. Hence, micro- and meso-level rights are subdued in special cases when macro-rights rule supreme. It is not difficult to understand that though the thesis is not exactly "organic" in nature (as in case of Mr. Sinha); it amounts to the acceptance of micro, meso and macro level harmony for greater welfare. Fr. Ekka, like others, do not agree that individuals and states enjoy overwhelming rights to bargain at any cost and following any trick in a game condition of profit making or seeking advantages. It appears that Fr. Ekka's conception of welfaristic duties overwhelms the conception of relative rights. In addition, the means for seeking advantages must be non-violent and thus ethical in nature. In any case, like others, Fr. Ekka does not believe that the bargain for political power for regions, for their good, notwithstanding the national good, is ethical as means if and only if it is non-violent, discursive, backed by readiness to curtail narrow advantages and egoism for the sake of greater advantages conducive to welfare. Fr. Ekka argues based on these ethical perceptions that there is no unethicality and fear in providing special status and packages to some regions for their legitimate and constitutional aspirations and needs. The point of merit based regional demands thus comes to the fore, the neglect and suppression of which results into a negative movement of secession, which are violent and anti-federal. Hence, secession of states are unethical if and only if they are anti-federal and thus anti-welfare. Fr. Ekka thinks that the federation must be authentic in suppressing negative secessionist movements for carving out states even if our rights for legitimate demands need not be suppressed. It is interesting to note that Fr. Ekka justifies, as did one of the previous speakers (by quoting Woodrow Wilson), that "positive secession" of states is ethical as far as a nation colonises, debauches the people of a region or regions, and destroys their welfare.

It is, therefore, educative on the part of those in the federal political power to learn that though our states are in essence federating, there may be voices of discontent and negative calls for secession, which turns out to be positive when there is a real feudal and colonising power-tracking at the pinnacle of the federal politics. The majority colonisation and power play on minorities is equally unethical and for that matter secession stands a good case. To be precise, holistic national welfare rules out power tracking at the helm it.

While going through the replies of Mr. Sudhir Prasad (Mr. Sudhir henceforth) of the Communist party (Marxist), one finds hardly any disagreement with what other speakers have said thus far though their views are not politically biased. Mr. Sudhir agrees that regional and federal harmony is a means towards complete social, economic and political welfare of people. He agrees that regionalism amounting to isolationism of egoistic welfare is unethical. However, he thinks that on merits of socio-linguistic, cultural and economic aspirations of regions, separate statehood may be granted, which is not secession in its usual negative sense because it guarantees regional and federal welfare. He thinks that the communist ideology of integration and unity is possible through grassroots economic progress, and in that case, regions need to be cared for better uplift programmes and effective federal integration. Mr. Sudhir does not think that in India an armed revolution is deemed to be necessary at this point when it comes to fight for rights of people of deprived regions, though armed revolution is not completely ruled out as a means to greater justice and good. This must be in disagreement with almost all the speakers particularly Fr. Ekka. Yet, the main tone of argument is not different because armed revolution in India is not an effective means for justice in any region at this point of time, says Mr. Sudhir. He is thus emphatic that a secessionist movement that is negative or anti-people, anti-national and anti-welfare is unethical. He is emphatic about the unethicality of petty emotions in seceding states though for effective governance and well-being despite qualified democratic centralism, regional autonomy and decentralisation is ethically just.

The moral opinions of Mr. J.P. Choudhary of the Congress Party (Mr. Chaudhary henceforth) are radically different. Interestingly for him the conception of regional and national welfare and harmonising them are the means and end of people and the states of a nation. He agrees that for regional uplift, social and cultural identity, and the good of common people, regional secession is not unethical provided that is not seceding from the Union itself because ultimately it contributes to the greater good. Hence, the states in the Union and the Union itself should not strive for negative secession. For Mr. Choudhary, in a democratic setup, for better governance seceding regions followed by dialogue and consensus are ethical alternatives than armed uprisings.

A close and careful look at the intersubjective corroboration debate reveals that despite normative disagreements, which is not so stiff, and disagreements regarding value of means in achieving the desired end, there is overwhelming agreement in "the rejection of negative secession which is breaking the Indian federal structure, though for different legitimate merits, regions of the Union may be allowed to secede under the constitutional prerogative not forgetting the basic need of general human good, and for which people's participation in dialogues with the agencies in power and the emergence of a consensus is needed. There should be thus a close watch on the micro and meso-level well-being contributing to the macro-welfare". There is no doubt that despite stray cases of idealism and ideological differences, the normative thesis most dynamic in the discourse has been "ethical welfarism", which amounts to the holistic well-being of nation though clear references to environmental, religious and spiritual well-being were not taken care of.

With this, we come to the end of the resolution of the value-laden practical problems of "secession of states" through intersubjective corroboration, which is a testimony to what application of ethics is in the field of politics and what political ethics is in part at least. The discussion reveals the way in which application of ethics does not remain anchored to ethical theoreticism and ethicists' chauvinism though that does not justify a role for the trained ethicists. The leadership in arranging debates, framing a questionnaire, conducting debates, and finally analysing the debates for points of agreements and normative dynamics demand some role for the trained ethicists if that does not mean trained only philosophers, rather all interested parties who want to partake in the process of ethical resolution following the method I have spoken about, the person may be a political scientist or a politician but versed in ethics if the analytic vocation is needed as well.

Let us now consider the value-crisis we face in India when the sections of the diaspora from time to time and for reasons best suited to them, "protests" in various ways against social, political and legal authorities or agencies. We might call this a crisis of "viable modes of protest". It is understandable that crisis of ways or modes of social, political and legal protests extends to crisis in "rationality" or "grounds" of such protests because in any form protest, apart from its nature and dynamics, the moot issue is *justification* of such protests, which range from practical to ethical. Hence, the crisis is one of justification of why and how protests against social, political and legal agencies should be brought out by sections of the diaspora (in this case by the sections of the Indian diaspora). Further, the issue of why and how *should* protests be staged against these agencies is not overwhelmingly ethical, the "should" covers the non-moral sense, that is, the stark factual/practical grounds that invite such protests.

However, in most of the "stark cases" the moral should or ought is unavoidable. Hence, we can say that cases of protests beg pragmatic and ethical grounds or justifications. It is due to this that there are social protests against the social organisations and institutions, for instance, against the malpractices of public health care units or educational institutions by a section of the population. In such cases, more often than not there are pragmatic-ethical reasons. Again, when people protest against the government (state or central) for political foul plays, the political protests are pragmatic-ethical. The same is the case when people stage legal protests to counter the judicial misgivings most glaring in cases of biased judgements, the same is pragmatic-ethical. This is to say that in cases of protests though there are strong practical grounds for instance, in the first case, corruption in distribution of public goods, we may ask deeper ethical questions such as, "why protesting against public welfare malfunction at social strata be ethically desirable or good or just?" We may reply that such malfunction should be protested on the ethical ground of "production of greatest balance of good than evil in society", which fortifies the pragmatics of public welfarist mechanisms to succeed at the ground level. The political protest against government's foul play in framing partisan laws for governance is pragmatically protested on the ground of corrosion in their public support and thus future political debacles, but the same have distinctive ethical reason of "gross egoistic morale" in governance only to be protested. The pragmatic ground to protest against judicial malpractice in being partisan in punishing someone harshly than others is that the common people of the nation lose faith in the judiciary, though the deeper ethical reason may be that the judicial or legal justice uphold the "principle of fairness and equality" in distribution of legal justice. Hence, social, political and legal protests are grounded on the pragmatic-ethical reasons, which answer "why", protests hold good. However, in what ways or how protests need to be staged is another important question, taking us further to another sphere of the pragmatic-ethical because we now ask, for instance, whether an armed upheaval practically fits to the purpose of protest against social, political and legal machineries or the civil ways of disobedience are more fitting. More deeper ethical probing is whether armed protests *vis-à-vis* civil disobedience is ethically desirable because it may be argued either that armed protest is production of social good by crushing the evil or that civil disobedience is production of greater social good by changing the evil to good; hence, the former ethicality is the one of the pragmatic ethics whereas, the latter belongs to the Gandhian pragmatic ethics. However, it may be said that armed or "violent" mode of protest and civil or "non-violent" mode of protest are not the only ones, we might conceive of the "conscientious mode of protest" as different from both. It is very difficult to be arrogant in saying that armed modes are violent and for that reason, "*un*civil" than "civil". There may be arguments that rabid dogs are evils inviting violent steps to be crushed for social good and the same may be true in some cases of social, political and legal crimes against society. Hence, armed or violent mode of protest as ethically grounded need not be anti-human or rogue or *un*civil, it may be "*non*-civil" in a way, if that means a mode, which is *different from* or *does not belong to* the category of "civil disobedience or protests" or "conscientious protests". Hence, the term "civil" in "civil disobedience" as a mode of protest is not the same as "humane" or "ethical" or "social" or "cultured" because other modes of protest demand similar status for them on pragmatic-ethical grounds. Nevertheless, "civil" is closer to mean "non-violent" or "non-armed" as well as "non-conscientious" (not unconscientious) to distinguish as a category of protest, which is different from other categories of protests. It is clearer that as civil or non-violent protest is different from violent and non-conscientious methods of *public protests*, a civil protest need not be taken as anti-human or unconscientious, for instance, no one will risk the argument that civil protestors are "unconscientious" people, they are rather non-conscientious in adopting a methodology. Hence, there is a risk in saying that some methods of protests are anti-civil and anti-conscience, and there is only one civil protest, which is pro-people, pro-civility, pro-humanity and pro-conscience. It may be also noted that the expression "public protest" suits best in cases of violent and civil methods because using the expression "social protest" raises clumsiness in understanding the proper meaning of "social protests". Any mode of protest is "public" in this case as we are here not concerned with an individual's protest against other individual or other individuals, we are considering here the ethicality of protests of the people or the public or the group or groups of people of a society or nation, whereas, such protests of the public or groups of people when directed towards the "social agencies" or the organs of society responsible in the management of the public and public institutions, are called "social protests". Hence, "public protests" are "social" at times, but they may be political and legal for their *intentions* or *directedness*. All protests are then public (in this case avoiding reference to what an individual does directly in society), or collective (whatever may be its size) which are also directed to social, political and legal agencies. In this sense, all social protests of the public are said to be public protests but not all public protests are social; they may be political, legal and so on. We come to conclude that while considering here the value-crisis in "modes of protest" we are considering value questions in modes of people's protest which are at least three, social, political and legal and each of them demand care for why are such protests needed on ethical grounds (though there are practical grounds as well), and how should (ethically speaking), such protests be staged by the public towards the said agencies considering the cases of armed or violent (non-civil) and non-violent or civil protests. It is also important to note here that the use of "protests" has comfortably replaced the term "disobedience" in the expression "civil disobedience" or "non-violent disobedience" because the term "protest" in its negative import here is hardly any different from "disobedience", though positive imports of the term suggest that "not obeying" or "not abiding by" or "not succumbing to" or "not subdued by" amounts to "intending to do a good to", though that may be ethically contested, yet such possibility of contest does not suggest that "protests" means a negative act and not positive in any case. It is more comforting to use the term "protest" and discuss about its methods etc. than using "disobedience" because that causes further ambiguities in understanding what if any is the meaning of "armed upheavals or actions". In fact, armed resistances are different from mere "disobedience" or "not obeying" what an agency has imposed on us wrongly, as we deem it. Armed resistances are better understood as modes of intentional human actions, which are "much more than" or are "beyond the limits of", "not obeying something", they are moving to the realm of "acts of violence". It might be for the nature of these intended acts, their ethical evaluations are needed on different cognitive planes. This problem in evaluating act of disobeying and enforcing brute power having social, political and legal directedness of the public is best solved, as I think, by using a more consuming or broader term covering disobeying, and using brute power for their resemblances in the context of public actions said above, which is "protest". Hence, the use of "public protests" and their ethical evaluation (as they raise questions of ethical value), is deemed to be more appropriate, it does help in a comfortable understanding of the public disobeying and using force for some reasons in different ways though they are all modes or forms of "public protest" where "to protest" is to *"negate"* and to *"assert"*. It negates decisions, orders and acts of agencies on the public having pragmatic-ethical reasons, and it "asserts" decisions, orders and acts of the public on the agencies having pragmatic-ethical reasons answering "why" to protest and "how" to protest. Hence, "public protest" as value crises is not only disobeying and being non-violent, they are many, and the use of "protest" in its overreacting stature is "violent disobedience", though the concept needs careful treatment for meaning clarification under the broad heading of "public protest".

It is then important to clarify the nature and justification of "public protests" and then try to resolve why one form of protest than others are *ethically* more desirable. It is of some importance to note that we make no reference to "conscientious refusal" as a mode of protest in the "public" domain because such "refusals" are by and large "individual" and "isolated", having least community direction and does not assume the status of "protest" we have just seen because it is more like "refusing" than "protesting" in an organised way whether that is violent or civil. It is also important to note that community or public protests need not be taken as unconscientious, whether that is violent or civil because that bereft the protestors of minimum "rational conscience" to evaluate why and how to protest, though the protestors may have little or no regard for a theory of divine or spiritual conscience, and may not like the idea of "moral conscience" if that means a queer faculty inherent in us or given to us by virtue of divine intervention which is absolute in moral evaluation of the why and how of protests. In fact, each protestor in isolation and communion can allow public protests when their common rational conscience is activated to find out why should I/we protest and how should I/we protest socially, politically and legally? Thus the activation of our common rationality allows us to apply our common moral experience and knowledge of good, right, just and so on apart from applying our common pragmatic experience and knowledge of good, right, just, and so on to find out, as said before, the "why" and "how" of protests. It is an over simplistic conception that protests demand our rationality for their ethical evaluation because public protests are matters awaiting complex evaluations on pragmatic-ethical bases, that is, the why and how of protests are evaluated on practical grounds not overlooking why such practical grounds are themselves ethically permissible.

Hence, blank talks on practicality of public protests do not stand on a firm basis if they are not ethically confirmed. It is exactly for this complexness of talk of public protests, we need the ethical evaluation of why and how something is deemed practical as protests. No one really contests the idea that public protests whether violent or civil awaits sociological, anthropological, legal and political evaluations because these are many interesting and important ways to judge why on practical levels something is done and how something is done. We are thus adding another perspective that considers why on moral grounds available to us is something done in different ways, the performance of which nevertheless, goes against some agencies.

Clearly, if public protests are not evaluated for desirability on moral grounds, it will be extremely difficult for us to justify why, despite sociological, political, economic and legal compulsions to protest against agencies who are essentially disturbed and try to repel such things for grounds available to them, such compulsions are still justified as desirable or good or right or just. Hence, ethical evaluations are the compelling justifications of protest. Hence, ethical justifications allow us to speak out clearly, why are we compelled to take steps, which are against some agencies who do not like them or who are disturbed by them causing utter turmoil in society. In this sense, the ethical justifications of our *intended entropic acts* at the social, political and legal spheres, involving agencies therein are ways to see for ourselves why such acts have "positive" desirable effects. Quite often in the cases of entropy in states, the lattices of equilibrium emerge gradually. Ethical evaluations of public protests are thus overreaching evaluations of the pragmatics, which, though avoidable, should not be avoided in civil states. In this sense, it is difficult to see why violent protests should be touted unethical and only non-violent protests be touted ethical provided, the logical strengths of ethical bases of such evaluation does not fix up non-violence as the only universal ethical form of protest. Nothing is really arbitrary in ethical judgements of protests; ethical evaluation in reality reveres the logic of evaluation of an act over other acts and therefore, why and how of public protests are open ended issues in ethics, we have really not found one good solution but we are trying to find some good solutions *in and with the public*.

It is interesting to find out whether it is imperative on us to consider the public in protests and then ethically justify and evaluate public protests. Why should we not concentrate more on the individuals than on the community or the public while discussing ethics of protests? Is it not true that individuals constitute the public and for that reason, the ethics of right and just of intended violent or non-violent protests of individuals should be cared more for evaluation? If this were true, why should we speak about "public protest" and not "private protest"? No one has really stopped us from considering the ethics of private or individual protests and why and how of protests on practical and ethical grounds. Individual torchbearers initiate more often than not public protests. In many cases, there are lone fighters against overwhelming agencies who are at the wrong side and the meek and mute diaspora watches the ignominy of torture and decay of the valiant. However, in other cases, as we forget, the lone fighters are joined by the public, and it is the masses that gives protests the shape and stature that is desirable of it. In many cases, individualism ends up in Robinhoodism, adventurism, or even chauvinism if the public do not join and that, such protests are not organised. Hence, for sheer power, stature and the ethics of community morality, public protests are given greater value. Without taking anything away from the valour of great individuals charged up ethically to protest against mighty powers, protests succeed when they, though organised and led by one or few individuals, are joined by group or groups of fellow men, when private and public ethicality merge to give the needed power and direction to protests, which if ethically and practically desirable, outsmarts the mighty agencies much comfortably than individuals do. It is thus one thing to *lead* a protest and another thing to *organise* a protest; protests may be led all alone, but a leader is he who organises the masses for an effective protest. It is in vain to argue that Rammohan, Gandhi and Subhas were vital in the great Indian socio-political protests than the public; the members of the public that these visionaries and leaders were, succeeded in their protests doubly so when they were *ethical* to organise a mass protest rather than championing their valiant solo efforts. We remember these great protestors fighting against injustice with reverence because they "led and organised people's protest". Hence, it is public protest not individual protest that becomes the focus of our attention in ethical evaluation though it is extremely important to evaluate the practical and ethical features of leaders in organised protests because it is important to find out whether they misled, ditched, or were mistaken or simply bossed in public protests. We still heatedly debate the ethical faces of great public protestors, the ways in which they carried on protests and why they did so because individualism in public organised protests are never lost, they should not be lost. The same is true of the public, a large chunk of it, if not the whole, who are watched if they went wrong, unethical, foolish or ethical and wise in protests. Obviously, for sociologists and ethicists, Marxian and Gandhian activism, Naxalism and counter Naxal activism are issues for constant evaluation. We thus continue with "public protests" and their ethical evaluation.

Let us now come to the "why" of public protests on ethical grounds. The crux of the ethical debate about public protests is that much worry is not about who participated aggressively, the leader or the public, much concern is about the nature of "protests". Protests, whether violent or civil (non-violent), bear resemblance as far as they are modes of organised and methodical negation, prevention and resolution of blatant "injustice and unfairness" done to the individuals, groups and the diaspora. More often than not unorganised and unmethodical negation, prevention and resolution of injustice and unfairness done to the population are hardly what we truly call, "public protests" because such protests turn out to be sporadic unrests and rage than protests. Protests of the public are generally not sporadic and accidental in nature, they do not rely mainly on public unrest and emotional outbursts and rage, and they rely on public's well thought-out, rational strategies to move along the path of negation, prevention and resolution of causes and outfalls of a planned or unplanned injustice meted out to population. Hence, in many cases, organised public protests are up against organised public exploitations and sufferings, caused mainly due to *unjust and unfair distribution of advantages rightfully due to the public*. Thus, unjust and unfair acts of agencies against the claim-rights of the public become *raison-d'être* of public protests, though there are many other reasons. Without going into the details of causes or reasons right now, we can reflect on three important points we have come across. First, analysis of the nature of "protests" in "public protests" reveals that apart from other things, "protests" of the public convey the sense of organised and methodical public actions against decisions and actions of other parties which are clearly unjust, unrightful and unfair (also illegal). The second point is that on grounds cited just now, public actions against the responsible trouble-shooters have enough bases to justify that protests are *unethical*, which is our concern. Finally, the said reason, causes or bases of protests are *not* the ethical grounds rather; ethical grounds are those overreaching grounds to evaluate the contributing causes or grounds for protests. Hence, public protests invites us to see that "protests" if public are by nature, organised; that such protests are based on concrete grounds and that these grounds may be evaluated for their *moral worth* (that is whether they are morally good, desirable right, just, duty, obligatory and so on). These amounts to say that public protests may be evaluated on factual and moral grounds to find "why" are protests good or desirable. It may well be that though on factual (or concrete) grounds some protests are deemed to be desirable, they are not so when we evaluate them on moral grounds. However, some thing that factually desirable may be morally desirable as well. Hence, it may be said that though it is factually desirable that claim-rights of public are not breached because that causes unrest and social protests appear to be legitimate in that case, it is nonetheless another inquiry to find why at all we *should* or *ought to* protect the claim-rights of the public even at the cost of some social turmoil caused by protests. Our inquiry of the "ought" of protests in favour of upholding the claim-rights takes us deeper in the realm of ethical validity or justification of the said intended mass actions. We may say violation of claim-rights that causes in the main public protests for inherent injustice and illegality, are themselves morally justified for they are based on the moral ideal or standard of "maximisation of public benefits". Then the moral theory of "public benefits", which as a theory of "maximisation" is likely to be a matter of calculus of benefits that serves as the moral justification of public protests, which are caused by breaching legal rights of the public for their benefits or advantages. In this sense, not all causes of protests of the public may be morally just because some causes may be fictitiously touted to be advantageous or of benefit to the public or are fictitious rights, which are claimed, but not to be legally claimed. For this reason, though we may conceive of public advantage in the introduction of entry of multinationals in retail business in the sector of agro-products, and that this is said to be legal right of those in business in the climate of free-trade and open economy, we may *contest* on moral grounds to evaluate whether such entry is morally right and just or such touted claim-rights are really so and they should be protected at some cost. I have said that there may be an "ethical contest" because we can always justify with the help of a con-argument that the same based on another ethical principle is unjust and undesirable. It is exactly due to this that on the same ground of "maximisation theory", multinationals' entry into retailing is morally permissible. Then there is a fierce "moral contest" between those who say that the maximisation theory is extended to the "public" in view of their relative powers to purchase goods of their advantage and therefore, the public enjoys the right and the business house does the same to buy and sell goods they would otherwise transact without other hitches, and those who say that the maximisation theory is in view of the disparities in powers to purchase goods of advantages, and therefore, a parity calls for extra-concerns or hitches in free transactions between those who buy and sell because they have the needed "power". When are the moral grounds manipulated, when are they corrupted and fictitious, and when are causes of protests fictitiously moral and when they are not, are important and interesting issues in what we call evaluation of ethics of public protests or simply, "public protest ethics", which is an aspect of *political ethics*. It may be seen that the factual ground of protest in the above case is *economic* by the parties crying for justice in enjoyment of public advantages and the deeper ethical probing is possible, the "protest" is in this case, "social" in nature that is, *directed to* the *social* agencies responsible in retail business. However, the protest is also directed to or at least most likely extends to the *political* agencies because allowing multinationals in retailing in agro-products is a well thought-out economic agenda of the state and/or the central government, for which the legislative and the executives are responsible. It is most likely that if the government has enacted a law towards free trade of this status, the protest may be directed to the *legal* agencies for its said interpretation of and support to the claim-rights business houses enjoy and which underpowered customers enjoy. In this way, simple factual grounds to stage a protest allows us to conceive of social, political and legal protests, but in any case, the underlined point is that there are debates about the moral or ethical validity of these grounds for protests which is never "final" because the whole society never comes to a finalistic moral solution to moral problems of these kinds with the help of a moral theory or theories. Surely, there are publ:c disagreements about moral values of social, political and legal justice and fairness, about justice done in the enjoyment of rightful advantages. Hence, analysis of the concept "protest" in "public protest" is so important, it takes us to the ethical inquiry of the matter notwithstanding factual queries. This is perhaps only one way to look into the case of "why" of public protests, where the "why" is a distinctive "moral why" over and above the "factual why", though they are related.

We have seen that though the principle of maximisation of benefits ethically justifies public protests, the principle takes two forms when conceived through egalitarian and non-egalitarian (sometimes called the capitalist) ways each vying to show that protests are desirable in some cases, particularly cases of breach of public's legal rights to gain advantages that are due to them. Another perception is that rather than fighting in favour of advantages for some at the cost of many others, we may toe the line of maximizing advantages for the most deprived in the spirit of a social *contract* among parties who would otherwise not like to do so or will fail to do so, because the fortunate few if they are not forced to give up some advantages or they are not compelled to be in some disadvantage due to the loss of unlimited advantages they will never be in a contract. In this sense, though there may be legitimate public protests if unfortunate people are not allowed to gain something at least, the same cannot be violent because neither social agencies can deprive *fortunate few* of their due advantages by virtue of their empowerments nor can they allow the unfortunate to rebel causing social tension. Hence, the civility of "contract" may be the answer when social agencies act as impartial agents under a veil of ignorance for distribution of advantages that are just and fair. This is something like John Rawls' conception of the "principle of maximin" as moral ground to justify why deprivation of our claim-rights cause protests and that protests are desirable. However, cautionary note is that the justification of protests is not the justification of violent protests. In his work, *A Theory of Justice* (1993), Rawls devotes separate sections to justify that though protests are morally legitimate they need to be civil or non-violent in nature, though not losing sight of conscientious refusals which are not "public" in nature and thus not important in this regard. The Marxists and the socialists argue that protection of fortunate powerful people in the climate of maximisation of benefits is never possible without a non-egalitarian scheme of distributive justice; hence, the theory is non-egalitarian or capitalist in the name of contractarianism. Yet, we cannot disregard the truism that the principle of maximisation still holds good in justifying protests whether violent or non-violent. The reason for this apparent contradiction is that though the "why" of protests may be similar, the "how" are different. This has far-reaching impacts on why at all should we morally justify a violent or a non-violent way to attain our cherished goal of maximisation. It takes us to the case of falling back on our basic principle of maximisation in each case of methods of protest because each method strives hard to show that violence or non-violence maximises public advantages and are thus desirable means or methods of protest. In any case then the principle of advantage is the key to justify the why of public protests. It cannot be any different if a contractarian line to do justice is followed. The non-violent means to do contractarian justice really falls back on the overreaching ethical justification. The same is again true of the communists, whose violent means to protest for justice takes us to the same principle for moral justification. Nevertheless, we have seen, they differ in not only the modes of protest but also in the ways in which differently empowered, needful and aspiring public for advantages be given what is rightfully due to them.

Sometimes, it is argued that *only the principle of benefits or advantages* of the public, which are due to them, is basic to judgement of right and good of public protests, whether violent or non-violent. First, we need to remember that the principle is a "rainbow-principle", that is, merging of theses of different lines each claiming to be monistic and omnipotent in the decision of what is just and desirable when public comes to protest. Such monistic theses in the main are either altruistic or welfaristic. Hence, the "rainbow-principle" consists of hedonic altruism, non-hedonic altruism, and welfarism. Thus public supports protest when they conceive of their benefits in terms of "pleasure maximisation" which is rightfully claimed by them or they conceive of their benefits in terms of "maximisation of a basket of *ideals* which are other than pleasures", for instance, maximisation of human values and virtues, self-fulfilment, and some bizarre ideals like collective *'nirvāṇa'*, if that is understood properly. The other conception of benefits may be "maximisation of human well-being or welfare" which may be deeply related to the conception of "overall wellness of the collective including the ecological community". In any case, when the "rainbow-principle" is taken in the distributive sense, it refers to any of these monistic theories justifying public protests, whether that is violent or non-violent. However, truly speaking, none of these monistic theories is valid; they are just the different myopic ways to conceive of an overreaching theory of "public benefit". Some care reveals that modes of public protest do not have an intrinsic value; they have extrinsic value so far as their directedness is to achieve an end or ideal that is taken either in the distributive sense or in the truly monistic sense of "maximisation of benefits". However, there are some problems. It is not that public protests as modes or means of benefit maximisation are truly "means". The reason is that even if the end principle is the "principle of benefits" the means of benefits are many concrete *decisions and actions*, social, economic, political, legal and metaphysical (or spiritual). Hence, public protests themselves are *not* means or extrinsically valuable contributors to the realisation of the end of maximisation of benefits, they are nevertheless, in a qualified sense, "means" to ensure that if an ideal is intrinsically desirable for humans in civil societies, then any step that disparages human pursuance to achieve such end should be protected. Hence, protests of the public are well-intended decisions and actions of organised humans in civil societies which are modes or *means of restoring justice and fairness*. In this sense, public protests have a *contributing or extrinsic value* in the "restoration of justice and fairness in the course of benefit maximisation of the public". Public protests are thus ethically justified as means to justice and fairness in civil societies though they are not means to the ideal of benefit maximization.

Again, there are some problems. Some ethicists are of the opinion that though some modes of protests are extrinsically good as means, not all of them have the same value. For instance, it is argued that violent public protests are bereft of good value, they are rather evil. Moreover, a means cannot and should not be evil, bad, or unjust to restore justice in the pursuance of higher ideal of benefit maximisation. We can thus say that public protests do not have value as means, only civil or non-violent protests have extrinsic value as means. It is exactly at this point that the ethical debate of good, right and just of violent *vis-à-vis* non-violent public protests are meaningful. We shall come to this moot point shortly but before that, we need to see whether a *deontic* ethical justification of public protests is conceivable. Can we imagine that public protests, whether violent or non-violent, is justified because they have *intrinsic value*, that is, they are not really valuable as means to restoration of justice in an ideal pursuance of the public, they are good or valuable themselves. Public protests are thus good *per se* because "protests" are as their nature goes, and what they intend to do, testimony to justice and fairness. Hence, protests are wrongly understood as means to restore injustice, right and good, they are in fact, bodies of or paradigms of good. It is due to this that protests are to be revered, they are intrinsically pro-good, and pro-legal (that is rights, justice and fairness). It hardly matters to argue whether violent protests are evil or bad because protests are justified legally and ethically as good and desirable. This is often an extremely strong ground to argue in favour of much-needed violent protests because as such, it is of value and not disvalue. Hence, in cases of need, the systematic use of a violent protest is good in itself. Perhaps this may be strong reason to support armed rebellion of the public, for the value of such public protests. Perhaps this may be one way to support why *just wars* are fought, why even gods resorted to violent protests when needed and why godly people did not favour continuation of wanton violence against the deprived, to go scot-free without meeting *counter-violence*, if that language is understood properly. Perhaps due to this the glory of performance of violent *duties* to counter violence, those of the military and the police is glorified. There are doubts that such a thesis will remain unchallenged because teleologists might argue that careful analysis reveals the purpose or *teleos* inherent in all the touted intrinsic duties. Moreover, others might retort saying that "protest" *per se* has no suggestion in it to deem it intrinsically valuable, it is only a bald assumption because not all negations or counter-actions of public have good value, not always or uniformly and eternally they have such value. It may be due to this that though violent peasants' protests against the East India Company may be seen to be good, for Gandhi it may be intrinsically evil as a sign of the coward. Pacifists throughout the history have been rejecting the intrinsic goodness of violent protests. Therefore, we are at hand a good ethical debate here about the ethical status of public protests.

Slowly but surely we have come to value public protests with civility and violence. Let us continue with this a little farther. To protest with civility is not to dissent, timidly or softly because the sense of "protest" is not mere "dissent", it is a clarion call to rise effectively against an establish law or set of laws of land which is expected to govern the masses effectively with a spirit of reverence and obedience. Hence, protests are disobedience to laws, which a section of the public or the whole population at one time thinks to be desirable, practically and more so, ethically because the laws are undesirable in the public perception, practically and ethically. In this sense, public protests are generally, "disobedience to established law or laws", and disobedience may be either civil in nature or it may be violent or armed as I said. I have said that my preference is not in favour of using the corollary "uncivil" for violent protests, in this sense, "civil" disobedience causes some ambiguities and hitches in mind because one doubts whether by that we mean disobedience which is not barbaric or nasty or rogue rather nice or gentle or social. If it means "social", that is, disobedience, despite its negative character of being "unlawful" and "arrogant in not abiding by law", is still a method, that is, socialised and socialisable than asocial or anti-social, that is, a method that is never to be socialised and socialisable. Hence, "civil" disobedience for going against laws of land remains a method of public protest that is neither asocial nor anti-social rather goes nicely along the social ways of our life; it is well accepted within our social fabric as humane forms of social life. If this were the case, despite similar negation of laws of land, the same arrogance to disobey them, "violent" protests, which by nature are another mode of disobeying laws of land, cannot be any different from being civil. There is no point in calling them asocial, anti-social, or not acceptable in the social ways of our life. Then there must be no point in calling violent protests "uncivil" meaning rogue or barbaric. By virtue of being violent, a public protest cannot be asocial, anti-social, or uncivil. It is extremely difficult for us to digest the truism that not all-violent public disobedience of the laws of the British during those dark days in India were acceptable to social psyche or social ways of life or socialisation. If we are not die-hard pacifists having obstinate assumptions, we cannot even imagine calling our valiant Indian violent protestor's rogues, anti-socials, and the method asocial or antisocial or barbaric and not civil. Thus, the main matter of dispute is why not call violent public protests "civil", if that is equally disobedience to law. In addition, why should we use "civil" to differentiate one form of protest, which is equally disobedience to law? Hence, the moot issue is what is the definition of or meaning of "civil disobedience" and "violent disobedience" of laws of land?

It is interesting to note here that for John Rawls "The problem of civil disobedience... arises only within a more or less just democratic state for those citizens who recognise and accept the legitimacy of the constitution."[1] This must be a near slap on Indian history of revolution for Independence during the British Raj wherein the several civil disobedience movements of pre and post-Gandhian periods were up against a completely autocratic and colonial Raj, not democratic to the least. Hence, anywhere in the world where disobedience is up against an autocrat or exploiter or coloniser, must be non-civil in nature, which is strangely not the case because civil disobedience may be movement of the public against "unjust laws" wherever in the world whether the land bearing the load of such unjust laws are under the pangs of a democracy or near democracy or autocracy or whatever forms of government we can imagine. In this sense, it is extremely out of point to say that in the said democracy or near democracy the public "recognises and accepts the legitimacy of the constitution" because during our bondage in the British era neither was there democracy nor recognised and acceptable constitution which, "we the people of India" abided in totality and thus the laws therein. The uprisings were really against the uprooting of the pseudo-constitution and its laws which governed (misgoverned really), the Indians. If Rawls intends to say that "only" when there is a well recognised and accepted constitutional democracy wherein some "unjust laws" are objected to for validity and practice by the population, there is "civil disobedience", is to limit the sense of "civil" because in that case we forget that any land governed by constitutional laws *independently* whether it is non-democratic in nature, "civil" disobedience still makes sense. It is to forget history that in our times in Myanmar the civil protests against the military regime constitutional laws (unjust), is not protests against a democratic constitutional system, though it is equally "civil". In addition, this must be true of civil protests in communist China and of late, in independent Nepal claiming to be near democracy. Hence, rather than incorporating such clause to define "civil disobedience" as a form of protest, we can thus far say that it is an uprising of the public, whether a section of it or whole of it against forms of government that governs aided with either constitutional or arbitrary laws which are deemed to be "unjust" practically and ethically in the public evaluation. In both the cases, "practically" refers to what is "legal" and "pragmatic", and "ethically" refers to what is desirable, right, just and good in the moral sense or based on moral reasons or arguments. Hence, unjust laws are so called for they are under the evaluation of law, undesirable whereas public evaluation of unjust is based on the moral grounds available to us. Civil disobedience is then deemed rightful or just public uprisings against unjust laws of land governed by *laws of different status* by *different authorities* at different periods. However, this is for sure that any uprising of such nature must be grounded on or based on legal theses and moral theses which are deemed to be just in the public, at least the majority of them accepts the same, which though does not demand a democracy necessarily and sufficiently, but rests on the conception of a people's consensus on such matters. If this be the case, how is violent or non-civil protests as we said before, be any different is difficult to understand; hence, some distinguishing features needs to be incorporated in the definition provided by Rawls.

Now Rawls says: "I shall begin by defining civil disobedience as a public, non-violent, conscientious yet political act contrary to law usually done with the aim of bringing about a change in the law or policies of the government."[2] The distinguishing marks as we get them are "non-violent" and "conscientious yet political act". Arguably, though the former is a distinguishing mark to define civil disobedience as different from non-civil or violent disobedience, the latter is not because violent disobedient public protests may be or generally are conscientious yet political act when it comes to a rage against institutions as strong as governments and its supportive laws. Hence, the key distinguishing feature in this definition is "non-violence", that is, civil disobedience is a form of public protest essentially "non-violent" in nature though it is directed against enforcement of laws deemed to be unjust by an overwhelming government. It is interesting to note here that what Rawls observed before this definition to which we differed, has been quickly changed here, and now, we hardly differ to say that civil disobedience is nothing but *non-violent public protest* against unjust laws of land. Rawls shift to this, what he calls, "narrow or restricted" notion of civil disobedience revering the definition advanced by Bedau, Thoreau and Martin Luther King and not sticking to broader ones advocated by Howard Zinn. Anyway, we are more or less satisfied with this definition more so as it keeps us in avoiding ambiguities in evaluating the status of violent forms of public protests as "*non*-civil" but not "*un*civil". Violent or armed protests are then public protests against overwhelming governments or political agencies enforcing unjust laws to govern the public in no pacifist or non-violent ways. Violent protests are then counter-forces or repulsive acts in which use of political power is countered by counter power that is political but uses all physical means to aid the same knowing well those suppressive physical and legal measures are in the offering and overwhelming. So violent protests are countering a political power with powers, political and physical, and if our knowledge of such protests is to be believed, often they are backed up by counter legal powers. However, elements of political and legal powers and their use do not clearly distinguish features of violent protests, we need violation of laws *using* or at least *threatening to use* physical powers available to the organised public conscientiously. The use of physical powers is surely backed up by public's mental powers because intention, decision and determination of such violent powers, are all in the mind of man. Violence is thus said to be mental. Hence, we may say that violent disobedience to unjust laws are protests of the public against political and legal agencies which are *intended to devastate* the said overwhelming powers enforcing unjust laws by *use of physical means* because there are practical and ethical bases to be so pro-active. In any case, violent and non-violent protests or disobedient protests are directed towards overwhelming agencies for their enforcement of laws deemed to be unjust on practical and ethical grounds.

Clearly, violent and non-violent disobedience as modes of protests (as we may call them now), are justifiable on ethical grounds, which is our concern here, but as I have said before, we cannot overlook the legal or practical grounds for their justification because more often than not both bases to justify these protests are closely related and overlapping. Let us deal with these justifications. In a seminal essay, Tom C. Clark observes, "In my view civil disobedience necessarily involves legal and moral considerations. It has legal aspects because it openly dishonours law, and it deals in morals because it has to do with personal or collective passion. The theories that interprets the problem of civil disobedience into traditional norms of law and order must be based on both law and morals."[3] This may be comfortably extended to the violent form of protests based on our analysis of such protest stated above. The involvement of law in both cases is clear because such forms of protests are not "dissents", and no one is worried under the purview of law if public dissents in various ways in spheres of social life. Protests are conscientious, intended breach of law of land and thus public's legal obligation, which is constitutionally pronounced. For this matter, protests are acts inviting *punishments*, whether they are violent or non-violent. Hence, blatant violation of law succumbing to punishments bring protests to legal purview. In any case, violent and non-violent protests cannot be a legal matter if someone protests for a law being unconstitutional, it is a legal matter if protests are for laws deemed constitutional though targeted for defiance conscientiously and intentionally knowing punishable consequences. This case of defiance of law is deemed to be just by authorities and not by moral agents for they are unjust or immoral and thus conscientiously unacceptable, brings law and morality basic to acts of defiance or protests. It is important to see that "laws that are *seemingly* just" for authoritative reasons need not necessarily be deemed just laws without a thorough legal critique, which is secular, positivistic enterprise based on hard facts, proofs and uniformities in the theoretical structures which the science takes on seriously without subjective and relativistic opinions or faiths. Hence, protests may be well justified within the context of a secular critique of "seemingly just laws" which were enforced by authorities as just laws for various reasons. In this sense, constitutionally justified laws, which are said to be *sacrosanct* in the light of uncritical acumen of experts, needs to be protested inviting punishment. The other face of the issue is that the justification of the unjust as sacred by the imposing authoritative powers may be ethically unjust under the ethical critique. Hence, protests may be well justified legally and ethically. The basic problem in this regard is how the public comes to violent or non-violent protests in a morally just manner because they have counter-legal reasons to justify that the enforced so-called just laws were unjust. The problem is acute because the "public" as we call it, consists of individuals or moral agents each having moral and legal grounds to allow his or her conscience to protest unjust laws. Personal evaluations like these cannot be the justification of public evaluation of the same and thus of the subsequent protests. For Ronald Dworkin[4] moral agents enjoy rights to evaluate laws as just and unjust according to their moral conscience and protest against the unjust though "seemingly just laws". This is a queer subjectivist and relativistic position, which being permeated in emotivism results into no collective evaluation and action. In addition, if discrete individual morality touts legality as they like. just laws are difficult to shape in the public; a society will thus have tyrannical ways to what they call justice. In this case, all public protests are individual tyrannical protests, not consented to the least and thus morally and legally unjust. The Dworkin thesis of "individual conscience" thus leads us nowhere in public protests as morally and legally just. Nevertheless, an apologetic view of Clark to justify that even non-violent protests do not have sufficient public support morally and legally, because such protests in our civil societies are intrinsically derogatory to social harmony and breaks us from within. As such, any seemingly unjust laws should be better left to the competent constitutional critiques for reversal, renewal, removal or any corrective measures that are just and those causing social harmony. It is a matter to be seen whether in despotic and anarchic states where the constitutional machinery has been tattered to pieces as evident in today's world, the public could wait for such apologetic approach. The greatest problem with this approach may be that it sees off legitimate public protests as anarchic and disharmonious when the "legitimacy" is due to clear and distinct anti-human and anti-social laws deemed and enforced to be just. The apologists would survive only in the climate of ideal democracy wherein a false fear of disharmony allows fortunate powerful authorities to go along unjust laws because they rely merely on the sacred positivistic wisdom of hard law that they believe would prevail on them by any Divine intervention or Divine conscience provided unrests of protests be kept aside. This is, however, not the position of Rawls seen before because he finds some legitimacy in public protests though in a climate of ideal democracy. Rather it may be urged in the line of Rawls that protests, particularly the non-violent ones is justified desirable because it sidesteps personal whims, group and self-interests, religious predilections and arbitrary points of justice. By enforcing civil protests, for instance, "a minority forces the majority to consider whether it wishes to have its actions construed in this way, or whether in view of the common sense justice, it wishes to acknowledge the legitimate claims of the minority."[5] However, Rawls has interesting things to say about violent or militant protests and its moral justification *vis-à-vis* non-violent protests. He reasons that organised militant protests against the majority is different from the non-violent one is so far as the former is "more deeply opposed" to the political system because the system pursues a misconceived course in justice and in the judgement of the opposer, the system is unjust. In addition, Rawls construes from this an emotive, predilection and arbitrary conception of justice by the militant overlooking "the sense of justice of the majority (or those who have effective political power)". Now, for one thing, militant protests cannot be unjust on a bald declaration of "deeply opposed" because a protest that is civil though "shallowly opposed" is nothing better, it is worse as the teeth and bite is missing and with it is missing the power to bring the guilty to fall in line quickly. Next, there is no problem in the militant finding that the majority's conception of justice is fallacious if it really is, the point is the judgement cannot be fallacious because the militant conception of justice is true. Well, this may be the case in some instances of judgements of militants, but from this assumption of a likely militant fault does it logically follow (what Rawls draws from it), that militants are unnecessarily "deeply opposed" because the majority's view was overlooked? The problem is that somehow Rawls imagines that militant perception of justice must be wrong because that may be prejudiced by a militant thesis that overlooks majority's thesis of the same. Now, the same may be put on the heads of the civil disobedient because they must in essence be so good to follow a thesis of justice (perhaps one of Rawls), and then argue that majority's conception is wrong and needs redressal though non-violently. The force in civil ways to press on the majority to see its blatant misconceived justice, their deep felt opposition to it as based on a more logically *strong* thesis of justice is no less "deeply opposed" and no less falling back on a sacred thesis. Does Rawls imagine that the militant thesis is never as logically sound as the non-violent theory? It appears that without reason he draws a conclusion that their thesis is weaker than any other is. Why this should or must be the case? The militia may be so good in logically thinking that gross injustice is done to the public by the majority in power out of their arrogant readings of social, economic, political and legal justice, which in most cases the non-violent agents agree to. Both wants to vehemently (deeply) oppose gross injustice, the only difference may be then in adopting methods or means to attain the end of compulsion for redressal of justice, and it may be argued here with some theoretical prejudice that only if means are noble, they are desirable, particularly the noble end of protests justify a nobility of means, not its barbaric status. We are acquainted with such end justifies means thesis, but it may be argued by the militant that the means being violent cannot be intrinsically evil because its underlying intention and end are both desirable or good, and the means (of violence) itself is desirable as it is pragmatically or instrumentally good in the realisation of the said good end. Rawls further argues that violent protests are unjustifiable, as they are "never bound to fidelity of law" as they are strongly apathetic to the constitution and laws enforced thereby, and for that matter "evades punishment". Now, this appears to be a strong argument, which is not the case because many violent protests are staged with perfect respect to the law of the land barring one or more, which needs redressal. It will be extremely difficult to say that violent peasant's protests in the recent times in India or the protests of the tribes calling for urgent redressal of exploitative laws for compensation in the face of forcible acquisition of land are those against the entire law of land, and that the poor people are infidel in our democratic system. The point may be raised in another way, that is, were they just in resorting to arms for they were pressed beyond the limits of non-violent protests? That some people go against the law, that one should resort to force against the system skipping the legal course that was available to them, be sufficient to justify that they are infidels. The ethical evaluation of violent and non-violent protests in a democracy and in autocracy or anarchy must be different, when we take a more or less stable democracy, for instance, public protests should be better evaluated for ethicality and for likely legal flaws that needs redressal in the climate of public debates and subsequent consensus.

Hence, both violent and non-violent options are open for us to take but not before the basic critique of laws that we want to oppose, and the system we want to change on practical and ethical grounds available to us. For us, then critiques at public spheres are most important than suddenly jumping in an action. It is exactly due to this that violent and non-violent protests open wide ethical debates in democratic India lest we recognise the reality that we are still with situations when our system enforcing constitutionally supported laws need to be placed in the practical and ethical scanner, because these laws are never sacred and obsolete with changing times. However, I must say that in autocratic and despotic or anarchic states, public critiques are no less important before taking recourse to violent or non-violent courses of action. A good sum up of what I have maintained thus far is what Professor D.P. Chattopadhyaya mentions in the opening paragraph of his essay, "Civil Disobedience: Its Necessity and Limits". He writes: "It is not of much use discussing civil or political disobedience in an abstract or unhistorical manner, disobeying the laws of a dictatorial regime is not the same thing as disobeying those of a democratic one… the principles of moral and political philosophy depending on our attitude, affirmatively or negatively towards civil disobedience have of necessity to be discussed at general level."[6] However, Chattopadhyaya's later observations are different from what I say in his use of "general" in the above statement. He thinks that it is proper to follow Rawlsian "veil of ignorance" in order to determine which *general principle* justifies a recourse to civil public protest because a form of protest which is otherwise taken to be negative against the ruler cannot be justified as morally positive on the part of the protestor (ruled), unless we put a veil of ignorance of a historical pure theoreticism and extreme historical relativism in view of information specifications. It is better then to put extremes of a history and history aside in order to abide by a more methodologically sound principlistic approach (as I find it), that is, "to fall back upon and follow the light of *general* principles, which if acceptable, will be in the common interest"[7] (my italics). But abruptly, as I believe, Chattopadhyaya concludes much to my liking, that "The ends of all interest groups, the ruler and the ruled, the exploiter and the exploited, etc. prove elusive if a minimal *consensus* is not available regarding the means to be employed…. Every game presupposes more than one party marked by difference or conflict of interest. A human society quite free from conflict is utopian, i.e., not to be historically found anywhere."[8] It is interesting to note that despite conflict among the ruler and the ruled whether in democracy or anarchy, there may be or should be "consensus" built across varying opinions which is amenable to "common good", but that is possible when public under the veil of ignorance "follows the light of general principles". Though I have said in all the volumes of this series and in earlier chapters in this work that public effort to build a consensus on matters that are value-laden before anything is decided and made functional, does not necessarily and sufficiently beg a principlistic stance, in the light of general principles under a spell of deliberate ignorance of spatio-temporal relativism and flow of information. The reason is that the contesting public on matters of value such as desirability of protests of any kind does contest for the same as based on and influenced by spatio-temporal relativism, flow of information and common value related experiences and knowledge. It is a utopia that they can or they should put a veil on their cognition of what exists, what happens and what things are desirable, good, right, just and so on. The public just cannot do so on ground levels of reality because those under terrific pressure of ethical and practical disagreements tending to cooperate in finding consensus, are never cognitively able to overlook history, because space-time relativism and information of stark truth unless a queer technique of overlooking these things has been taught to the common men is ever possible. Such queer practices since a long time belonged to a clan of theoreticians and philosophers who are trained in putting mind over matter. Moreover, putting a veil *should not* be allowed in cases of conflict to consensus because that prevents moral agents' value experiences and knowledge to flow out freely and with them their informal critical acumen which is logical to find out how in the light of history, relativism and informational details, our evaluations of right and good of matters like protests come to a consensus. This is the simple peoples' way of ethical consensus on value affairs where *non-principlistic approach* is the key, that is, an approach that does not try to cling to or put stress on one or more norms of just, right and good though all normative opinions are at free play in and with the contesting public. The approach unlike the historical blunder of theoreticism and passionate clan-based work of ethicists does not find out any general thesis for procedural justice as sacred guiding principles on all value matters pertaining to society, polity, law and economy. It is both impossible and unethical that some norms are put on heads of contesting public on matters of protests because a clan of intellectuals have found them to be so good to crush the freedom these concerned people enjoy to *apply* their experiences and knowledge gathered in history, space-time relativism, information and in the waves of public actions and interactions in ecological community that testifies the right, good and just. Hence, here I stress on a non-principlistic, non-artificial, non-intellectualistic mass participation on matters like protests, whether violent or non-violent against any form of government.

It is exactly in defiance of ethical chauvinism (see Vol. 1), the author of this work attempted to resolve value-crisis in the choice of *mode of protests* in India whenever they are deemed either most effective or least effective. In the year 1999, I arranged a public debate on the following issue: "Which socio-political mode of protest do you think to be ethically more acceptable: fast unto death or armed rebellion?" The focus was shifted from broader debate on non-violent *versus* violent modes of protests to more specific "fast unto death" and "armed rebellion" as the state of Bihar at that point of time (1999) was undergoing quantum socio-political turmoil owing to the demand of creation of a new state and tribal areas noticing rise in mass movements of peaceful and violent natures. Despite such real-time focus, the modes stated here has been under public scanner for ethical value since the time of Gandhi or even before that. In fact pre and post-independent India has been constantly facing the value crisis in application of these modes of protest because we have been enforcing laws and to keep social unrest under control whenever there were participations in fast unto death and militant actions of common people against the rulers of the periods. For the debate, as usual, I selected the following participants:

1. Sri Tridib Ghosh, Senior Member of C.P.I. (ML), Ranchi Unit.
2. Dr. Rajendra Prasad Chaudhary, C.P.I., Ranchi Unit.
3. Sri Amol Bhattacharjee, C.P.I. (M), Ranchi Unit.
4. Sri Brajesh Kr. Sharma, Commandant, III Battalion, B.M.P., Dhanbad.
5. Dr. K.K.L. Karma, Head of Philosophy, Ranchi University, Ranchi.
6. Dr. L.M. Prasad, Professor of Political Science, Marwari College, Ranchi.
7. Dr. Srikrishna Pandey, Professor of Hindi, Yogada College, Ranchi.

As usual, the debaters were selected keeping in view of balanced debate on the said violent and non-violent means of protest. On the one hand, we have three Marxists of different affiliations, having different perceptions on the use and quanta of armed rebellion in Indian contexts, and on the other hand, we have two pronounced Gandhians in Dr. Pandey and Dr. Karna. Dr. Pandey is a law graduate as well as a person who had experience of a fast unto death for quite some period for the cause of university teachers. Whereas we had two participants, Dr. Prasad and Brajesh Sharma, who had a more or less non-affiliated views as they had moral perceptions in the capacity of a secular, social scientist and political analyst, and an executive who stood for the cause of law and order in the state. The following questions were put to the participants:

QUESTIONNAIRE

1. What would be your evaluation of the value of human life *vis-à-vis* 'fast unto death'? Do you think that 'fast unto death' is a veiled licence for 'suicide'?
2. How would you evaluate the intrinsic value of human life *vis-à-vis* 'armed resistance'? Do you think that 'armed resistance' is a veiled license for 'homicide'?
3. Do you think that 'fast unto death' and 'armed resistance' are either essentially cruel, anti-human, and therefore, immoral or are they essentially benevolent, aimed at general welfare, and therefore, morally justifiable?
4. Under which circumstances do you think that 'fast unto death' and/or 'armed resistance' are ethically acceptable modes of protest in India?
5. What should be the morally justifiable courses of action of the police, the administration and the judiciary if the previously mentioned modes of protest are effectively undertaken?

It is clear that the first two questions intend to evaluate the value perception of the participants with regard to both modes of protest. Next two questions are aimed to find out in the context of the replies to two basic questions why at all any of these modes of protest are ethically justifiable and what are the bases for such justification. Finally, we need to see what are the value resolutions and likely decision-making rules suggested by the participants.

As I have said before, I will refrain in this case from detailing the debate and analysis of the debate for normative findings. Nevertheless, my experience is that none of the elevated participants was able to press on others a normative or general theory of morals to resolve this crisis though there were consensus on some points despite stiff difference in value perceptions and application of knowledge of the participants. It will be extremely interesting to see how readers apply this methodology to find something new, and for this, any improvement in the questions is welcome.

Notes

1. Rawls, John, *A Theory of Justice*, OUP, 1973, p. 363.
2. *Ibid*, p. 364.
3. Clark, Tom C., "Philosophy, Law and Civil Disobedience" in *Ethics and Social Justice*, Kieffer, H.E. and Munitz, N.K. (ed.), State University of New York Press, Albany, 1970, p. 243.
4. Dworkin, R., "A Theory of Civil Disobedience" in *Ethics and Social Justice*, *Ibid*, pp. 225-239.
5. Rawls, John, *Op. Cit.*, p. 366.
6. Chattopadhyaya, D.P., "Civil Disobedience: It Necessity and Limits" in Roy, Krishna and Gupta, Chhanda (ed.), *Essays in Social and Political Philosophy,* I.C.P.R. in association with Allied Publishers, New Delhi, 1989, p. 201.
7. *Ibid*, p. 202.
8. *Ibid.*

5

People's Ethics and Legal Ethics

Many things have been said about social and political ethics, which includes among important issues, the most important issue of the application of ethics in social and political affairs because those affairs draw our ethical attention before a careful resolution. We have seen that value-laden social and political affairs awaiting ethical attention for most legitimate resolution is not an exclusive business of trained ethicists. It is equally true that the same does not depend only on trained social and political scientists or scientific experts. We have argued that people owing to community participation or sane human ways of life face many practical problems in the social and political fields, which are value-related or ethical problems asking for participation of the concerned public for effective application of their ethical experience and knowledge. I have argued at length throughout the Series (in all six volumes dedicated to different areas of practical and professional ethics) that application of ethics or what is the practice of ethics in occupations, professions and sub-professions, demands people's participation, and therefore, practical ethics is people's ethics in some sense or the other. I have reservations in accepting that practical ethics is arbitrary and linear application of academic normative theses by experts, whether they are ethicists or non-philosophers trained in ethics or a party consisting both of them. Throughout the Series I have argued that though the "justifications" or the "logic of practical ethics including the branches therein" is an interesting academic field of study most suited to the ethics experts, nevertheless, the practice of ethics "transcends" academics and academia to cover the huge body of the public, their ethical reflections, ethical disagreements, arguments, the force of their heuristic understanding and agreements that are broad based, provided amicable social and political conditions prevail in a given society wherein ethical resolutions are urgent. It is in a sense that I call practical ethics, people's ethics.

In volumes One and Two of the Series, I have argued that any amount of justification of application of ethics as a sensible study within ethics and any amount of stress on people's participation in ethical matters are meaningless unless the outcomes of the entire exercise are backed up by adequate empathetic involvement of the government. Let us now clarify why at the end of social and political discourses, particularly at the end of social and political ethics, this point emerges as most crucial. Ethical practice involving the public demands to know why something should or should not be done before abruptly jumping into deciding and acting at the broader social level because that allows us to evaluate how well we are ethically equipped before intending to act that affects society and environment positively or negatively. Our humane attitudes towards life, society, beings and things count most as humans because bereft of these, what it is to exist *qua* humans is difficult to assert. If this be the case, the public is expected to be active in the resolution of ethical dilemmas concerning practical affairs because that is one important aspect of our being humans in civil societies. But our ardent efforts to be involved in value-resolution does not bear any fruit on the ground level of social reality if the political power that rests with those governing the society are not equally involved in not only value-resolution but implementation of what has been corroborated by virtue of resolution, that is, implementation of the most humane decisions, policies, rules, laws and functions. Suppose widespread ethical debates in India come to a broad consensus that public-private participation in welfare programmes are most desirable (ethically speaking) on grounds available to the participating public, what on earth does the consensus amount to if following the same, at the political level and subsequently at the social level policies, rules, laws, decisions and dynamics of implementation of the same are not enforced with urgency and purpose? What is great in ethical debates concluding to consensus but never cared for real-level implementation, which were otherwise desirable and thus desired by the public? What is great if governors of the public do not pay a little pittance on what the public thinks is desirable to do? Hence, practical ethics as people's ethics is a futile exercise if the findings of the public in communion and consensus are not paid adequate political attention, and thus lack political will to implement what is otherwise desirable to do in the society because the population wanted the same on moral grounds. Practical ethics as people's ethics is thus dependent on ethical governments and their ethical governance because ethically charged political power-holders and their functioning cares for what is desirable to do than what things were done so that governments are not turned to fictitious entities; they are for real, in and with the public, they are the representatives of a population. If this be true then it is difficult to see why those responsible for effective social governance be not *participants* in resolving ethical crises in practical matters and effective parties in implementing what has been resolved for the social good. It is simple to follow that government *acting-at-a-distance* never participates in value-resolutions in and with the common people whom they govern, nor do they follow what people resolve in communion. There are then at least two forms of governance and governments in our civil States—that *acting-at-a-distance* and that *acting-without-a-distance*, though that never amounts to acting without any distinction because not keeping a distance from the public is not keeping any distinction as a functionary. The government is in essence distinctive body of functionary at political, social, economic, legal, administrative and management levels which is easily distinguished for the same from what the masses are with whom perhaps they joined to resolve ethical dilemmas and came to consensus; there are then two ways of social and political governance, one is *dominant* or *power-tracking* or *patriarchal*, and the other is *empathetic* or *involving* or *matriarchic*. We may call them *chauvinist* and *feminine* governance, if we wish to be precise. The former type of government deem it wise to rely on the political, administrative and legal powers they have assumed by virtue of coming into existence, whether by exclusive use of authoritative powers or by a process of election that may be anything like the farcical or mock election to a serious affair having methodologies to select people's representatives involving the people of a State. Hence, it will be unwise to say that only authoritarian governments act-at-a-distance or that only dictators or autocrats act-at-a-distance; it may well be that a government existing by virtue of popular franchise in a more or less fair governments of the latter type, the empathetic, feminine in nature, are those who assume power by virtue of fair or just methods of election wherein people's free choice or representations are neither abused nor prevented, and hopefully it happens best in a democratic set-up. It is not that any democratic government in modern times show feminine face, it can be equally chauvinist. Hence, there is for sure impostors in democracy who *act-at-a-distance* than acting for the people, involved in their affair and participates in and with them. Nevertheless, in other forms of government, the method of election may be very sound and fair in the sense in which we have just seen, but that does not guarantee that the people's government assuming power will not turn to chauvinism because patriarchal mode of governance may be built in the State's constitution and thus in the social psyche and forms of social and political life, unless the root of patriarchy itself is destroyed or eliminated by people's revolution. The likelihood of such basic and revolutionary constitutional changes that eliminates the patriarchal psyche and ways in governance is extremely difficult but not impossible to imagine because the moving power of State's governance that the constitution is, remains as usual a human affair, always possible to be amended or even drastically scrapped. Hence, patriarchal government succeeds only when constitution is absolute and sacrosanct, not likely to be flexed, amended, or changed. As such, acting at-a-distance in governance succeeds only in modes of governance, which is subsequently guided by an absolute, inflexible constitution because the constitution is thought to be divine, or divine-like, suited best to the select race of wise men, more like Plato's Philosopher King or the absolute centralised power which has corrupted the power suckers. In any case, an ideal democracy neither imagines power to philosophers or any such Kings or divine-like people or corrupt centralist whose inflexible laws would never be flexed at the *ethical and practical probing* of the public. In democracy, the ethical and practical probing of the public shakes or should shake those corrupt laws invoked in constitution that corrupt the public psyche and ways of political life of the public. Hence, the government elected from among the population should be always spirited to remain pro-public, ethical and practical, that is, the public always scan laws and functions of government. It has to be on the empathetic feminine line or else, the democratic system is non-existent. The question is "do we have such a democratic system on earth or in India?" It is matter of pity that most so-called democratic modern States including India, cares little about the active and effective involvement of common men of various occupations and professions in the ethical probing of practical social problems, which raise distinct questions of moral, ought, just, right and so on. The public in these democracies are hardly involved in such matters, which is a great failure from which the philosophical diaspora cannot shy, nor the organs of the government whether independently or totally can shy from such failure. It is a great shame on the philosophers if they believe that *qua* analysts they have a pure theoretical academic work, which contributes some way or the other in the growth of knowledge of sections of the public allover the world. In this sense, the philosophers surely apply their academic skills and that they are not impractical by any imagination. Nevertheless, there is no point in thinking that the skilful academic people should refrain from taking any practical responsibility that comes on them partly by virtue of their training and partly by virtue of being members of a society and a nation fraught with huge problems, most haunting for them being the practical problems needing careful ethical scrutiny. In a democratic set-up as in India, no one has really prevented philosophers to get involved into participating and/or leading a people's movement for "value-resolution" in and with the common men. If philosophers take on this responsibility and then follow up with their academic analytic work of normative study of public ethical discourses, they will not be cursed lesser philosophers. Some old-fashioned sceptics argue that *per se* philosophy is never an empirical inquiry and philosophers are not suited for such an inquiry, hence, they owe nothing to the society to study value crises therein and attempt at resolving them. This is a queer conception of a division of labour in which the philosophers are not allowed to act even as a section of conscientious, civil citizens of modern world who do not prefer remaining in a purely theoretical comfort zone but comes closer to the hot zone of public discourses about moral dilemmas that disturbs the social fabric to find some solution in consensus. Our democratic rights and our philosophical task-performances cannot and should not prevent us from applying our ethical experiences and knowledge in resolving moral dilemmas. It is different issue whether we assume leadership or only we need to do such things in the name of philosophy. In fact, we have been scathing in our criticism of philosophers' solo effort in resolving value crises. We have been constantly harping on the truth that value-resolutions are open to parties who have desire and some training to lead the discourses, which is of course done most ably by philosophers, but non-philosophers can do it equally efficiently provided they have the same desire and training expected of leaders. We have argued that philosophers and non-philosophers should get involved with public perceptions and opinions with a learner's mind to learn how to frame relevant questions for moral discourses, they should be equally competent in learning from philosophical writings on value-laden practical issues, they should have the élan to moderate and corroborate moral debates and if needed, they should be able to analyse moral views for logical strengths and weaknesses and for understanding real-dynamics of normative theories. Nevertheless, for non-philosophers and prospective philosophers, it is a pragmatic exercise in philosophy education to let the learners know the intricacies in applying ethics in its completeness, though the education needs to be anchored on ground level of reality than classroom pedagogy and/or mock debates. Therefore, applied ethics as people's ethics is ethics as highly useful enterprise for philosophers and non-philosophers alike. Equally true is that applied ethics as people's ethics calls for participation of those non-coopted common men who otherwise have no philosophy or ethics background and no ability to take up lead in value-resolution, but when called upon, are open and upright in contributing what they know is desirable, good, right, just, obligatory and duty when faced with moral crises. In this sense, applied ethics as people's ethics is active social participation of occupations and professions in value resolution whether the participants have least academic knowledge of ethics or desire to know them. However, applied ethics as people's ethics is not bereft of theoretical effort to find out normative involvement in value-resolution, but that is not the whole of applied ethics. We have argued that applied ethics as a social enterprise transcends pure theoreticism in a number of ways, which may be true of other enterprises in philosophy. Hence, moral philosophy or ethics should be distinguished from logic, epistemology, or metaphysics as far as it cannot avoid application of ethics as social enterprise dragging us to do a number of things stated above in and with the public, which is trans-theoretical. In this sense in civil societies, no one has really prevented philosophers to be trans-theoretical when time calls on them to do the needful, and then they will be no less philosophers, they will be rather social beings.

For those who do not take a lead in value-crises resolution but participate in resolution assumes a place in society which is democratic, so that they debate on moral issues, resolve them and then press the organs of the government to take care of them. In other instances of governance, we said, the pillar being an overwhelming sacred inflexible constitution or arbitrary body of rules and laws it bereft the masses of the needed freedom to participate in value affairs, the equal status for the academia and the common men to resolve value crises.

Along with this, social and political justice that allows the most concerned parties of society to speak freely and fearlessly on value matters irrespective of their castes, creed, faiths, incomes and status is disparaged if the constitution is arbitrary. The greatest point among all is that it is in the ideal democracy that people's moral probing can be pressed hard on the heads of those in government, as they were participants in moral discourses and therefore, corroborated points should be accepted now without any contradiction and moral blemish. The legislators should try to incorporate what public feels "should be done" even if that demands quantum shifts in constitutional provisions and laws. The point allows us to say that democracy is ideal for application of ethics because moral probing find pathways in the organs of government, the legislative, executive and judiciary to be expressed in reality or in practice. Without such expression, what it is to apply ethics as people's ethics is difficult to say. Applied ethics is thus of value in an ideal democratic set-up which is not merely a body of argumentative people on moral matters, it is a body of people pressing hard for implementation of moral findings on critical social, economic, political, legal, administrative, ecological, biological, educational and many such issues. It is extremely difficult to say that whether in India or elsewhere we have such an ideal set up for the said application of ethics because an ideal set up is the one that succeeds in avoiding patriarchal chauvinism in matters of social concern that have moral features. When the organs of the government are least interested in what people urge about value issues, when members of the organs of government are least interested in actively participating in public debates on moral matters, and when people are corrupted by those powers because they make a clan who can only imagine that they are absolutely valid on matters of value, there is a democracy faltering to the core and with it, there is no application of ethics as people's ethics. The point is whether being blind to the moral perception of the public that is, when people in power become moral islanders strengthened by virtue of a sacred body of laws and professional powers bestowed upon them there is any ethicality left for them. Hence, the powerful imagines that only they who are custodians of constitution, society and polity, should decide on moral questions on practical affairs. In association of such moral islanders and arrogant chauvinism, there is only unethical governance at-a-distance, which is itself a value-laden issue for our resolution. We should as starter in glorious democracies invite the population that includes the people in power to debate and agree on a broad base whether moral islanderism and action-at-a-distance are desirable attitudes and strategies in democratic governance.

We are thus in the final run in applied ethics as people's ethics facing the question that drags us to legal ethics, the one that asks whether the laws of the land, the lawmakers, the implementers of laws and the custodians of laws are subject to ethical inquiry for what they variously decide and act at the social plane. It may be apt to say that applied ethics as people's ethics succeeds when the makers of law and their implementers and custodians have minimal respect towards the moral dilemmas of public regarding laws and task performances of those in government. This requires us to go briefly indeed through what is legal ethics, how it is justified, what issues concerns us most instantiated by a major value-laden case in India today. However, I must say that this work does not require to deal with the problems at length because it needs a full-length work on Legal Ethics. Anyway, I take up this task at least briefly because I have said before, without doing so, a yawning gap is left for us in applied ethics. Let us now continue with "legal ethics". Without any detailing of what is ethics and what is legality, we can say that "legal ethics is ethical scrutiny of legal matters", that is, on the one hand we try to analyse the ways in which metaethical and other tasks of ethics find relevance when non-moral or factual matters such as the legal matters are in consideration, and on the other hand we try to analyse the ways in which non-moral legal matters invite ethical inquiries of desirability, good, right, just, duty, obligation and so on. In this sense, we speak of legal ethics when we consider (as we are now doing), the meaning, significance and justification of legal ethics as a study in the field of ethics, which is in one way of studying the sense and relevance of moral inquiries of non-moral matters (such as legal matters). Further, we inquire whether normative ethics has anything to contribute in an ethical inquiry of legal affairs. We also inquire how ethics in application tries to resolve value questions in legality, and what ethical virtues or values are relevant in legality and for legal experts. All these amount to metaethical, normative, practical and virtue-related inquiries that make some sense in relation to legal affairs. We have just seen that the other way round, we can inquire why and how legal issues such as the violation of human rights and capital punishment opens opportunities for their ethical evaluation. Legal

Ethics is thus ethically relevant inquiries of matters pertaining to legality. The point is what matters pertain to legality? In our earlier discussions, it was clear that most of the modern civil States are run by popularly elected governments, though the methods of election varies greatly and the forms of government and their functioning varies as well, but it is difficult to imagine a rudderless nation. Coming to democracy, particularly in India, we found that the government is popularly elected at the centre, states and union territories through secret ballot, though the party or coalition parties in charge elect the heads of states, the chief ministers and the head of central ministry, the prime minister in consensus. The president is here the supreme commander of armed forces, who is the statutory head of the States and the custodian of the written Constitution of India. In this structure of our democracy, the governments in the centre and the states are run as effectively as possible by the three organs of the governments; the legislative, who is responsible in making laws for social governance and assuming that the constitutional provisions for effective governance are neither abused or neglected, though for several good reasons the constitutional provisions or laws may be amended. The other organ of the government is the executive, who assures implementation of laws, plans and programmes framed by the legislature. Whereas the judiciary, which is the third organ sees that the constitutional provisions and the laws of the land are not breached or violated, and in cases of abuse, breach and violation, adequate punishments through free and fair trials are meted out to the guilty irrespective of their caste, creed and colour. The same organ also settles disputes in centre, states and centre-states in relation and attends to the manifold disputes of civil and criminal nature among the population. It is exactly in the sense of attending to manifold dispute settlements and meting out prize and punishment after trials based on the laws of land available to the legal agencies that we speak of legal justice of which judicial justice is a part. In this sense, the judiciary, its functions and the justice it does in the society is a part of the broader "legal justice", which is however, not merely justice done in the judiciary or the civil, high and supreme courts of justice. Hence, "legality" should be understood along with "legal justice", that is, inclusive of and broader than judiciary and judicial justice. In fact, legality covers all aspects of law, starting from its framing to its implementation, upholding, and protection which may be as broad as law taken in the international perspective or in the national perspective.

However, judicial justice is somewhat narrower in its purview as it sees the individuals, institutions, organisations and even States get what is due or rightful to them in view of what established laws of nations or international forums prescribe. Legal justice, in this sense, is then arranging, implementing and meting out what is rightful or due to individuals, institutions and organisations whether nationally or internationally. Legality also covers assurance of what is rightful or just in our constitutionally established laws, penal codes and functioning of organs of governments throughout the world, though its stature, nature and workings or actual dynamics vary greatly given the socio-political structure of a nation and what the guiding constitution lays down. It is easy to realise that ethically relevant inquiries would cover matters pertaining to legality in the above sense, which includes, judicial legality as well. Hence, we may inquire into the ethical right, good, just and so on of what is "given to us by States and International Forums" as laws or the guiding principles of conduct and the rules that forms parts thereof. We may thus inquire into what is ethical right, good and so on of what is "agreed upon by the individuals and communities as guiding principles of conduct and the rules that forms parts thereof". It must be basic to legal ethics that an inquiry is allowed to evaluate on moral or ethical grounds what States give us and is agreed upon by us as principles of conduct, breaching which is to invite problems. It is always important to see how legal and/or judicial evaluation of our conducts (those of individuals, institutions and organisations), be correlative to moral evaluation which have different grounds. If the "given laws and the rules that to which we more or less agree as basic to judgement of our conducts" are so important, can we at all evaluate these laws by virtue of the "given moral principles or norms agreed upon more or less generally by us as basic to judgements of our conduct"? How can what is given by States or Individual Forums as basic to evaluate our conducts be doubly evaluated on different norms that State or International Forums did not give us? This question is crucial in scepticism regarding "legal ethics" and "judicial ethics" because we have to justify why *non-normative grounds* of conduct become subjects of evaluation on grounds alien to it, that is, grounds which are normative in nature. Such justification takes us to the metaethical task of providing reasons in favour of possibility of "legal ethics" and "judicial ethics", and we perhaps cannot avoid falling in the realm of "legal ethics" as a relevant ethical discussion on matters of law.

There is no way to forget that after all laws that are "given" to us are laws that some humans have handed to us to obey them for our good or social good. Then laws have a purpose, they are not without a reason and that laws have not dropped from the blue, they are results of human deliberations, which most expectedly others agree to for their intrinsic and extrinsic values. However, some others might believe that laws are Divine; they are Commands of God though useful for the society. In any case, laws are not given arbitrarily to many of us by some of us for good. If "our good" or "our well-being" is the cornerstone of laws that are framed, then those who decide in framing a law and not another one, those who deliberate on the contents of law, their interpretation, application and justification (reasons), are guided by the ethical *principle of well-being* which is meant for a diaspora and not for the few or for a class. It may be argued that they are guided or influenced by the moral principle of utility or duty and many others. Hence, framing, enforcing and upholding any law are human affairs meant for the masses to accept and obey as paradigm of conduct, they are nevertheless, related to, and to some extent based on certain moral principles. Jeremy Bentham in *The Principles of Morals and Legislation* (1948) and John Austin in *Utilitarianism* (Lecture, 1962) vehemently argued this. However, the relation of ethics and law does not amount to their equivalence; they have clear distinction as both thinkers stressed law concerns itself with "what is the case", whereas ethics is concerned with "what should be the case". As seen above, as law relates itself to human deliberations in construction, enforcement and respect of rules of law or what as matters of fact are required for social good, whereas ethics relates itself to inquire why something that is/are required should at all be required or is/are *desirable*. It may be that on ground levels or reality and hard facts judiciary lays rules of law on homicide, ethics inquires whether what the law requires us to do *should* at all be done, and then if the law touts social good as the ethical goal of capital punishment for homicide, there may be an inquiry if that really should be the case on available moral grounds. Hence, the making of laws required for ground realities or stark facts never sidesteps and should not sidestep concerns for why laws at all "should" be made, implemented and respected. This is stated clearly in one of the seminal piece by Prof. H.L.A. Hart: "What both Bentham and Austin were anxious to assert were the following two simple things—first, in the absence of an expressed constitutional or legal provision, it could not follow from the mere fact that a rule violated standards of morality that it was not a rule of law and conversely, it could not follow from the mere fact that a rule was morally desirable that it was a rule of law."[1] Hence, in case of law, it is crucial whether one or more rules of law "should exist", this is *moral justification* of law itself; whereas it is another thing whether one such rule of law by any *positive standard* was formulated, accepted and enforced on us. The question of legal ethics is thus why any law founded on positive standards be at all deemed ethically desirable? This basic metaethical inquiry justifies why at all we should discuss legal ethics as an aspect of ethics though legality is a non-moral domain. No one has or can logically prevent us from inquiring into justification of legal ethics and thus answering the sceptics who thought this was not a business of Philosophy.

It is interesting to note that more and more we explicate the reasons or justifications in favour of having a rule of law, we are taken to the different moral standards or norms, which we have just seen. In case of Bentham, the standard was of utility and in case of Austin, the mixed standard of Divine Commands and Utility. This is to take us to *normative ethical* inquiry of what they amount to and why are they justified. Further, the justification of one norm over others, that is, weighing the logical strengths of egoism, utilitarianism, deontology and so on in the context of evaluating the ethical value of rules of law is nothing but *metaethical* in nature. In the recent times in the same context the discussion of basic human values and virtues, for instance, what are basic virtues expected of the lawmakers, implementers and custodians of law have gained some importance. The questions of benevolence, sympathy, empathy, honesty, fairness, neutrality towards caste, creed, and status and many other basic human values and virtues have assumed centre-stage for those who have the great responsibility to see through fairness and justice in legality. Hence, *virtue-based* ethical discussions gain importance in legal affairs. We will reserve details of the ways in which *applied ethics* comes closer to legal matters. In any case, we were trying to justify that the basic tasks of ethics make great sense when we come to consider the field of legality, which is nevertheless, non-ethical in nature. The reasons for an entry of ethics in non-ethical legal matters are many, this takes us to the various ways in which legal matters or matters relating to making, implementing and upholding rules of law invite ethics for a closer inquiry. To start with, we have for us the problem of these clarification and justification of legality, morality and ethicality, that is, what exactly do we mean by these terms and why should we use them in association though legality, morality and ethics are different. One can easily find that the posing of the problems amount to some solution and for that we should allow metaethical entry because the analysis and resolution of this issue is naturally taken up by second order ethics or metaethics. Stated simply, legality pertains to rules of law enforced at any place in the world by either a *supreme authority* or lawgiver whose laws we abide by as sanctions of the *natural law* or by sovereign powers of states as *positive laws*. When we come to "morality", we mean that either norms of conduct laid down by a group or groups, which has become a tradition or a custom for us to abide by because they are taken to be right and good in particular groups or societies without any critical evaluation or norms of conduct laid down contextually, and those needed for decent social behaviour. In any sense, "morality" concerns itself with laid down non-legal norms of human conduct by social groups as customary and/or needed for decency according to the situation, though such norms remain sacrosanct within closed uncritical groups. "Ethics", we have seen, is far different from legality and morality because unlike both it concerns itself with principles or standards of evaluation of moral good, right and so on irrespective of particular contexts and has nothing to do with either uncritical acceptance of such principles as laws given by authorities sacred or social or uncritical acceptance of customary norms of groups or societies. Ethics must be then a body of *critique* of norms as social customs, traditions as well as rules of laws we get from various sources and follow them obediently. Ethics is thus a critical inquiry into both legality and morality, where criticism is philosophical in nature. Ethics is then philosophical morality or philosophical scrutiny of morals, and philosophical scrutiny of rules of law. For instance, ethics takes to evaluate or critically evaluate on standards available to it whether contextual moral norms in vogue in societies are at all desirable, good, right, just and so on. It may be that law has it own positive grounds to justify why some provisions are right and good, such as, why capital punishment is right and good on grounds of deterrence. Nevertheless, ethics has the purpose to inquiry on what grounds "deterrence" is itself a desirable course in punishment, that is, what overreaching grounds of deterrence could be right and good. At times utility theory is needed to justify right and good of deterrence or another ethical principle for evaluation is needed to decide whether for such and such crime, capital punishment is needed as deterrence because that is customary in legal practice in a society. More often than not a dragging ethical question for "end-thesis" leads us to see why (on what grounds or ideals), should or *ought* we take a "deterrent" path even if sanctioned by law and social tradition. Can we say that it is the ideal of maximisation of social pleasures or good for which we take a deterrent way to punish because the intrinsic value of deterrence allows us to take recourse to an extreme form of punishment. We can easily see now that an analysis of nature and justification of legality, morality and ethics takes us to a close relationship among the three because more often than not rules of law bearing authoritativeness and wide group acceptance assumes the status of moral laws or codes and influences moral agents in contextual decision making which are good and just. Much like this happens in our societies even today when law's sacredness imposed on us uncritically and authoritatively as a way of social life becomes basis of moral decency and decisions. However, as seen before, though both legality and morality can be put to ethical tests, their affinity is no less emphatic as both legal rules and moral codes have some implicit or explicit ends or ideals, which are assumed to be of worth, or are epitomes of value, not disvalue.

If philosophical critique of legality and morality are important, we can find out a number of cases in legality (particularly for the purpose here), which invites for ethical scanning, justifying the validity of legal ethics. One important inquiry is the value of law in civil societies. If laws are in essence put on our heads by political authorities and always policed for abeyance, does it not disparage our autonomy, civility, pride and freedom? Are we so corrupt in being compelled to follow rules of law framed and pressed from outside not to the least taking our own lawful and fair intentions and actions to count most? Is it not ethically unjust to have laws and then find them from our own rational acumen whether they should be followed? One reaction to such ethico-legal scepticism is that only egoistic thinking about human nature allows us to say that we tend to bend laws that suit us best, but social life, which is cooptive, needs many personal or egoistic sacrifices, including the tendencies to bend laws from our so-called "nature" that benefits us. Prevention of moral islanders and sceptics from disparaging altruistically oriented civil laws for the responsible agencies to frame and others to implement and uphold is urgent. Rules of laws are thus imperatives for cooperative, civil life, the one clearing off hegemonies, whims and autocracy. Hence, the ethics of legality is the acceptance of a *system* that functions for or at least intends to function for the maximisation of social well-being than anarchy. One might argue that most touted good laws in the above sense are not needed because they make us moral adolescents. It is ethically just to be more and more mature in our inner or intuitive moral reflections for better, lawful, civil living—it is we who find lawful conducts. This does not prevent having rules of law because any morally mature legal anarchist would agree that unless human societies are not full of divine beings at a stroke of time, noble souls won't find for them uniform codes of conduct. Hence, all so-called discovered legality from within would be as good as the other, each fighting for absolute divine worth. Finally, anarchists would fall back on an *agreement* to establish a sacred legal system or they agree not to agree to any system causing complete failure of a civil society. Therefore, legality is absolute necessity for social existence wherein individuals' conceptions of worthwhile laws are never trashed completely because ethically, social good is supreme. In fact, not merely maximisation of social well-being, the rules of law seen mostly as "rules of convenience" are agreed upon by egoistic members of society because "keeping trust" is another extensive ethical conception that allows us to accept duties for us as social beings to cooperate with others and try to fulfil the legitimate human expectations in society. It is due to this that a person of plenty still has to perform a social duty to cooperate with those living in abject poverty to allow them to have their share of basic amenities and not grab everything available at some price. This is to remember the principle of trustworthiness. Hence, coming to respect laws for non-exploitation and aggression stems from ethical thinking, which does not mean we follow moral codes of our society rather dynamics of social interactions, moral agreements and disagreements or simply the dynamics of moral thinking enable ethical critique of laws stated above, and then in the midst of the said dynamics we discover principles of ethical evaluation whether that is the maximisation principle or any other. This point takes us to see what exactly practical ethics is doing the needful in the field of legality. In cases of legal dilemmas that raise distinct questions of moral ought, it is exactly the social dynamics of moral inquiry that enables us to resolve the said crises in communion, in which is implicit, the active principles of ethical evaluation. Practical ethics is getting involved in this social dynamics and subsequent discovery of normative functions implicit in the dynamics. In any case, as social cooperative is basic to legality and morality, the same is basic to ethical reflections or critiques of resolution of legal dilemmas. In the midst of everything, we find the role and value of legal ethics, which is in one sense, matters of legality awaiting ethical reflections.

However, some thinkers are of the opinion that *relativism* in our value systems, that includes social and moral values, does not allow cooperation and social agreement on legality and thus rules of law as basic to social good are impossible. However, in the recent past Professor H.L.A. Hart in a number of works on legal ethics have argued that an agreement in moral ought and desirability allows us to conceive uniform and time tested rules of law. The well agreed upon ethical standard of "public welfare" enabled us to justify "worker's welfare" throughout the globe at any place where people are contributors in production, distribution and profits at the cost of limited wages. We have seen the relevance of people's welfare as the evaluative standard for goodness of worker's rights and well-being. If this were the case, we needed laws, those well in tune with the ethical principle that prevents egoistic people or organisations to exploit labour at some price for their good. Similarly, we needed laws those well in tune with the ethical principle, encourages working people (wage earners) to earn the rightful without being exploited or exploiting others. Hence, it is the ethical orientation of the social beings that enabled modern men to have stringency provisions as rules of law. It is this way in which ethical conception of humans have led to legality. The relevance of legal ethics could be thus well noticed. We can now see that despite radical and continuous relativism in moral conceptions of people about human welfare and worker's welfare, that is, relativism in social value systems, we need laws more than ever because we found that relativism never allows us to shift from the social ways of life. Hence, our universal need to community life allowed criticism of partisan relativistic morality at different epochs in the history of human societies for acceptance of *objective values* and the much-needed *positive laws* that are anchored on these values. Is it not true that despite all changes in values in the capitalist, socialist and communist states, wage earner's welfare should not be defended vehemently by imposing stringent laws? Hence, relativistic value perceptions regarding human labour, profits, wages and just distribution of what is due to the labour class does not prevent us from conceiving laws that favour the class on rights they enjoy and for that the overriding ethical standards may be equally important.

The issue of personal and public emotions and attitudes towards value systems of persons and public influencing them to express pro-con views on rules of law are equally important in legal ethics. One way in which a mater of legality opens to ethical scrutiny is whether pro-con attitudinal expressions of an individual or sub-groups or groups on legal matters such as rules of law are ethically good and right even if the expressions are largely induced by nothing but the personal and group moralities that have become obsessive to the said people. It is extremely important to evaluate the morality of individuals and groups on legal issues. If we fail to do so, any individual, sub-groups and groups in societies would disagree forever on rules of law, but we have seen that societies still sustain existence of cooperative living despite pro-con emotions on legal matters because certain objectivity and authoritativeness that comes with consensual ethical evaluation are found to be overriding. However, the problem becomes stiff when we consider the morality of minorities (the sub-groups), and their attitudinal expressions on certain laws which they find unacceptable. The point is how the minority should find an ethical way out of the impasse provided the well-being of the society be at stake. More often than not, it is the case that what the minority groups demand concerning a law, is right. In such cases, it is all the more important to transcend the minority moral perceptions on available ethical principles which are group-based and which may not be sufficient for the evaluation of minority morality and their pro-con expressions. When we "transcend" on ethical grounds, we do not press on *our moral reasons and arguments* rather, we are in *association* where majority, minority, ruler and ruled, the empathetic parties seriously want a resolution on widely acceptable ethical basis. If the group's ethical exercises succeed, they may well ratify sub-group's moral position to be right on broader ethical grounds which do not belong to any one individual, faith, or group. In this sense, moral emotions and reasons that the public display in association in a heterogeneous climate is ethically more cogent. It is startling for any one who has participated in any such exercise to find that theory non-co-opted people of majority and minority, ruler and ruled in a free flow of their ethical knowledge and ethical arguments thrash out popular moralities for their validity, ratification and rejection, and subsequently enable us to ratify rules of law on minority matters. In the methodology of ethical application, we have seen in earlier chapters that social, political (and even legal matters) may be resolved in social association where morality gives way to ethical criticisms. However, it is important to repeat as I did before that ethical evaluation of moral reactions on legal issues is not the same as deliberately applying any one or more standard ethical theories. Rather, the standards are applied informally but freely, which is of course a matter for discovery by virtue of ethical analysis of public discourses. Naturally, therefore, legal ethics on the one hand is justified when some legal issues as mentioned just now awaits ethical scrutiny and when practical ethics comes to justify how a discussion of methodology of application takes on legal matters such as the one we are considering here. This focuses that though rules of law are framed, implemented and upheld by professionals in different capacities in our society, the common people who are related to the impacts of implementation of these laws, have some moral authority to speak on them when ethical scrutiny is so important. It is due to this that though penalty by hanging unto death is legally viable in extraordinary cases of criminal justice, in India, there are many individuals and rights groups who generate a lot of ethical heat on this issue. It is interesting to note at the time of famous ruling by the Supreme Court of India in the recent past to hang a criminal to death and the victim applying for clemency to the President, both the President and the Chief Justice went public against such penalty on their own strong ethical arguments which they wanted should be widely discussed. Hence, no one has really stopped the diaspora to thrash out ethical aspects of such criminal justice though for that, personal or group moralities if they do not hold ground on broader and more stringent logical grounds of ethical analysis, should be given up. It is important to value many rule of laws this way in our times in India.

To continue here what has been said before, in cases of civil disobedience and violent protests, the rules of law available to us needs to be put to constant public scrutiny if that amounts in some cases to offend the judicial justice. It needs to be remembered that anarchists and archaic legal experts have always prevented their sacred system and rationality from being revaluated on ethical basis by the non-experts. It is always ethically open to inquire whether anarchic and archaic experts are at all ethically desirable in our judicial system. It is difficult to imagine the right to express and freedom to speak out what is believed to have some logic at least in a climate where the judiciary has become arrogant and apathetic to criticism, the legislative headstrong and anti-people to neglect value-systems of the public and the executive unmethodical and lacklustre to care public opinion. It may be thus said that even if law rests on hard evidences and not emotions, moral approbations and ethical judgements, rules of law should not be prevented from non-legal or extra-legal evaluations because that does not bereft law of its inherent inclination to be anchored to facts and evidences, and of course to what has been well debated and framed as rules to be followed. Rather, extra-legal or ethical evaluation of legal rules, rulings, provisions and punishments in social cooperation enable its framers and implementers to find out whether the law of the land is at all pro-human, that is, does it have a human face. A system of law with a human face always sticks to basics of law but never loses sight of public value perceptions about law to weed out anti and inhuman features of law. Law should be ethically right, just, good and desirable.

After a brief justification of legal ethics in two ways: the way in which ethical task performances relates them to the field of legality and the way in which legal issues or problems related them to the field of ethics, particularly normative and practical ethics, we are now poised to consider the most important value-laden legal problem for resolution. This may be done in two ways: One is the traditional misconceived way to show how ethical principles are useful in resolving the value-crises and the other is the way to show how ethical discourses lead to resolve the value crises in legality which reveals functions of ethical principles implicit in the discourses. I have said before that the second course is preferable but in this work, I will refrain from detailing the debates leading to consensus and the analysis of the normative involvements in those debates. Let us now consider the sense in which concerns in *capital punishment* is value-laden practical problem, inviting ethical criticisms for resolution and the set of questions needed for discourses along with a list of participants giving us an idea of how ethical discourses on such matters should be conducted. I take this issue more as importantly as it demands a discourse on ethics of punishment, which is one way to see how legal ethics is a justified account. I think it is always good to proceed with brief account of ethics of punishment and then turn to the particular form of punishment in consideration, its ethical evaluation and resolution. The entire exercise we said before is following the model of "intersubjective corroboration". Capital punishment for its nature exploration demands a few words on crime, punishment, objectives and types of punishment, and related conceptions of guilt.

In the common parlance, crime is logically antecedent to punishment because first we have to find out why the problem of punishment arises at all. Punishment is deemed necessary when there is a criminal act by a person or persons, or a group of people or a society or organisation or institution and even a State, which is in essence an intended act of a person or some persons against established laws of the land or the international community such that by those acts humans and/or non-human beings and things are either affected negatively or if they are not affected distinctively in that manner, those acts violate the agent's bindings or obligations to abide by the said laws *qua* agents belonging to the said land or the international community. Though punishments are deemed "necessary" as covering or back-up measures by competent legal authorities to see that laws are neither breached nor overlooked, it is a matter of debate whether they are both *necessary and sufficient*. Hence, it will be a matter of debate whether any type of punishment as covering up legal measure can be at all sufficient though they are necessary. In the recent times, punishments are often backed-up by subsidiary measures such as counselling and other psychological treatments. In many cases, thinkers prefer giving way to self-evaluation and self-realisation of the undesirable acts and a change of the character. However, in the legal parlance, criminal acts being injurious to the legal system, and the individuals and society, criminals cannot and should not be left scot-free encouraging more crimes and great harm to the persons of character, who are obliged to rules of law. In fact, the social superstructure demand laws, which has to be followed. In this sense, "crime" is not merely an intended act of breaching law and thus non-obligatory to the prescribed rues of law; it is an intended act of injury or harm or production of evil, that affects the society. The introduction of an element of social harm or production of social evil as undesirable or unethical allows us to realise that crime should not be explained merely in the traditional positive or natural terms (of breaching laws), because the set of laws may be a set of arbitrary, unjust, unethical and illegal prescriptions forced on unwilling people to follow. Hence, crime is really against reaching those laws, which were otherwise pro-people, pro-society and pro-production of good over evil. It is said that if we miss the crucial unethical aspect of crime, we miss the ethical aspect of punishment because punishments cannot be touted good unless it is ethically good to cover-up as legal measure that which was unethical or evil, that is, "crime". However, it may be debated whether the goodness of punishment begs the production of good over social evils produced by crime because, among other things, one may argue that punishments are intrinsically good and not good for a higher social ideal, and it is the "duty" of legal authorities to punish that overwhelms their ethical reasons to justify punishment. In this sense, it may be said that certain things such as "crime" are intrinsically evil or bad and it needs our ethical intuition to find this truth to justify why a cover-up punishment (which is itself good) is justified. To say this is to argue that even if crime and punishment were not socially harmful and useful, they should be seen to be ethically unjust and just, and for that matter, unjustified and justified. In an extreme sense, as crime is inherently an evil, it cannot and should not be repelled or covered-up by counter measure of legal punishments if that amounts to counter the criminal in reality than the criminal intentions and acts. Hence, there may be no usefulness and even intrinsic goodness of punishment though it may be true that crime is an evil in the society. This may take us to a debate about the limited use, if not complete rejection of good of punishments. It may be argued that though an evil should not cover-up another evil, the evil of crime should be covered-up by a punishment as *means* that is itself good and not an evil. However, the goodness is something that demands our moral intuition to "see" for itself. In any case, both "crime" and "punishment" may be explained in *teleological* and *deontic/intuitive* terms, and punishments may be justified or rebutted on both these terms, provided we concentrate on the ethical aspects of these concepts than the social, economic and positivistic legal aspects. Clearly, "crime" and "punishment" are concepts demanding different social, economic, political, legal and ethical explanations for their complete understanding, and the justification of punishments demands the same explanations than any one because that would be too narrow, unsatisfactory and thus practically undesirable. More so, as we have just seen, it will be unwise to leave out the ethical justification of punishment even if crimes are ethically unjustifiable for the unethicality charge on punishment is always worth considering, taking us to the interesting debate of positive or natural justification of punishments being themselves ethically just. This is to consider the legalised institutional punishment being legally right and obligatory at the cost of ethical rightness and obligatoriness. Such a consideration takes us to find out whether it is ethically right and just to abide by social or legalised institutional rules of law even if we do not accept the rules of law on legal and/or ethical grounds.

This is the problem of moral system or legal superstructure despite the inherent positive and ethical flaws. This is nicely explained in Socrates' debate with Thrasymachus in *The Republic*. There is also a moral dilemma in abiding by criminal laws that are fragmentary in nature because such fragmentariness, incompleteness, imperfectness and unjustifiableness of laws fail to reason why or for which "crime" are they needed. Such laws in fact, fail to define "crime" and thus fail to explain why an "injury" to a person that is touted to be criminal, be caused. This might demand revision of punishment as "injury" to agents amounting to *non-injurious* punishment (if that is possible) because we are neither sure of the status of an act as "crime", nor sure of the status of an act as "punishment" to cover-up that "crime". Most of us who demand that "non-injurious" punishment should be justified legally and morally may be really in the tenterhooks of ambiguity of understanding crime and punishment. We may thus argue that as a "rule" we need to respect laws of land for the ultimate *use-value* in society. Or, we may argue that as a "rule" we need to respect laws of land for their intrinsic value because *per se* laws are incorrupt and are paradigms of right, just and good; those that are debatably so or not so, are "laws wrongly so called", they are not laws by any imagination. This is to conceive of system of laws that are sacrosanct, which persons of sharp intuitions can construct. Much like this was in the mind of Plato when he spoke of the Philosopher Kings constructing just laws as they *knew* "goodness-itself". In any case, if laws are not sacred, they are relatively right, good and just, as positivists would believe, no one really stops the *abolitionists* to argue that punishments should be done away with. In the midst of all this, we come to see that talks of crime and punishment pops up many questions of ethical right, just and good, which are unavoidable, and therefore, we are here speaking of "legal ethics" that justifiably contains "ethics of punishments" and "capital punishment".

When we come to consider the nature of "punishment", we find that unlike "crime", it expresses both negative and positive features because in reality the "act" of punishing can be pro-agent as well as con-agent. Hence, the act of punishing someone may be right and good for the one who punishes and the one who is punished, and the act may be wrong and evil for the punisher and the punished. In this sense, though "crime" is an exclusive "con-concept", "punishment" is a "pro-con-concept". The reason is that punishment is a "social act", that is, an act of an individual which affects social beings or other beings in society both positively and negatively, and being social, the punisher is affected positively and negatively. Whereas crime, despite being acts of individuals, affects negatively but not positively both the criminal and the society. Crime is thus con-law, con-people and con-goodness. However, punishment when *justified* can be both pro and con, and not otherwise because if an act is not at the social level justified to be an *act of legal stature*, that is allowed under the provisions of law, be understood as having both positive and negative values. Equally true is that if an act of crime at the social level is an *act for judgement of worth based on legal statutes*, only then can it exclusively have negatives but no positives. A deliberated crime is thus under "legal justification" a negative act and not otherwise. However, a crime that is legally a crime and evil can be ethically evaluated for the similar values. Similarly, a punishment that is legally a punishment and good in some way and evil in another way can be ethically valued for the good and evil worth. In this sense though in the eyes of law deliberated crimes are essentially negative, on ethical judgements, the definition of the said crime may be different. It may be argued that though stealing is a criminal act, well-organised stealth by the spying agents for national safeguards is not a crime eligible for punishment. To an extent one might argue that in cases of famine and hunger it will not be a punishable crime to steal food grains hoarded by black marketers. There is tension between non-legal evaluation of the pro-con aspects of crime and the legal evaluation of the essential con-aspect of crime. A defined crime is "negative", but under ethical scanner, the evaluation may be different though well debated. It cannot be said that legal declaration of crimes as essentially negative has no ethical basis, the declaration itself may be ethical, but the point is that when based on *an* ethical basis and legal provisions crimes are seen as essentially "negative", it is *fixed*. There is thus "fixity" in the legal evaluation of crime, which owes to "fixity" in the back-up ethical evaluation of the same. For any crime therefore, irrespective of relativism, legal evaluation is uniform provided we are sure that the act is a criminal one in the eyes of a *fixed* set of rules of law at any given space and time. However, the case is completely different in case of punishment because the act in the eyes of law or ethics is both positive and negative or good and evil, because it negates crime, that is, it strives to take crime head on to replace it by some positives of goodness. It is clear that therefore, punishment strives to be positive or good to the agent who commits it and the society as they are assured of criminal justice and safe living. No doubt then, that punishment valued legally is good for one reason and evil for another reason. It is good for the social existence and evil for the deliberate committers of criminal acts. Despite being in essence good and evil, punishments are evaluated for ethical worth differently. In the ethical scanner, punishment as a legal act can be evaluated in many ways thus objecting to what has been imagined legally and non-legally desirable. In this sense fixity of law allows us to state that "even if punishment is basically good and bad, legally speaking" in confirmed crimes, it is always good and not bad for which there are enough grounds for justification". Then the non-fixity or relativity of ethics allows us to state that "even if punishment is basically good or bad to social systems and criminals, it is not necessarily and sufficiently good and not bad for which there are good grounds for justification". Again, in case of this tension between law and ethics, the key is "fixity" in legal perception of value of punishment (and crime as well). Ethical relativity than fixity allows punishment to be evaluated as act of evil or bad even if one accepts that it contributes positively to uphold law and order in society and negatively to banish crime and criminals. We can see that the fixity of law may be ethically grounded, but that too is fixed ethicality or simply an obsessive morality but not open, flexible and relative system of ethical evaluation. Clearly, only under an ethical system can punishment be good or bad, which is clear arrogance to disallow other ethical systems for evaluation and then look for logical strengthens and weaknesses. In this sense, often legal system may be at great fault in judging crime and punishment for their value in the light of *fixed* legal and ethical systems. This brings in the debate of legal relativism in spatio-temporal or contextual conditions and its possible values. Conflict between the customary and the relative punishments are worth evaluating.

Keeping these basics in mind, we can now analyse the nature of "punishment". It can be said that unlike the *classical perceptions* of punishment, it is not merely "an evil", whether that is hedonic evil or moral evil or physical evil. Thus, punishment is not an epitome of badness or evil caused by competent public Authorities. This is to refute the classical idea that not anything that is not partly or wholly evil can be punishment, and for that matter, punishment can be nothing but an act of organised violence or "punitive violence". We have seen that punishment should not be seen as a purely negative act or punitive violence. To take the *hedonic* conception of punishment as evil a little farther is to call it a "necessary suffering" inflicted on an offender of established laws by competent authorities as a "token of censure" so that someone can be brought to a moral way of life, which is privation of pain and suffering. It is important to note that not only is punishment a necessary evil inflicted from outside on agents causing privation of pleasure, it is not to do away with the offenders as such, rather, it is mere "token of censure" to lead a moral way of life. A number of utilitarians and Prof. A.C. Ewing prefers to argue like this. This gives punishment its ethical basis and tries to give it a human face, which otherwise tended to go against the offender without giving him any chance of revival. Still, the "positive" side of punishment is visible, at least a glimpse of it, in this way of interpreting its meaning. And we have urged that it cannot be wholly negative or evil, it contributes "positively", and does a lot of good in *reforming* an offender, *preventing* possible offenders from criminal acts and threatening or *deterring* offenders by exemplary punitive acts. In any case, it is said by many thinkers of a "non-violent" theory of punishment (Gandhi and Tahtinen Unto, to name a few), that punishment are in essence negative and never positive in contribution (which is to forget our explanation). The reason is that even a number of ways to explore the nature of "punishment" that aims at the *objectives* (reform, deter, prevent and so on) all take punishment to be deliberate act of negation or evil, though the terminologies and explanatory phrases differ. For instance, some modern day thinkers explain it as inflicting *positive harm* by means of preventing an offender from enjoying erstwhile freedom to fulfil his desired desires. This is then a great social function. C.A. Baylis and S.I. Benn support in this way. Others like Antony Flew and J.D. Mabbott think that punishment is a deliberate act of authority to "deprive" offenders the needed freedom for offence by thus inflicting necessary suffering for which only he is responsible. Hence, the infliction of suffering by depriving someone of something is glorified for a noble *moral intention*. In any case, in the midst of all, the "positive" of punishment has been missed. The same is true of what has been analysed in this regard by K.E. Baier, A.M. Quinton, W.G. Mac Lagan and many others. Tahtinen Unto aptly remarks: "It becomes obvious that the common element in all reformatories is the 'infliction of pain on a person'. The ground or motive of this infliction, but not the essential content of punishment, is different in each theory."[2] The author thus comes to conclude that these ways of understanding the nature of punishment is encouraged by the "violent" theories of punishment, where punishment is *nothing but negative* as it is nothing but infliction of harm, pain and suffering. We have seen that without being an ardent supporter of the "non-violent" theory of punishment, in saying that the intention of punishment should be realisation of the guilt, shame and self effort to change ones intentions, character and acts, we can comfortably say that in all so-called violent thesis was implicit in the "positives" of punishment, that is, upholding the cause of lawfulness and fairness in society by meeting offenders face to face without any preconditions or reservations. Can non-violent theory negate this truth that there should be some rights for us to get legal justice if we are deprived of it, and that whatever noble the intention in non-violent theories may be, allowing someone for self realisation and correction demands a legal course to convict someone and then to confine the guilty with some freedom for the noble acts said above? If minimal judicial courses are not ruled out and the pragmatics of conviction and confinement accepted, does not everything go *against* or *negate* offender's wishes to move along an egoistic and derogatory ways in life? It does; even a noble man has to show someone what it is to live in guilt and crime and *prevent* the person from the further derogation of moral life. The negation in positives of non-violence is always there to be realised. It will be then difficult to accept purely positive or negative explanations of punishment. Anyway, let us find out what Tahtinen writes, "We may thus clarify the concept of punishment free from violence. Punishment is non-injurious measure applied on a responsible offender for breaking a morally justified rule. This 'measure' refers to the way society treats an offender. Minimally it involves a denunciatory pronouncement. Censure is as such not intended to be painful and, although made by a social authority, it may not necessarily even be public in the sense of making the offender known to the public."[3] It is interesting to note that Tahtinen finds "non-injury", "responsibility" and "moral justification" as the pillars of non-violent explanation of the nature of "punishment" and reminds us that the "non-injurious measures" are many, mostly morally neutral in character such as psychiatric treatment. In any case, what he forgets to highlight is the measures, he says, "involves a *denunciatory pronouncement*" (minimally). As we have said before, all noble men of non-violent punishment needs a course of "denunciation" and "conviction" before actual confinements and amoral courses for the renovation of character. These courses are in essence derogatory or negative to the offender's wishes (not will). There is no way to forget that in any form of punishment, one aspect is to negate certain undue or unrightful advantages to a person. Hence, we will stick to our explanation of "punishment" as a pro-con well-deliberated act of authorities competent to do legal justice in society, an act that is rightful causing much reprieve to the society. We will, go by the idea that punishments need not be merely an act of "harm" or "evil" because it all depends on the *objectives* of "punishment".

While we consider the "objectives" of punishment, we generally confuse certain well-intended ends or *goals* of punishment with the *means or methods* of punishing. No doubt, we should always have a clear objective or end in mind while punishing offenders and then deliberate on the permissible and most effective methods or means in reaching the desired (and desirable) end. In this sense, there is no way to equate the means with the end, but we tend to do the impossible when we argue that the ends of punishment are reformative, retributive, or deterrent, and therefore, there are three types of punishment. The truth is that punishment does not aim at any of these things; in fact, it aims at expressing *our disapproval* of certain acts through the legal system and thus their representatives. In this sense, punishments do not try to reform an offender or banish them from undesirable exemplary harm or prevent them from undesirable acts. Punishments are thus well thought-out measures taken by those on whom *we* rely to dissent and denounce certain actions, which *we* did not consent to be desirable, just and rightful. In this course of our dissent through a system, it becomes imperative to take concrete steps or obtain concrete methods to express on ground realities our said denouncements, and only then authorities need to do this or that. At times the authorities deem it necessary to deter or reform or retribute or to combine two courses, that is, to deter and to reform and so on. Hence, punishments are basically (as we said), *our* conscientious *dissents* and *denouncements* of criminal acts expressed through a system and its representatives, showing its basic "con" or "negative" aspect. At the same time, we want posterior justice which is positively constructive or "pro" aspect of punishment. In any case, we need not target the criminal as such to finish him off because whosoever does unjust things stands ground to be punished after a just trial under rules of law. Punishments are deterrent, reformatory, retributive, character transformation, man-making or educative, and so on. This is aptly expressed by a noted legal expert and scholar Fali S. Nariman in these words (in *The Statesman*, Calcutta edition): "It is a mistake to consider the object of punishment to be deterrent, reformative or preventive... but it is the denunciation by the community of a crime the judge or magistrate represents the conscience and good sense of society. Some crimes are so outrageous that it is said that society insists on adequate punishment because the wrongdoers deserve it. The idea that we may punish offenders not to prevent harm or suffering but simply as a means of expressing our condemnation is uncomfortably close to human sacrifice as an expression of righteousness. Hence, the need in any scientific system which turns the focus at the sentencing stage not only the crime but the criminal and personalises the punishment so that the reformatory component is as much operative as the deterrent component."[4] It has to be remembered that rules of law needed for criminal justice are not framed at the will of the judiciary but in consensus of the legislative representing the masses who are nevertheless well informed about the pros and cons of the system of law. Further, our expression of denunciation at the stage of sentencing becomes personalised in forms of fines, incarceration, death and so on. However, here the moot point is we can still debate on ethical lines why the said objective or justification, which is largely legal, is ethically desirable or good. We can ask, why at all the expression of denunciation of a crime be called right, good and just? That people agree on certain points cannot be sacred forever, and for that matter, laws framed show under circumstantial relativism, ethical gappiness. This is why we go on putting rules of law under scrutiny of pragmatics and ethics even if at some points they are broadly taken as legally justified. Hence, even if punishments under law are legal matters needing legal justifications, they cannot be mute and blind to pressures of non-legal justification or ethical justification. In any case, when we talk on the legal and the ethical validity of forms or types of punishments such as the deterrent etc. we should not confuse it with talks regarding the object of punishment but take it as a talk about the means of punishing the criminal for a definite objective though we can go on debating about the ethical justification of both the said objective and the means. For example, legally speaking, capital punishment is justified when the crime is "outrageous" or gruesome against humanity and society, but as we say now, whether the said justification is ethically well accepted is another issue not to be overlooked.

Without going into the finer points of nature of the different types of punishment and their relative merits and demerits we now come to discuss why at all capital punishment has caused our ethical attention. Throughout the discussion of crime and punishment, we have been maintaining the unambiguous position that issues are not merely legal in nature, they raise many ethical questions, most importantly, why should these legal issues be discussed under ethical light? Why should types of punishment be discussed under the ethical light? Why at all is capital punishment legally desirable if it is or is not ethically desirable? The question of ethical values, those of ethical rightness, justice, and good and so on are extremely important and unavoidable is our conclusion thus far. It is in this sense that "capital punishment" as doing criminal justice demanded by the public denouncement of a crime becomes a *value-laden* legal problem or ethico-legal problem. Next point is whether the problem is of great concern in India. If it is not of much concern, we might give more importance to other value problems. For instance, cyber-crimes of late have become great problems for us in India but the ethical questions therein may not be so instigating at this time for the Indian legislature, judiciary and the public. What is the reason for such comparative importance? The main reason is that certain value-laden practical problems in India demand more attention given a particular time and social, political and economic tensions. Capital punishment has grown in such importance for ethical inquiry because we are living in India in an era of quantum growth in outrageous acts of criminality amounting to loss of human life taken in a well-planned or cold-blooded manner owing to a number of factors. We are also in an era of smart executive and judicial activism under public pressure causing more arrests and convictions of gruesome crimes by ordinary criminals to extraordinary criminals enjoying power, post, position, money and so on, who would otherwise avoid any conviction erstwhile. We feel today that there are some public and organisational activism that keeps the three organs of government on toes due to the scrutiny on the functioning and flaws. For instance, all of a sudden with the conviction of Dhananjay in Hetal Parekh case and subsequent death sentence, we started talking about the ethical validity of death sentence of someone who has suffered long under the bars during long years of conviction and trial and that the person belongs to an extremely poor class, whose family would be under great tragedy if he got death penalty. There was renewed debate over classism in awarding death penalty until *Jessica Lal case* fuelled it and then with the conviction of the powerful criminal who went scot-free, there was revision of the classism-talk. One after another case, those involving powerful politicians, terrorists and minorities who were tried and convicted to death stirred the common people and experts alike to find out whether death penalty was ethically viable even if it was legally desired. Even the judges and the president of India came out publicly on their moral opinions and wanted a public debate *de novo*. Well, this is nothing new because repeatedly in India there has been some reservations against the death penalty. Instead of the details of ethical arguments in favour and disfavour of death penalty in general, let us first find out where we stand in India with regard to this issue. It is believed that death sentence has been in the Indian Penal Code since a long time (Section 53 of 1860) but always with a gamut of alternatives which were given more value in the Amendment Bills of 1972 and 1978 because death sentence was greatly restricted though not abolished in what Supreme Court observes is deemed in the "rarest of the rare cases". However, it has always been a decisive test for the Indian judiciary to identify such "rarest of the rare cases", and thus the debate of ethics of the justice done has ever lived. There are proofs for the long debate. Perhaps one of the most noted anti-death penalty row was staged in the public forum in 1931 when the debate heated the Delhi legislative assembly. Further, in 1956, Mr. Mukund Lal Agarwal moved a Bill on the validity of death penalty in the parliament, which witnessed more sessions on the matter in 1958 and 1961. The result of constant debates might have influenced the Supreme Court of India in 1980 to note that only in "rarest of the rare cases" death penalty is needed. With this the identification of the said case came to the fore, it was researched and found that in majority of the cases of extreme cruelty to life and dignity of individuals, the convicted and sentenced were poor and underpowered whereas in cruelty of equal proposition, the powerful and rich were acquitted of crime though that was evidently clear. This is then the prime point in the heated moral debate reflecting the value-laden character of the issue. Clearly asked, why is capital punishment ethically desirable if it amounts to awarding extreme penalty to a class of people even if they are found guilty of a rare type of crime, whereas other classes remain free of the same type of crime? In an excellent feature in *The Sunday Statesman* of 3 May, 1998, Somenath Mukhopadhyay asserts that though Law Commission or any other body in India have done least research about the social, economic and other empowerment status of the convicted for death penalty, it has been researched and reported by Dr. U. Jadhav in his work *Is Capital Punishment*

Necessary? (1979) that out of 30 accused and convicted for murder in Maharashtra, 70 per cent of them earn a paltry Rs. 100 per month, only 3 per cent attended school, 22 per cent passed the fourth standard and 23 per cent reached the senior secondary classes. It is accused that most people in India, who perhaps could not fight their case well or just gave up the case even if in some cases there were ample doubts in conviction, were people belonging to poor or not so well off class. Something like this happened when one Kishorilal was given death sentence for 1984 riot though instigating politicians were not convicted. There are citations of cases of powerful men, the politicians in the main, who in connivance with those in power, went scot-free in cases of crime amounting to the rare type. As such, the author remarks, "the privileged middle class, the movers and shapers of the Government and other institutions have hardly been affected. Except for one or two stray cases... Krishna Iyer's plea for an ethical re-examination of the death sentence or when pardon was sought for a suave killer who was an employee of the Merchant Navy in the *Nanavati case*, in almost every incident judgement was tailored to suit the demands of the ruling middle class."[4] The author then corroborates his view based on what Rajeev Dhavan (a Supreme Court lawyer) has observed in an article in *The Hindu* to conclude that the ruling and powerful class never cares for an intersubjective agreement on death penalty because the said provision under law is "their" or it is "them" who have enforced this law for them. The "us" is terribly absent in the whole affair because many among "us" might point this unfriendly truth that capital punishment is a test of the ruling class against underpowered guilty class who threat our lives and thus essentially partisan or divisive and *unethical*. Hence, the ethical charge against a class-oriented award of capital punishment is that it is bereft of *social interests*. The punishment really divides the society from within and fails to do the expected, that is, either to deter or to prevent and reform the criminals. This is clear from several instances of crimes of rare types, which went either unpunished or severely punished depending on social status. All these raise important ethicality questions of vengeance than deterrence or any other strategy in punishing a person until death. Moreover, it raises doubts over the coming of an ambiguous "rarest of the rare" phrase, easily falling prey to the linguistic manipulations and interpretations of the empowered middle class for their good. This middle class egoistic legal chauvinism allows ambiguity than legal clarity in cases of extreme punishment, which is charged for its basic unethicality. Strangely, in the midst of all this, the empowered have forgotten one of their legal obligations to abide by the Article 14 laid in the Constitution of Indiastating "equality before the law or the equal protection of the laws". The myopic vision of Constitution's fundamental rights by competent authorities cannot be a lesser crime and thus cannot be less than unethicality.

If the Constitution of India has to be relied, "right to life along with basic human dignity" is of utmost importance. It is not that while the Constitution was adopted the concept of death penalty was absent, but we found more value in strengthening the human life and dignity. Hence, anything that went against them were met with appropriate justice, knowing fully well that even the same human life could be taken in extreme cases of criminal acts. The glaring problem is, why at all life be taken if life was so valuable? In many countries as in India, death penalty was seen of value for its *deterrent effect* on the criminals. This is then the other key point of attack by those opposing death penalty as unethical. Though there are dearth of researches in this field in India, many criminologists believe that if a case is well attended by the public, particularly if the accused has been convicted for death penalty, only then there is a noticeable though minor slump in crime rates such as rate of homicides. However, there is again a steady increment in the rate of homicide and rape followed by murder because the public's and the criminal's memory are short lived and in particular, criminal's habits are incorrigible. It is interesting to research on the matter of fall and rise of homicidal cases in West Bengal and India after a lot of media hullabaloo and public attention in the Dhananjay's execution for rape and murder. One argument for ethical undesirability of capital punishment for deterrence is that least to be deterred, the die-hard or habitual criminals often live on crime and never have a chance to reform not particularly, if they are caught, convicted and executed because at the end, chances of deterring him or reforming him has ended with the death of the criminal. Whereas, there are some chances of prevention and reformation (even deterrence) when such criminals are put in jails for life (at least 14 years) under rigorous labour, counselling, psychological treatment, alternative therapies for mental health, education and courses in socialisation and decriminalisation. Therefore, death penalty goes against the chances of a revival of human values and socialisation whereas, life imprisonment gives chances for such a revival, and thus ethically desirable than killing. To be precise, murder cannot be cured by the like act. It *should* not be cured by a like act for it is anti-human and anti-socialisation of derailed humans. Thus, unethicality of death penalty lies in the intended "vengeance" and "violence" inherent in it. The point must have been noted by the United Nation's Commission on Human Rights, which voted strongly in disfavour of death penalty and called for a global debate on abolition of death penalty. Mr. Sam Rajappa observes, "Though India is a signatory to the declaration of human rights, it is dragging its feet on the issue."[5] Mr. Rajappa observes that though a number of countries have completely abolished death penalty and in India many persons of esteem favour a debate (ethical inclusive, as I believe)*, to abolish death penalty for all practical purposes, it has not been in favour here until date. He cites in this regard the staunch abolitionists Dr. Radhakrishnan, Mr. E.M.S. Nambudiripad, Justice Krishna Iyer and Chandra Babu Naidu. He argues that apart from the constitutional duty of the authorities to respect human life and dignity, it is the duty of the state (as laid in Article 51A) to be compassionate and humane to subjects. He further cites a number of disputed cases and judgements to show that it is extremely difficult to assert the so-called "rarest of the rare" cases to punish until death. Hence, complete abolition could be the best pragmatic and ethical course of action in this regard.

Not long back (in 2003 precisely), the Law Commission of India, which is accused of not doing the most needful studies on issues like capital punishment suddenly jumped the track to initiate a debate on "the most humane way of carrying out death sentence". Now this must be in the wake of some important sentences for death for rarest kinds of crime though the brutality in hanging unto death remaining unconcealed. Mr. Rajappa reports a jail warden's experience as this: "The day before an execution, the prisoner is weighed, measured for length of drop to ensure breaking of the neck, the size of the neck and other body measurements. When the drop springs, he dangles at the end of the rope. There are times when the neck has not been broken and the prisoner is strangled to death. His eyes pop almost out of his head, his tongue swells and protrudes and the rope often takes large portions of skin and flesh from the side of the face. He urinates, he defecates and dropping fall to the floor while witness look on."[6] This must have disturbed those in the legal system to be a little "humane".

---

* My inclusion.

To be "humane" is to have minimal respect for human life, dignity, values and of course ethical analysis of decisions and actions. Taken together, the Commission must have in mind the most "painless" ways, avoiding external damages which are perceivably agonising to the observers and family members to finish off life albeit effectively. The other thing in mind must be the least possibility of asphyxiation and follow-up brutal acts in case breaking neck has not been successful. Hence, "painlessness" and "effectiveness" are the two issues standing for us in death penalty though the said Commission never cares intersubjective agreement on abolishing the penalty when India is a signatory to ending brutalisation of punishment. We remember that few days before Dhananjay's hanging, there were graphic details in the print media about ways of death penalty, which are in use or may be used most "humanely". Is it poisoning, electrocution, or any other? The ethical debate starts exactly at this point. It is argued by the abolitionists that there is nothing "humane" in awarding a death penalty, and for that matter, there is no humane way to carry on that penalty. How can "effectiveness" and "painfulness" as well as "public's non-agonizing observance of the act" be the factors for evaluating "humaneness"? Do the definition of right to life and dignity state how can we be "humane"? Can it be more than crocodile's tear in killing? If killing for justice is itself well debated for ethical validity, how can methods of killing be a valid question at all? It may be a spurious or fictitious question. Or, better said, it is a false question that *asserts* that as death penalty is valid, there are best ways to do so, which we are in search of. It is the same unethical question asking, what is the most effective way of revenge on a criminal so that the authority does not have least burdens of failure, moral guilt, shame and above all, the egoistic designs to bear with alien pain that do not rock from within? This is the fall out of the *fear* of failure in executing the moral guilt that I am a party to homicidal act in which the system has unarmed the opponent and the *shame* that I am a killer of the helpless. However, all this is nicely covered by the false *sympathy* for the killed because (as Hobbes said about 'sympathy'), sympathisers fear "if they were in the other side". Hence, false sympathy or simply antipathy, favouring the act of punishment to be inhuman and thus the point of humaneness is useless. The truth is that sanctioning death sentence is unethical as it is indirect criminalisation of the society. The recommendations of brutality by social authorities is against social harmony and thus unethical.

Not everything said here really takes credit out of death penalty because we have still not weighed the logical strengths and weaknesses of pro-capital punishment. We have thus far seen that death penalty is accused of failing to achieve any of its touted objectives, the deterrent objective in the main along with prevention of crime and in many case reformation of criminal attitudes. But we have seen that it will be completely out of point to say that capital punishment aims at deterring in the main and other things as well because such punishment rests on an ethical conception of end or objective, namely, striving to do appropriate legal justice to weed out injustice and unjust acts of individuals thus doing a lot of social good or social well-being. In addition, no one can contest the goodness inherent in the encouragement of social well-being through meeting injustice and unjust acts. It is said that the value of punishment (which is a legal decision followed by appropriate steps) as intended by authorities depends not on what are the emotive factors influencing the authorities or their preferences or whims or gains; hence, they do not try to avenge death or express rage and hate or become psychopaths or petty hedonists. The authorities try to abide by the given rules of law, which are consensual public rulings against gruesome crimes, and thus they remain *neutral* to or aloof from all extraneous considerations or extra-legal or non-legal considerations, though they are not blind to the basic ethicality of this essential "neutrality". To borrow from Rawls, the legal authorities strive for legal justice by means of death penalty with a pure ethical intention to do social justice free from personal emotions, gains, and so on. It is much like punishing the evil by God for universal justice whenever humanity is endangered and goodness is at stake. The punishment meted out by the Omnipotent to weed off evil elements is thus not "murder" (as we call it in our *śāstras*, *hatyā*), but it is justice done in weeding off evil (or in our *śāstras*, *vadha*). Hence, the Lord in the Gītā did not counsel Arjun to commit mass murder but urged for a "just punishment", the call of the hour for restoration of good and right. If our intention is pure, that is, what we decide and plan keeping in mind the nobler in it even if that is "killing", it is not unethical. It is exactly in this sense that a judge does not order for a homicide by ordering death penalty. It is not order for "*hatyā*" rather an order based on sufficient evidences of crime for the "*vadha*" of the criminal. The ethicality lies in this purity of intention that is good intention. Nevertheless, how can death penalty, be called "good" as means? How can "*vadha*" be good if it is a negative act of killing? The pro-people argue is that for the achievement of a greater good, allowing but not weeding off an injurious life cannot be any nobler. Hence, a rabid dog or an aggressive poisonous snake dangerous for society has to be killed: Even Gandhi was not in the side of allowing such dangerous life on earth. If we truly have love for humans and human values and society, agents who have turned out to be advanced psychopaths, killers and extremely aggressive for society, peace and love, they need to be "killed" where all such killings are not "murders". Truly, by any logic, not all killings are murders.

Another pro-argument is that unless we have the right wisdom to place ourselves in the place of a victim or his near and dear ones, it is very easy theoretically to argue in disfavour of capital punishment. Those who have never been affected by wanton injustice and gruesome murder of close ones, cannot realise what it is to be befitting in justice if the criminal is beyond doubt a wrongdoer. It is very easy for us to feel the dread of death given the real pictures of a person put to the gallows and have some shame and guilt. It is equally important to have feeling of the dread of death and agony when an innocent girl has been tortured, raped and murdered. The ethics in befitting justice is not equality in revenge but letting the criminals realise what it were to torture, agonise and put to death. During this, he will never reform but prospective criminals have a chance to realise the dread of death attached to gruesome crimes. We can only judge the value of death penalty in extreme cases of criminal acts when we have the human heart to empathise with the victim in pain and agony and not when we shower theoretical wisdom. In a famous parable Sri Ramakrishna Paramhansa said that no one really takes any disvalue in a snake to act habitually to hiss if not bite unnecessarily. No one really takes off any credit from deterrence shown in rare cases of gruesome killings of the innocent and unarmed even if that amounts to punishing unto death because that may be truly a legal way to empower the innocent who are likely to be victimised by criminals. The value of deterrence lies in the indirect empowerment of the underpowered by social authorities. It is thus good for human modesty, dignity, self-esteem and self-defence.

Further, the pro-argument considers the economy of life imprisonment *vis-à-vis* death penalty when cases of extreme forms of crimes against humanity or national integrity are under consideration. The point is how can it be economically wise to put die-hard criminals in prison for life than not awarding them death penalty? Can we really be so ethical in bankrupting the exchequer by feeding those who were against life, dignity and national integrity? Is it not the unethical way to encourage crime by withstanding the criminals for a long time at our own cost? How can we be so noble in sponsoring our own enemies? If we hope to be noble by giving them a chance to reform their character at our cost, it is nothing but betraying many of our own economically downtrodden and unwell people as well as the taxpayers whose hard-earned money goes in vain. Is it in anyway ethical to be so unwise practically to take great risks within the prison climate to feed dangerous and habitual criminals who can spread any nuisance among others just for the sake of our touted ideal of reformation? With the already overflowing jails in India, can it be wiser and ethical to tax ourselves to bear with inhuman people? The answers to each of these questions should be in the negative because reforming inhuman to human is not only ethically undesirable as it corrodes our economy and the jail climate, it is undesirable as the ideal itself is living in a fool's paradise because "reformism" is another name of slow but sure torture physically, mentally and spiritually of the convicted to life and thus for the rest of the life. It may be said that the unethicality of "reformism" through life imprisonment, which may be equally conceived of as deterrent and retributive, is nothing but "sadistic" acts of otherwise pretending holy men. A person is put to jail for life, thus finishing prospects of life in freedom with the unusual hope that one day a reformed person will walk out with a fresh lease of life. In reality, we sadistically finish life gradually but surely and the worse person is worst. The terrible thing in imprisoning is that it is a serious ethical offence because we intend to do something what we do not reveal but pretend to be so good. Living a dual character of evil and good is not ethical either. The better course is not to pretend in weeding off undesirable elements from society to establish nobility and good.

Thus far, we have been following a course of arguments that flow from the typical Indians in favour and disfavour of capital punishment. Before our readers are instigated to take the challenge on their own, let us now try to be a little more academically argumentative though some of them have already appeared in other words. However, we will now try to be brief and avoid repetitions. In an excellent paper, *In Defense of the Death Penalty* (1978), Earnest Van Den Haag enlists the "popular arguments" against death penalty:

(a) The one we have seen before is the unethicality charge of barbarisation in awarding death penalty because the penalty is nothing but 'legalised murder'. The counter argument of Haag is that if this be so, penalising by imposing fine would be equivalent to legalised extortion of money, which is not the case because in some cases the resemblance of crime and punishment awarded is merely physical than legal. Hence, murder and death penalty are not equal even if they are physically similar, the real difference lies in the moral intention (as we have mentioned)*, and the legal intention (that Haag asserts and we mentioned it as well)*. However, Haag denounces public display of execution as unethical because that may be cruel and also illegal for being derogatory to human psyche than deterrent.

(b) What are crimes called rarest of the rare type or intolerably inhuman and gruesome are often not well intended or planned rather at the heat of the moment, passionate irrational acts demanding sympathy. Hence, the real blame is psychic and not ethical demanding legal protection for criminal's life than taking it. Haag argues that crime as such is not committed with a deliberation or at the heat of the moment by rational beings because only irrationality allows crimes in any condition. Further, the deterrent effect on rational beings and those who can fall prey to irrationality at the heat of moments are undeniable. Death penalties for this pragmatic value, which is also for the general good of the population, is said to be ethical. Being passionate and irrational does not call for its abolition. Again, there is no point in public execution for the deterrent effect because in any case execution's effect bears on some not all because some people are ever undesirable and it is still valuable for it *reduces* crime than tries to eliminate it.

(c) Another popular argument against death penalty by the abolitionists is that it is done with motive of "revenge" (we have seen this and countered it)*. Haag quotes interestingly from Bible (Romans 12:19 and Numbers 35:16-18) to show that even vengeance in eliminating the evil is Divine (For us it was *vadha* of Ravana by Rama or Pandavas eliminating

* My inclusion.

Kauravas and so on). Haag does not hesitate in agreeing that death penalty does involve an element of vengeance but he points out that the act is human (not Divine) and still ethically good as it does a lot of social good or it is legalised way towards 'social solidarity' (*sic*). Further, it is ethically permissible because it is not the motive but the intention behind an act of punishment that needs to be evaluated for worth. It is completely out of way to cure bad motives in death penalty because it has been confused with ethically charged legal intentions to do many social good that justifies the act.

(d) We have seen that equality of humans in terms of enjoyment of rights assured in respective constitution of one's country is an ethical idea, any act therefore, that bereft such enjoyment is ethically repugnant. One among this basic right is to live unharmed in natural existence, and a so-called legal act that takes one's right to live for any crime whatsoever must be ethically repugnant. To this Haag argues that by parity of reasoning both murderers of innocent and the victims have right to live in dignity and freedom. If this is true then for the respect of an undignified life the murderer should, nevertheless, be respected and not killed by legal provisions, which is unacceptable ethically as that amounts to respect for lives both lived in dignity and indignity. The latter life should be thus looked down. Now comparing other lives lived in indignity such as theft and swindling they should be ethically equally cursed. But the lives of indignity of a murderer of the innocent and that of a thief and swindler demands punishments though not equally because common sense of justice for criminal acts tells us that being qualitatively different, the crimes demand qualitatively different punishments. Hence, for theft, a petty crime not amounting to lives of innocents, death penalty is ethically repugnant but the same penalty is appropriate in case of murder. This focuses the weakness in the call for an egalitarian view to treat life equally valuable and thus arrange for equal punishments irrespective of nature, extent and intensity of the crime. No one really takes the argument that Harshad Mehta and Dhananjay should have been both awarded capital punishment even if Mehta is powerful in many ways, whereas

> Dhananjay is poor, and that Mehta's swindling is no less gruesome than that of Dhananjay (but surely not the same as raping, torturing and killing an innocent girl child). Thus, even if life is valuable as such, lives lived may be both extremely unethical and ethical, and we capitally punish the unethical ways of lives of criminals. In doing so, we remain egalitarian in justice. Most utilitarian would argue this way because in the end it is the production of maximum good over evil in society through legal justice that counts most.

Haag then reminds us that awarding capital punishment is not merely based on an ethical conception of "equality" because it cannot overlook the conception of legal "justice". It is important to note that capital punishment does more or less appropriate justice and is injustice only if in the name of "equality" it puts justice at stake. Hence, abolishing death penalty is to encourage "misdistribution" of legal justice, which in turn is ethically unjust as well. Haag thinks that as all arts (as Plato says) are capacity for opposites, doctors, sportsmen are all likely to fail in many cases and thus some way or other there are "miscarriages of justice" (*sic*). However, if that is not intended or deliberate on the part of the professionals, it is not unethical either. In the same way, though criminal justice depends largely on evidences and other delicate factors for judgement by an expert professional judge, there are injustices even when death penalty is awarded. However, in no case, the erratic judgement being deliberate can be called unethical. Moreover, not one court but other courts deliberate on the pros and cons of the judgement passed minimizing errors until the whole system is rotten, vindictive and whimsical. Haag concludes stating: "To refuse to punish any crime with death, then, is to avow that the negative weight of a crime can never exceed the positive value of the life of the person who committed it. I find that proposition unpalusible."[7]

Taking a cue from this inherent possibility of error in awarding a death penalty because no person or system is fool-proof rather they may be equally cunning in deliberations, it has been argued by most experts, including ethicists that though in "rarest of the rare cases" death penalty must be reserved and awarded only after thorough unbiased judgement of facts and evidences, it should be by far avoided in any legal system that does not fall in the trap of being cursed "arbitrary" and unjust to distribute what is rightful or due to someone.

This must be then the key in understanding why in India there is great hesitation in agreeing to either abolitionists or pro-death penalty proponents. When we say that there is hesitation in agreeing with the pro-proponents, we mean thereby those "qualified" supporters of the penalty who deem it necessary only in rare cases which have been justified beyond doubt to be cases of cold blooded murder of the helpless and the innocent involving torture, agony, and inhuman and undignified acts. This position has been nicely explained by Stephen Nathanson (1978) in his paper: "An Eye for an Eye: The Morality of Punishing by Death", Nathanson argues that as both assertions that (a) people who commit murder do not deserve to die and (b) even if people who cannot murder deserve to die, it is pertinent to say that the "argument from desert" stating "rightfully due to the wrongdoer" is not appropriate. Therefore, "an eye for an eye" is not good enough, ethically speaking. He reasons that it is not *always* the case that people committing homicide "deserve" to die because not all homicidal acts call for extreme deterrent punishment, they should be reprieved for other punishments, which may be equally effective. Moreover, in such cases, it is clear that death penalty would be an unethical "brutalising" law. Hence, even if what is due to a criminal we need not be brutal in justice because that is a brutal avoidance of possibilities of other options to do justice. This is followed by the argument that the government organ (the judiciary) is obliged to weigh value of the general and basic governmental duty to protect the lives of people and distributing justice at the cost of taking lives. It is basic and ethical to protect lives than taking lives even if it is due to some. Such weighing enables us to see that the state is on the wrong side when it executes death penalty rather than focus on protecting the innocent live. Again in some peculiar criminal cases the legal system in totality (in India we may call it a failure of justice from the lower to the apex court), fails miserably to justify an act of homicide by a criminal, which is well thought-out, with malice and rarest of rare violence on innocent. Famously, in the 'lack of crucial and enough evidences' the whole system acquits a criminal, and then he accepts the crime off the record. Though extreme punishment is due, can he be legally punished after the acquittal? In such cases then what were due could not be awarded. Then it is ethically just to concentrate more on effective protection of citizens from criminals than run after capital punishment. Hence, death penalty brings forth an ethical dilemma in government obligations, in which unethicality lies in concealing basic obligations and highlighting the secondary ones.

To show that even if what were due to an actor of homicide, he should not be awarded with death, Nathanson argues against Haag's argument that though at times justice is 'arbitrary' in cases of homicide, and thus erroneous and unequal, it is still not appropriate for the system to award extreme punishment. In the midst of the argument, thinks Nathanson, Haag forgets that though in individual cases some *impositions* are arbitrary; it is not the same as *judgements* being arbitrary. Hence, we have to keep in mind the difference between "arbitrary judgements" and "arbitrary impositions". If we do not keep this in mind, we tend to say that though someone has been wrongly imposed of homicide, still one who commits homicide deserves to die. The problem is one that really "deserve" to die is itself "arbitrarily judged" (a case of homicide) because he himself says that there is always a possibility of "arbitrary imposition" in such judgements. Then without being obstinate in saying that the deserving one's need to die, one should better attend to the problem of *judging* who deserves to die. If this is problematic, probabilistic, erroneous and unjust at many cases, it is ethically improper to attend to such issues and concentrate on our general and basic obligations in justice.

Therefore, we have to either agree to what some people as if Charles Black says that the system is essentially arbitrary in judgements of crime because it skimps the essential and unavoidable complexities and subjectivism. Alternatively, we have to say as Haag, that the system is arbitrary in judgement in many cases, but "so what", we need to award that because justice requires death at times (as if that was a fixed dogma). Alternatively, as we think that despite complexities and threats of subjective determinations, the system overall is *not* arbitrary. For this we need to be thorough, scientific and threadbare in our analysis of *facts* than maxims which have become dogmas, and only through the better revelation of truth can there be proper determination of which cases (rare) demands capital punishment because that is true to the legal science itself and not against or beyond it, and thus ethical. All said and done, capital punishment has in the main to deal with the problem of "arbitrariness" to face the ethical challenge that after all what are our standard of rightful judgements?

Having said this we come to the end of showing our readers that people's ethics needs some care at least because legal ethics is not all theoretical jugglery, intersubjective discourse involves display of moral reasons in and with the public, though it is not to forget important expert analysis of the issues. I have said that in this work I will refrain from the discussion that was arranged by me regarding resolution of this issue. Nevertheless, for our interested readers, here is the Questionnaire, which may be used for a debate.

QUESTIONNAIRE

1. What in your opinion is the value of a human being? What rights should the human beings enjoy? Should they enjoy the right to take someone's life or should they enjoy the right to pass necessary legal orders to end someone's life?
2. What in your opinion should be the aim and objective of the judiciary while it is responsible in either framing or upholding and acting in accordance with some such laws which may be as extreme as ending one's life?
3. What in your opinion is the status of an individual *vis-à-vis* society and circumstances when he or she commits homicide?
4. Should killing as an act be sometimes glorified and sometimes punished? Give reasons.
5. In what ways is capital punishment humane as well as ethically justifiable?
6. What would you suggest with regard to the existing law providing capital punishment?

The participants in the discussion were:

1. Mr. L.P.N. Shahdeo, Retd. Judge, Patna High Court (Ranchi Bench), Ranchi.
2. Mr. D.C. Sinha, Retd. IPS, Advocate, Patna High Court (Ranchi Bench), Ranchi.
3. Mr. V.K. Verma, Research Officer, Bihar Tribal Welfare Research Institute, Ranchi.
4. Mr. M.M. Banerjee, Advocate, Patna High Court (Ranchi Bench), Ranchi.

With some welcome risk of repetition, I would like to end this book and thus the Series on Practical and Professional Ethics with the remark that legal ethics or any other application of ethics in fields beyond it demand intersubjective corroboration. There is no application of ethics without ethical discourses and resolution by virtue of *public participation*, and there is no application of ethics without *theoretical analysis* of a problem in consideration, value-related questions that the problem gives rise to and a post-corroboration analysis of the normative dynamics and related logic of norms, their relations and pros and cons. In this sense, the Series reveals in at least five different ways in which the public having occupations and professions might be actively engaged in reflecting and resolving practical issue of ethical concern. With this was revealed the social-scientific vocation that is needed in application of ethics that is in some ways empirically grounded. It also reveals a return to philosophical critique of ethical theories. Most importantly, we have seen in this volume in particular that application of ethics is a complete value-free affair if everything is said and done passionately, not pragmatically, that is, not with an idea what lies beyond the esoteric groups of thinking people because without involving the masses, the debates and findings have no pressure on the organs of government. This is tragic because in a democracy of some experience and maturity we expect of Indian government to be careful about what ordinary to extraordinary people have thrashed in communion about what courses of decisions and actions taken by the legislature, executive and judiciary are ethically desirable, right and just. It is not always true that in democracies those in power are the most appropriate representatives of what a large chunk of population thinks is desirable. Hence, an avoidance of chauvinism at the levels of the planning, deciding and functioning of the different organs of the government is extremely important. To do this, there must be some nodal agencies in our society who work in a declassed, fearless and selfless way to care for the value problems and their resolutions involving a large number of our professionals. I have some reservations to appreciate the idea of having an ethics committee headed by a member of parliament or having such committees in our state legislature because more often than not, such committees are "cosmetic" or "decorative" working in the shadows of what power brokers decide are "ethical". More often than not, people living in false esteem, pride, prejudice, malice and fear do not have the guts to face the ordinary people for their moral opinion. People's ethics is never possible when people living in glasshouses or in comfort zones that are palpable to outer dangers imagine that what "intellectual" or "power trackers" decide on ethical matters and thus on practical matters must be final. There is nothing sacred and absolute in a democratic decision making that is value-oriented. It is due to this that debates and resolutions through intersubjective corroboration are not sacred and final. One who has read carefully the debates in all the volumes of the Series comes to know the basic underlying relativity in the methodology I have followed. It is due to this that I have left so many things for interested parties to decide and do for themselves. Starting from analysis of problems to arranging a debate, reaching a closure and analysis of normative dynamics, everything demands constant scrutiny, and the more we spread them and change them, the more information we get. With this, the doors of knowledge and pragmatics of application of our ethical experience are wide open. With this, we come to realise that governmental decisions and actions are not matters for easy go merry. We realise that unless rules of law are value oriented, their implementations and safeguard are value-charged, and of course, if people involved in these obligatory functions are not careful about value questions and public opinion about such questions, there is complete lacklustre governance. It has to fail in the end because gradually public disagreements would give way to rage and ravage. It is not difficult to assume why in democratic India there are so many non-violent public protests and armed rebellions. The responsibility has to be taken by boastful and mindless government chauvinists who care least for value crises and their public resolutions. Ethicists and philosophers taking interest in other branches of philosophy should participate in the societies in resolving value crises. No one has really stopped them to do their bit when social crises are looming large. There is no point in crying foul that "in the name of philosophy" public work cannot be done because "in the name of philosophical ethics, for instance, we have seen a lot of sensible things should be done" of which the justificatory chapters of the six volumes of this Series were sufficient evidences. Equally true is that philosophers should not suddenly get interested in people's ethics because "it pays". I have not invented another successful job for the philosopher friends by virtue of a division of labour because it was always right below our nose, which we forgot in the flurry of a long trend of theoreticism but no application. The wise men of east and west always reminded us though that philosophy and ethics are good to read and apply in life. They always reminded us of a lurking threat which should be reminded finally—"Philosophers need not pat their backs in the enthusiasm of the idea that they have the tasks of making a whole nation ethical, that they should teach values and virtues". Ethicist should be careful of the danger that they should apply ethics and ethical techniques of application to build great characters. The whole course on practical and professional ethics, therefore, does not aim at making us great people. However, if some of us become value-charged in social life after going through what has been written, the credit does not go to me because it is the person who has applied what he has learnt; he is in reality a person of great practical wisdom who knew that knowing certain things and being informed vastly is not the same as being educated.

Notes

1. Hart, H.L.A., "Positivism, Law and Morals", *Essays in Jurisprudence and Philosophy*, Clarendon Press, Oxford, 1983, p. 50.
2. Tahtinen, Unto, *Non-Violent Theories of Punishment: Indian and Western*, Motilal Banarasidass, New Delhi, 1983, p. 61.
3. Nariman, S. Fali, "Crime and Punishment—1: Deterrence or Reform" in *The Statesman*, Calcutta edition.
4. Mukhopadhyay, Somenath, "For Whom the Bells Toll", *The Sunday Statesman*, Calcutta edition, 3-5-1998.
5. Rajappa, Sam, "Right to Life", *The Sunday Statesman*, Calcutta edition.
6. *Ibid.*
7. Haag, Ernest Van Den, "In Defense of Death Penalty", *Ethics: History, Theory and Contemporary Issues,* (Part II) Steven M. Cahn and Peter Markie, (ed.), OUP, Oxford, 1998, p. 847.

Appendix I

List of Participants of Intersubjective Corroboration Debates

I take this opportunity to provide the list of the professionals, who were kind enough to devote their precious time for Intersubjective Corroboration debates. This list has been prepared according to the value-laden issues considered under following headings. The list is as follows:

(I) Bonsai: An Ethical Issue in Horticulture

1. Dr. Ram Dayal Munda, Former Vice-Chancellor, Ranchi University, Ranchi.
2. Dr. B.P. Jain, Director, Deptt. of Horticulture, Birsa Agricultural University, Ranchi.
3. Dr. K.K. Nag, Vice-Chancellor, Vinoba Bhave University, Hazaribagh & Ex-Head, Deptt. of Botany, Ranchi University, Ranchi.
4. Dr. T.K. Ghosh, Professor of Taxonomy (Formerly), Ranchi University, Ranchi.
5. Dr. N. Dayal, Professor & Head, Deptt. of Botany, Ranchi University, Ranchi.
6. Dr. P. Dey, Pathologist and Bonsaist, Ranchi.
7. Mr. A. Chatterjee, Development Officer, L.I.C. and Bonsaist, Ranchi.
8. Mr. S. Chanda, Officer in the S.B.L. and Bonsaist, Ranchi.
9. Mr. S.K. Sengupta, Officer in C.C.L. and Bonsaist, Ranchi.

(II) Should we use Chemical Fertilizers, Insecticides and Pesticides in Agriculture?

1. Dr. S.K. Sarkar, Professor & Head, Deptt. of Soil Science, Birsa Agricultural University, Ranchi.
2. Dr. D. Prasad, Professor & Head, Deptt. of Entomology, Birsa Agricultural University, Ranchi.
3. Dr. B.K. Roy, Professor, Deptt. of Toxicology, Ranchi Veterinary College, Ranchi.

4. Dr. K.K. Singh, Reader, Deptt. of Pathology, Ranchi Veterinary College, Ranchi.
5. Sri D. Mahto, Farmer, Boreya Village, Kanke Block, Ranchi.
6. Dr. N. Dayal, Professor & Head, Deptt. of Botany, Ranchi University, Ranchi.

(III) Narcotic Cultivation and Morality

1. Dr. B.P. Jain, Professor & Head, Deptt. of Horticulture, Birsa Agricultural University, Ranchi.
2. Dr. M. Borde, Psychiatrist, Davis Institute of Neuro-Psychiatry, Ranchi.
3. Dr. A. Sarkar, M.D. (Medicine), Cardiologist, Ranchi.
4. Dr. B.L. Das, Controller of Drugs & Pharmaceuticals, Ranchi.
5. Mr. A. Karna, Society for Rural Industrialisation, Ranchi.
6. Dr. M. Prasad, Ex-Professor & Head, Deptt. of Botany, Ranchi University, Ranchi.

(IV) Should we harness rivers for Power Generation?

1. Sri S.K. Chand, I.A.S. (Retd.), Ranchi.
2. Sri M. Bhattacharjee, Social Activist, Ranchi.
3. Dr. I. Dey, Asstt. Director, S.R.I., Ranchi.
4. Mr. D. Prasad, S.R.I., Ranchi.
5. Dr. R. Sharan, Professor, Deptt. of Economics, Ranchi College, Ranchi.
6. Dr. S.K. Sinha, Professor & Head, Deptt. of Botany, J.N. College, Dhurwa, Ranchi.
7. Dr. N. Dayal, Professor & Head, Deptt. of Botany, Ranchi University, Ranchi.
8. Sri Sriprakash, Social Activist and Film Maker, Ranchi.
9. Miss Dayamani Barla, Social Activist, Ranchi.

(V) The Moral Basis for the Nuclear Option

1. Fr. Johnekerre, S.J., St. Albert's College, Ranchi.
2. Dr. A. Ranjan, Psychiatrist, R.I.N.P.A.S., Ranchi.
3. Dr. K.R. Banerjee, Major (Retd.), Director, R.I.N.P.A.S., Ranchi.
4. Mr. P.R. Bose, Major (Retd.), Director (Personnel), H.E.C., Ranchi.
5. Mr. R. Kumar, 'Veer Chakra', Brigadier (Retd.), Ranchi.
6. Dr. N.R. Roy, Nuclear Physicist, Professor of Physics, Ranchi University, Ranchi.

7. Sri A. Karna, S.R.I., Ranchi.

(VI) Is "logging" ethically desirable in India?

1. Dr. O.N. Pandey, Professor & Head of Forestry, Birsa Agricultural University, Ranchi.
2. Mr. P. Shiva, Reader, Deptt. of Forestry, Birsa Agricultural University, Ranchi.
3. Sri S.K. Singh, Deptt. of Environmental Engineering, M.E.C.O.N., Ranchi.
4. Sri S.S. Chaudhary, Forest Research & Conservation Officer, Ranchi.
5. Dr. S.K. Sinha, Professor & Head, Deptt. of Botany, J.N. College, Dhurwa, Ranchi.

(VII) Urbanisation and Moral Crises

1. Dr. S.D. Singh, Ex-Professor & Head, Deptt. of Political Science, Ranchi University, Ranchi.
2. Dr. N. Dayal, Professor & Head, Deptt. of Botany, Ranchi University, Ranchi.
3. Dr. D.K. Tiwari, I.A.S., Director, B.P.D.P., Ranchi.
4. Sri R. Kumar, I.A.S., Ex-D.C. & Chairman, R.I.A.D.A., Ranchi.
5. Dr. C.R. Laha, Ex-Vice Chancellor, Ranchi University, Ranchi.

(VIII) Experiments on animals and the human beings, some moral questions

1. Dr. P.N. Labh, Ex-Head, Deptt. of Anatomy, R.M.C.H., Ranchi.
2. Dr. A.K. Roy, Ex-Head, Deptt. of Ophthalmology, R.M.C.H., Ranchi.
3. Dr. R.P. Yadav, Chief Research Officer, Homoeopathy Research Centre, Govt. of India, Ranchi.
4. Dr. P. Dey, Pathologist, Ranchi.
5. Dr. M.P. Sinha, Professor, Deptt. of Zoology, Ranchi University, Ranchi.
6. Dr. U. Sahay, Professor & Head, Deptt. of Zoology, Dean, Faculty of Science, Ranchi University, Ranchi.

(IX) The Ethic of Psychotherapy

1. Dr. S.H. Nizami, Central Institute of Psychiatry, Ranchi.
2. Dr. (Mrs.) A. Nizami, "Deepsikha", Home for the Mentally Challenged Children, Ranchi.
3. Dr. A. Ranjan, R.I.N.P.A.S., Ranchi.

4. Dr. Masroor Jahan, R.I.N.P.A.S., Ranchi.
5. Mrs. Mamta Berheria, Psychotherapist, C.I.P., Ranchi.
6. Ms. Sharmila Saha, Psychotherapist, C.I.P., Ranchi.

(X) Euthanasia and moral dilemma
1. Dr. Ram Bali Sinha, Ex-Head, Surgery, R.M.C.H., Ranchi.
2. Dr. M.S. Bhatt, Professor, Deptt. of Surgery, R.M.C.H., Ranchi.
3. Dr. N. Dayal, Head, Deptt. of Botany, Ranchi University, Ranchi.
4. Dr. A. Sajjad, Head, Deptt. of Urdu, Dean of Humanities, Ranchi University, Ranchi.
5. Fr. C. De Brouwer, S.J., St. Xavier's College, Ranchi.
6. Sri P.C. Roy, Advocate, Ranchi High Court, Ranchi.
7. Dr. K.K. Sinha, Neurologist, Ranchi.

(XI) What is moral in privatizing education?
1. Dr. K.S. Iyer, Professor, N.I.I.F.T., Ranchi.
2. Dr. J. Ashraf, Ex-Professor of Management, X.I.S.S., Ranchi.
3. Fr. C. De Brouwer, S.J., Retd. Head, Deptt. of Physics, St. Xavier's College, Ranchi.
4. Dr. N. Datkeoleyar, Retd. Principal, Govt. Teachers' Training College, Ranchi.
5. Dr. Ramesh Sharan, Professor of Economics, Ranchi University, Ranchi.
6. Mr. S.K. Chatterjee, Ex-teacher, Guru Nanak School, Ranchi.
7. Dr. S.N. Prasad, Professor & Chairman, Academic Affairs, N.I.I.F.T., Ranchi.
8. Dr. Mithilesh Kanti, Ex-Principal, Netarhat Govt. School, Netarhat.

(XII) Are spiritual and religious teachings desirable in educational curriculum in India?
1. Dr. Md. Hasan Razaa, Professor of Urdu, S.S. Memorial College, Ranchi.
2. Dr. Icchapurak, Professor of Botany, Ranchi Women's College, Ranchi.
3. Fr. Johnekeere, S.J., Rector, St. Xavier's School, Ranchi.

4. Dr. Malancha Ghosh, Professor of Zoology, Ranchi Women's College, Ranchi.
5. Sri Tej Bahadur Sinha, Advocate, Ranchi.
6. Dr. K.C. Prasad, Head, Deptt. of Mathematics, Ranchi University, Ranchi.
7. Dr. K.K. Nag, Head, Deptt. of Botany, Ranchi University, Ranchi.

(XIII) Computerisation, Mechanisation and some moral questions

1. Dr. J. Ashraf, Ex-Professor of Management, X.I.S.S., Ranchi.
2. Mr. V.K. Sharma, Head, Deptt. of System Analysis, S.A.I.L., Ranchi.
3. Mr. U. Krishnamurthy, Regional Manager, Central Bank of India, Ranchi.
4. Mr. Manoj Kumar Tiwari, Director, Samadhan Group of Companies. Ranchi.
5. Dr. Ramesh Sharan, Professor of Economics, Ranchi University, Ranchi.
6. Mr. Samir Kumar Dass, Jt. Secretary, B.S.S.R. Union, Ranchi.
7. Dr. R. Badrinarayan, Ex-Head, Deptt. of Physics, Ranchi University, Ranchi.

(XIV) What is the moral basis of reservation in jobs?

1. Dr. P.C. Oraon, Director, Tribal Research and Welfare Department, Ranchi.
2. Dr. R.K. Jha, Professor of Political Science, Ranchi College, Ranchi.
3. Dr. B.K. Sinha, Lecturer in Political Science, St. Xavier's College, Ranchi.
4. Sri S.K. Chand, I.A.S. (Retd.), Ranchi.
5. Dr. A. Sajjad, Ex-Head, Deptt. of Urdu, Ranchi University, Ranchi.
6. Mr. Ratnakar Bhengra (Advocate), Convener, "Johar", Ranchi.

(XV) Some moral hunches in capital punishment

1. Dr. U.K. Verma, Sociologist, Tribal Research & Welfare Deptt., Ranchi.
2. Sri M.M. Banerjee, Advocate, High Court, Ranchi.
3. Sri D.C. Sinha, I.P.S. (Retd.), Ranchi.

4. Sri L.P.N. Shahdeo, Retd. Judge, Patna High Court, Ranchi Bench.

(XVI) Which socio-political mode of protest do you think is ethically more acceptable—fast unto death or armed resistance?

1. Sri Tridibesh Ghosh, Senior Member, C.P.I. (ML), Ranchi Unit.
2. Sri Brajesh Kumar Sharma, Commandant, III Battalion, B.M.P., Dhanbad.
3. Dr. Rajendra Prasad Chaudhary, C.P.I., Ranchi Unit.
4. Dr. Lalmani Prasad, Professor of Political Science, Marwari College, Ranchi.
5. Sri Srikrishna Pandey, Professor of Hindi, Yogada College, Ranchi.
6. Sri Amol Bhattacharjee, C.P.I. (M), Ranchi Unit.
7. Dr. K.K. Lal Karna, Head, Deptt. of Philosophy, Ranchi University, Ranchi.

Appendix II

List of Contributors in Other Capacities in the Intersubjective Corroboration Discourses

1. Dr. A. Sajjad, Professor & Head of Urdu & Dean of Humanities, Ranchi University, Ranchi.
2. Dr. B. Kumari, Professor of Philosophy, University Deptt. of Philosophy, Ranchi University, Ranchi.
3. Dr. C.R. Laha, Professor & Head of Bengali & Former Vice Chancellor, Ranchi University, Ranchi.
4. Dr. Indu Parmar, Lecturer of Philosophy, Ranchi Women's College, Ranchi.
5. Dr. K.K.L. Karna, Former Head of Philosophy & Dean of Humanities, Ranchi University, Ranchi.
6. Dr. K.K. Thakur, Reader, Marwari College, Ranchi.
7. Dr. K.M. Jha, Former Head of Philosophy & Dean of Humanities, Ranchi University, Ranchi.
8. Dr. P.V. Lakshmi, Reader of Philosophy, University Department of Philosophy, Ranchi University, Ranchi.
9. Dr. R.B. Prasad, Reader of Philosophy, University Department of Philosophy, Ranchi University, Ranchi.
10. Dr. Raghav Thakur, Reader, Birsa Agricultural University, Ranchi.
11. Dr. Raj Kumari Sinha, Professor of Philosophy, Doranda College, Ranchi.
12. Dr. Raj Rajeshwari Verma, Reader of Philosophy, Ranchi Women's College, Ranchi.
13. Mr. Rajendra Kumar Singh, Student, Department of Philosophy, Ranchi University, Ranchi.
14. Dr. S.K. Paul, Reader & Former Head of Bengali, University Department of Philosophy, Ranchi University, Ranchi.
15. Dr. S. Mishra, Professor of Philosophy, University Deptt. of Philosophy, Ranchi University, Ranchi.
16. Dr. Sushma Priyadarshana, Student, Department of Philosophy, Ranchi University, Ranchi.
17. Dr. T.K. Chakraborty, Professor & Former Head of Philosophy, Jadavpur University, Jadavpur, Kolkata.

18. Dr. Y.G. Jha, Professor of Zoology, Ranchi College, Ranchi.
19. Mr. G. Kumarappa, Assistant Librarian, The National Library, Kolkata.
20. Mr. Gautam Nayak, Teacher, Cambrian School, Ranchi.
21. Mr. Purushottam Kumar, Student, Department of Philosophy, Ranchi University, Ranchi.
22. Mr. S.K. Chatterjee, Sole Agent, Veedol, Ranchi.
23. Mr. Sanjay Kumar Singh, Typist, Nagratoli, Ranchi.
24. Sr. Mary Paul, Lecturer of Philosophy, Nirmala College, Ranchi.
25. A number of Press Dignitaries of the dailies, Prabhat Khabar, Aaj, Ranchi Express, Hindustan Times, Hindustan & Times of India.
26. A Number of Students of Philosophy Department of Ranchi University during the Sessions 1997 to 2000.
27. The Librarian, Director & Staff Members of the National Library, Kolkata; I.C.P.R. Library, Lucknow & St. Albert's College, Ranchi.

Bibliography

Acton, H.B. (ed.), *The Philosophy of Punishment*; Macmillan, London, 1973.

Ahmad, Imtiaz, "Caste is Relevant" in *The Times of India*, Patna-Ranchi Edition, 11-6-7.

Bayles, M.D. *Ethics and Population*, Cambridge University Press, Mass., 1976.

Aristotle, *Nicomachean Ethics*; J.A.K. Thomson (Trans.), Penguin Books, Baltimore, 1966.

Baier, Kurt, "Is Punishment Retributive?" in H.B. Acton (ed.), *The Philosophy of Punishment*; Macmillan, London, 1973.

Baier, Kurt, *The Moral Point of View*; Cornell University Press, NY, 1958.

Benn, S.I., "Punishment", in Paul Edwards (ed.), *The Encyclopedia of Philosophy*; Vol. 7, Macmillan & Free Press, NY, 1967.

Benn, S.I., "Society", in Paul Edwards (ed.), *The Encyclopedia of Philosophy*; Vol. 7, Macmillan & Free Press, NY, 1974.

Blanshard, Brand, "Morality and Politics" in De George R.T. (ed.), *Ethics and Society*, Macmillan, London, 1968.

Boxill, Bernard R., "Equality, Discrimination and Preferential Treatment" in Singer, Peter (ed.), *A Companion to Ethics*, O.U.P., Oxford, 1991.

Cahn, S.M. & Markie, P. (ed.), *Ethics: History, Theory and Contemporary Issues*, O.U.P., Oxford, 1998.

Chakraborty, Sauvik, "For an Equal Justice" in *The Times of India*, Patna-Ranchi Edition, 17.01.07.

Chattopadhyay, D.P., "Civil Disobedience: Its Necessity and Limits", in Roy, K. and Gupta, C. (ed.), *Essays In Social And Political Philosophy*; I.C.P.R. in association with Allied Publishers, New Delhi, 1989.

Clarke, Tom C., "Philosophy, Law and Civil Disobedience" in Kieffer, H.E. and Munitz, M.K. (eds.), *Ethics and Social Justice*; State University of New York Press, Albany, 1970.

Coady, C.A.J., "Politics and the Problem of Dirty Hands", in Singer, Peter (ed.), *A Companion to Ethics*; O.U.P., Oxford, 1991.

Danielson, R.E., "The Right to Strike" in *Atlantic Monthly*, Vol. CLXXIX, No. 2, 1947.

De George, R.T. (ed.), *Ethics and Society*; Macmillan, London, 1968.

Deshpande, Satish, "Learning to Speak Caste" in *The Times of India*, Patna-Ranchi Edition, 03.05.07.

Dworkin, R., "A Theory of Civil Disobedience" in Kieffer, H.E. and Munitz, M.K. (ed.), *Ethics and Social Justice*; State University of New York Press, Albany, 1970.

Dworkin, R., *Taking Rights Seriously*; Duckworth, London, 1978.

Edwards, Paul, *The Encyclopedia of Philosophy*; Vol. 6 & 7, Macmillan & Free Press, NY, 1967.

Evans, J.D.G., *Moral Philosophy and Contemporary Problems*; Cabridge University Press, Cambridge, 1987.

Feinberg, Joel, *Social Philosophy*; Prentice-Hall, NJ, 1973.

Feinberg, Joel, *The Moral Limits of the Criminal Law*; (Vol. 1), O.U.P., Oxford, NY, 1988.

French, P.A., *Ethics in Government*; Prentice-Hall, Englewood Cliffs, NJ, 1983.

Fuller, Lon L., *The Morality of Law*; Yale University Press, New Haven, 1972.

Garvin, Lucius, *A Modern Introduction to Ethics*; Houghton Miffin, Boston, 1953.

Gewirth, Alan, *Reason and Morality*; University of Chicago Press, Chicago, 1978.

Glover, Jonathan, "Utilitarianism and Punishment" in Pojman, Louis P. (ed.), *Introduction to Philosophy: Classical and Contemporary Readings*; Wadsworth, Kolkata 2004.

Goldman, Alan H., *Justice and Reverse Discrimination*; Princeton University Press, Princeton, 1979.

Goodwin, R.E., Pettit, P., (ed.), *A Companion to Contemporary Political Philosophy*; Oxford University Press, Oxford, 1993.

Gupta, Chhanda, "Objectivity in Social Inquiry", in Roy, K. and Gupta, C. (ed.), *Essays in Social and Political Philosophy*; I.C.P.R. in association with Allied Publishers, New Delhi, 1989.

Gupta, Chhanda, "Value and Social Science", in Roy, K. and Gupta, C. (ed.), *Essays in Social and Political Philosophy*; I.C.P.R. in association with Allied Publishers, New Delhi, 1989.

Haag, Earnest Van Den, "In Defense of Death Penalty" in Cahn, S.M. and Markie, P. (ed.), *Ethics: History, Theory and Contemporary Issues*; O.U.P., Oxford, 1998.

Hampshire, Stuart (ed.), *Public and Private Morality*; Cambridge University Press, Cambridge, 1998.

Hare, R.M., *Essays on Political Morality*; Cambridge, MA, 1992.

Hart, H.L.A., "Problem of Philosophy of Law" in Edwards, Paul (ed.), *The Encyclopedia of Philosophy*; Vol. 6, Macmillan & Free Press, NY, 1967.

Hart, H.L.A., *Positivism, Law and Morals: Essays in Jurisprudence and Philosophy*; Clarendon Press, Oxford, 1983.

Hart, H.L.A., *The Concept of Law*; Clarendon Press, Oxford, 1961.

Hill, T.E., "The Message of Affirmative Action" in Cahn, S.M. and Markie, P. (ed.), *Ethics: History, Theory and Contemporary Issues*; O.U.P., Oxford, 1998.

John, L., *Second Treatise on Civil Government*; Hackett Publishing Co., Cambridge, 1980.

Kainz, Howard P., *Ethics in Context*; Macmillan, Basingstoke, 1988.

Keith, Graham, "Morality, Individuals and Collectives" in Evans, J.D.G. (ed.), *Moral Philosophy and Contemporary Problems*; Cambridge University Press, Cambridge, 1987.

Kekes, J., "The Injustice of Affirmative Action Involving Preferential Treatment" in Cahn, S.M. and Markie, P. (ed.), *Ethics: History, Theory and Contemporary Issues*; O.U.P., Oxford, 1998.

Kieffer, H.E. and Munitz, M.K. (ed.), *Ethics and Social Justice*; State University of New York Press, Albany, 1970.

Kipnis, K., *Legal Status*; Prentice-Hall, Englewood Cliffs, NJ, 1986.

Krishnan, P.S., "Rights Reserved" in *The Times of India*, Patna-Ranchi Edition, 12.12.06.

Lukes, S., *Moral Conflicts and Politics*; O.U.P. Oxford, 1991.

Lyons, David, *Forms and Limits of Utilitarianism*; The Clarendon Press, Oxford, 1969.

Mackie, J.L., *Ethics: Inventing Right and Wrong*; Penguin Books, Harmondsworth, 1977.

Mappes, T.A. and Zembaty, J.S. (ed.), *Social Ethics, Morality and Social Policy*; McGraw-Hill, NY, 1996.

Miltner, C.C., *The Elements of Ethics*; Macmillan, NY, 1959.

Morscher, Edgar, Neumaier, Otto & Simon, Peter (ed.), *Applied Ethics in a Troubled World*; Kluwer Academic Publisher, London, 1998.

Mukhopadhyay, Somenath, "For Whom the Bells Toll", *The Sunday Statesman*, Calcutta Edition, Kolkata, 1998.

Nagel, T., in Stuart Hampshire (ed.), *Public and Private Morality*; Cambrige University Press, Cambridge, 1978.

Nariman, Fali S., "Crime and Punishment: Deterrence or Reform", *The Statesman*, Calcutta Edition, Kolkata, 1998.

Nathanson, Stephen, "An Eye For An Eye: Morality of Punishing By Death" in Cahn, S.M. and Markie, P. (ed.), *Ethics: History, Theory and Contemporary Issues*; O.U.P., Oxford, 1998.

Norton, D.L., *Democracy and Moral Development*; Berkeley, CA, 1991.

Nozick, R., *Anarchy, State and Utopia*; Basil Blackwell, Oxford, 1986.

Parikh, Kirti, "A Fair System" in *The Times of India*, Patna-Ranchi Edition, 10.02.07.

Pears, D.F., *David Hume: A Symposium*; Macmillan, London, 1963.

Plato, *The Republic,* (Trans.), F.M. Cornford, O.U.P., Oxford, 1945.

Pojman, Louis P. (ed.), *Introduction to Philosophy: Classical and Contemporary Readings*; Wadsworth, Cal., 2004.

Rajappa, Sam, "Right to Life", *The Sunday Statesman*, Calcutta Edition, Kolkata, 1998.

Raphael, D.D., *Justice and Liberty*; The Athlone Press, London, 1980.

Raphael, D.D., *Problems of Political Philosophy*; The Macmillan Press, London, 1976.

Rawls, John, "Two Concepts of Punishment" in Pojman, Louis P. (ed.), *Introduction to Philosophy: Classical and Contemporary Readings*; Wadsworth, Kolkata 2004.

Rawls, John, *A Theory of Justice*; O.U.P., Oxford, 1973.

Roy, Krishna and Gupta, Chhanda (ed.), *Essays in Social and Political Philosophy*, I.C.P.R. in association with Allied Publishers, New Delhi, 1989.

Roy, Krishna, "Hermeneutics and Ethnomethodology", in Roy, K. and Gupta, C. (ed.), *Essays in Social and Political Philosophy*; I.C.P.R. in association with Allied Publishers, New Delhi, 1989.

Rudner, R., *Philosophy of Social Science*; Prentice-Hall, NJ, 1966.

Sadurski, Wojciech, *Giving Deserts Its Due: Social Justice and Legal Theory*; D. Riedel Publishing Co., Dordrecht 1950.

Singer, Peter, *A Companion to Ethics*; O.U.P., Oxford, 1991.

Stewart, R.M. (ed.), *Readings in Social and Political Philosophy*; O.U.P., Oxford, 1986.

Tahitinen, Unto, *Non-Violent Theories of Punishment: Indian and Western*; Motilal Banarasidass, New Delhi, 1983.

Ten, C.L., "Crime and Punishment" in Singer, Peter(ed.), *A Companion to Ethics*; O.U.P., Oxford, 1991.

Trusted, Jennifer, *Moral Principles and Social Values*; Routledge & Kegan Paul, London, 1987.

Velasquez, M. & Rostenkowski, C. (ed.), *Ethics: Theory and Practice*; Prentice-Hall, NJ, 1984.

Walzer, Michael, *Political Acton: The Politics of Dirty Hands*; Books, Chicogo, 1979.

Index